Praise for *Bodies of Subversion: A Secret History of Women and Tattoo*

"The insights [Margot Mifflin] brings are insinuating and complex . . . *Bodies of Subversion* is delicious social history."
— DWIGHT GARNER, *The New York Times*

"Mifflin's thesis is rooted in subversion. She asserts that tattoos in Western culture have always been subversive for women, especially in the 19th century when they violated the assumption that 'women should be pure, that their bodies should be concealed and controlled, and that ladies should not express their own desires.'"
— STEVEN HELLER, *The Atlantic*

"*Bodies of Subversion* . . . beautifully documented the evolution of women and tattoos from Victorian couture to mastectomy scar coverups in the nineties . . . [It was] the only book to chronicle tattooed women and women tattoo artists."
— LEAH RODRIGUEZ, *The Cut*

"More than just a photographic history of this deep subculture . . . [The book] is a close study of women during a period of historic limitations and social mobility, beginning to break barriers by exploring alternative ideas of beauty and self-expression."
— SYREETA McFADDEN, *Feministing*

"In this provocative work full of intriguing female characters from tattoo history, Margot Mifflin makes a persuasive case for the tattooed woman as an emblem of female self-expression."
— SUSAN FALUDI

"Essential reading for anyone interested in the subject."
— ED HARDY

Praise for *The Blue Tattoo: The Life of Olive Oatman*

The Booklist Reader, 1 of 150 Memoirs and Biographies of Women, by Women

Finalist for the Caroline Bancroft History Prize

Named a Best of the Best from American University Presses by the American Library Association

A Southwest Book of the Year

Named a Book of the Year by over a dozen regional publications including *The Kansas City Star, Anchorage Daily News*, and *Idaho Statesman*

Named a Book of the Year by *PopMatters*

A One Book Yuma community read selection for Yuma, Arizona

"Mifflin engagingly describes Oatman's ordeal and theorizes about its impact on Oatman herself as well as on popular imagination . . . Her book adds nuance to Oatman's story and also humanizes the Mohave who adopted her. Recommended for general readers as well as students and scholars."   —*Library Journal*

"*The Blue Tattoo* is well-researched history that reads like unbelievable fiction, telling the story of Olive Oatman."   —*Bust*

"An easy, flowing read, one you won't be able to put down."
                                    —JON STRAUB, *The Christian Science Monitor*

"An important and engrossing book, which reveals as much about the appetites and formulas of emerging mass culture as it does about tribal cultures in nineteenth-century America."
                          —CHRISTINE BOLD, *The Times Literary Supplement*

"Margot Mifflin has written a winner . . . *The Blue Tattoo* offers quite intense drama along with thorough scholarship."   —ELMORE LEONARD

Looking for Miss America

A Pageant's 100-Year Quest to Define Womanhood

♕

MARGOT MIFFLIN

COUNTERPOINT
Berkeley, California

Grateful acknowledgment is made to the following for permission to publish reprinted material:
"Miss America"
from THE MISS AMERICA PAGEANT
Words and Music by Bernie Wayne
Copyright © 1954, 1955 Bernie Wayne Music Co.
Copyright Renewed
All Rights Controlled and Administered by Spirit One Music
International Copyright Secured All Rights Reserved
Reprinted by Permission of Hal Leonard LLC

ISBN: 978-1-64009-223-5

The Library of Congress Cataloging-in-Publication Data is available.

Jacket design by Nicole Caputo
Book design by Jordan Koluch

COUNTERPOINT
2560 Ninth Street, Suite 318
Berkeley, CA 94710
www.counterpointpress.com

Printed in the United States of America

10 9 8 7 6 5 4 3 2 1

To Lawrie Mifflin and Lize Mifflin—my sisters, my lodestars

Contents

Looking for Miss America

American Beauties

To a girl, to a girl.

To a symbol of happiness.

To the one, to the one

Who's the symbol of all we possess.

"A Toast to Miss America," pageant theme song, 1949

WHO IS MISS AMERICA? SHE'S the kind of girl who enters a bar and orders an orange juice "just loud enough for everyone to hear her," said Yolande Betbeze, Miss America 1951. "She's a prom queen who wants to become the Statue of Liberty," wrote the critic Richard Corliss. She's "the body of the state, and the country is in her eyes," gushed the journalist and pageant judge Frank Deford. But no—she's "Miss Whatever She Wants to Be," Miss America's mission statement declares.

She was born in 1921, a "beauty maid" wearing a sash and a swimsuit in a parade in Atlantic City, conspicuously unlike those *other* parades, where women in sashes marched for suffrage until they got it in 1920. Sometimes she was the girl next door; sometimes she was America's ideal woman. A few Miss Americas became household names: the actresses Mary Ann Mobley and Lee Meriwether, the journalists Phyllis George and Gretchen Carlson, the singer Vanessa Williams—the most famous and beloved of all, despite getting dethroned in 1984. One Miss America regretted her win: Bette Cooper skipped town the night of her 1937 crowning, whisked off into the night by her dashing pageant chauffeur, leaving the mystified press staring at her empty throne the next day, awaiting her press conference. She just wanted to finish high school.

Looking for Miss America unzips the story of the pageant: an underexplored, curious, contradictory, ever-changing, entertaining piece of women's history. It spotlights the women who made it an inadvertent index of feminist progress, from Betbeze, who flatly refused to wear a swimsuit in public during her reign (so angering a key sponsor that it dropped Miss America and started Miss USA), to Erin O'Flaherty, the first openly lesbian contestant in 2017. It examines the controversies the pageant has ignited, the racial bias it has enabled, and the social mobility it has offered low-income winners.

Considering that neither a Muslim nor a woman of Hispanic descent has ever won, it's safe to say that Miss America does not represent America. But the pageant crystallizes many distinctly American impulses: a dual fixation on women's virtue and sexuality, a baffling fascination with royalty (is there anything *less* American than a crown?), the belief that education and intellect can be demonstrated in a twenty-second interview, and the unshakable conviction that young women are the best women and it's their duty to entertain you.

The state and national winners, judges, and pageant officials I interviewed for *Looking for Miss America* were open about the organization's weaknesses and persuasive about its benefits, from life-changing college scholarships and sponsorship jackpots to career-boosting professional training and networking connections. (That said, the title can also backfire. In an editorial for *Refinery29*, Crystal Lee, first runner-up to Miss America in 2014, said the "stigma of pageantry" hurt her professionally and that her company told her it "diminished my credentials as a businesswoman.") Though the number of contestants in its nationwide competitions has shrunk to about 4,000—down from 80,000 in the 1980s—the Miss America community is still a buzzing subculture. The network of volunteers who sustain local and state pageants includes contestants, "formers," friends, and families. Even state pageant judges and directors are unpaid. It's most vibrant in the South, where winners are in the greatest demand and pageants are well funded.

In its first half century, Miss America channeled the aspirations of women whose professional and economic opportunities were so limited that beauty was an attractive and potentially powerful tool of advancement. Their options broadened with feminism's second wave, which announced its arrival on September 7, 1968, the day activists protested the pageant's sexism on the Atlantic City boardwalk outside, then dropped a banner from a balcony inside demanding WOMEN'S LIBERATION!, releasing "women's lib" into the American lexicon.

Since then, the pageant has been in constant dialogue with feminism, though rarely in step with it. Most of the pageant people I interviewed for this book referred to contestants as "girls," evoking Playboy bunnies or cheerleaders, not the super-achievers touted in the organization's mission statement. And though the Miss America Organization promotes women's empowerment and vows to prepare them for professional success, the honorific "Miss" died out in the workplace decades ago.

Still, despite Miss America's socially conservative roots, many contestants consider themselves feminists (though most don't say this publicly, one state board chair confided, because they fear the word's negative connotations might be a turnoff for some fans). Broadway producer Eric Cornell, a veteran state pageant judge, is often asked, with a note of incredulity, why he supports Miss America. "I'm a huge feminist," he says, "and I do really think giving visibility to women who are pursuing higher education and professional careers is important." He believes that even if they never win state or national titles, Miss America contestants end up better off financially because of the prize money and professional training they get from competing.

Though there are "formers" whose pretty selfies and peppy Instagram bromides fulfill age-old beauty queen clichés, some winners have been iconoclasts, if not full-on rebels. Starting in the 1960s, Betbeze publicly decried the pageant's racism, boycotting the event until Vanessa Williams was crowned the first black Miss America in 1983. Miss Montana Kathy Huppe quit in 1970 after being told to muzzle her anti-war views. She posed for *Life* magazine in her gown and crown, a fist raised in defiance. Miss America 1998 Kate Shindle's AIDS activism brought her a standing ovation when she addressed the 1998 International AIDS Conference. Marilyn Van Derbur, Miss America 1958, went public with her family history of incest and became a proto-#MeToo activist in the 1990s. Now in her eighties, she's still fiercely advocating for abuse survivors. And there are symbolic subversions: though Gabriela Taveras, a runner-up in 2018, was advised to tamp down her Spanish accent during her introduction, she rolled the *r*'s in her name, sending a thrill of pride and a flurry of Snapchat videos through her hometown of Lawrence, Massachusetts.

The pageant's history encompasses not just the women who won or lost, but also those who were excluded, like the Native American beauty queens invited to join Miss America's court in the 1920s, standing as "guests of honor" in buckskin and beads, sidekicks to America's queen. Asian Americans, African Americans, and Native Americans staged their own pageants before and after Miss America barred them through its notorious Rule Seven, formalized in the 1940s, requiring contestants to be "in good health and of the white race." As chapter 1 confirms, the whiff of eugenics wasn't coincidental.

Likewise, Miss America's legacy belongs not just to its queens, but to the Americans they presume to represent as "ambassadors." It's a gauge of dominant regional and national values. Miss America 1960, Lynda Lee Mead of Mississippi, for example, was the face of the state with the highest number of lynchings in America, including one just five months before her crowning. At a homecoming lunch in Jackson that year, she affirmed her state pride by telling the press she wouldn't apologize for Mississippi. "We have nothing to apologize for," she said. Nina Davuluri's historic 2013 win as the first Indian American Miss America was both a triumph of diversity and an alarming barometer of American bigotry and cultural illiteracy: in a flood of social media vitriol, she was denounced as an Arab and a terrorist. But the pageant has also had a galvanic effect. When Bess Myerson was crowned the first (and only) Jewish Miss America weeks after the end of World War II, just as the scale and horrors of the Holocaust were fully registering, she spotted triumphant Jews in the audience shouting "Mazel tov!" and turning to embrace one another.

Whether we grew up loving its sparkle and spectacle or hate-watching it as a rhinestone relic, the pageant has wormed its way into our national subconscious. Its mythology runs through popular culture, from Mae West's withering 1927 Miss America teardown *The Wicked Age*, which she wrote and starred in, to the uproarious 1999 pageant mockumentary *Drop Dead Gorgeous*. In Philip Roth's *American Pastoral*, we meet the only Miss America contestant in literature who speaks—loudly and sympathetically— for herself. Pop stars from the Beach Boys to Leikeli47 have exalted and reviled Miss America. The pageant has also attracted a hodgepodge of celebrity judges: Norman Rockwell, Grace Kelly, Rod McKuen, Soledad O'Brien. In 1952, when Marilyn Monroe served as its parade grand marshal, her publicist claimed she "murdered those poor little Miss Americas" with her beauty, but she said she was intimidated by theirs.

As a cultural institution, Miss America is impossible to categorize. If it's not a beauty contest—or not *just* a beauty contest—what is it? It's neither a variety show nor an athletic event, though it has elements of each. It's not a government-sponsored ritual, though winners are invited to meet presidents and address congressional committees. (North Dakota governor Doug Burgum was so jazzed after his state's first Miss America was crowned in 2017 that he signed a proclamation dedicating an annual Cara Mund Day.) Early on, as a kind of middle American debutante ball, it propelled women toward marriage. Today it trains them for careers, but the lingering requirement that they be unmarried and childless makes this elimination extravaganza look a bit like *The Bachelor*. Now, with the swimsuit portion abolished, it's a talent show wrapped in a scholarship program decked out as a job interview.

Any Miss America fan will trumpet the contest's most impressive achievement: it awards $3 million in scholarships each year, more than any nonprofit scholarship organization for women. Unlike other pageants, it charges no entry fee. What goes unsaid is that 85 percent of this money is generated by the contestants themselves, who must raise a minimum amount—by soliciting donations—to compete. These women spend months or years drumming up funding, volunteering (to enhance their résumés), dieting, exercising, practicing a talent, and paying for coaches, trainers, wardrobes, and travel in the hope of winning a $10,000–$50,000 scholarship. Most are working or attending college while they prepare. Some state winners even have full-time jobs while they serve. Why do they do it? Why *did* they do it? Does it matter?

It does. The pageant's history reflects the often ludicrous demands made of ambitious women and the canny ways contestants have both exploited and subverted them. It also shows how visions of ideal American womanhood have been shaped by social forces since the pageant's inception, whether immigration and the Great Migration in the early twentieth century, wartime and postwar consumer culture in the 1940s and '50s, civil rights and feminist activism in the 1960s and '70s, or the late twentieth-century culture wars we're still fighting. And though Miss America might seem like something only men could have dreamed up (which they did), it was a woman, Lenora Slaughter, who redesigned it for the most part as we know it today, running it for nearly three decades starting in the 1930s. She was a tangle of contradictions—prudish but flamboyant, independent yet socially conservative—a Southern Baptist who gussied up a seaside skin show so her "girls" could get a college degree, partly because she'd been unable to afford one herself. She hoped some of the winners would become doctors and lawyers one day, which some did. And she dearly wished they would land rich, dreamboat husbands, which many did.

Today, in our increasingly multi-ethnic, multi-gendered nation, the myth of a single paragon of authentic American womanhood has faded. Even the winners themselves have trouble saying exactly what they represent. Many explained it by telling me how well competing had served them personally or how it helps women economically or educationally, instead of expressing what the title signifies nationally.

But the pageant's fluctuating symbolism has never meant just one thing to one group anyway. For some, it's a cherished expression of regional pride; to others it's harmless fun, like Barbie, not to be overthought. Still others see it as a pre-feminist pathology, forever pushing women as fetishized commodities. ("The sooner you realize you're a product, the better," said Miss America 1962, Maria Fletcher.) Its messy, mercurial, wacky history reflects our class anxieties and cultural biases, our faith in beauty as a virtue and in virtue as a measurable trait, and the truism, as the historian Rosalyn Baxandall put it, that "Every day in a woman's life is a walking Miss America contest."

ONE

Bathing Beauties

S HE WAS JUST OVER FIVE feet tall, weighed 108 pounds, wore her hair long, came from a respected Georgetown family, and was fifteen years old when she was named Miss Washington D.C. in August 1921. Her photo had been chosen from a thousand submitted to the *Washington Herald*'s local beauty contest, which meant she would enjoy a paid trip to Atlantic City to compete in a sensational new pageant. When two *Herald* reporters set out in the sweltering summer heat to interview her, they found Margaret Gorman on her knees in a playground, shooting marbles in the dirt.

Gorman and nine other finalists had appeared in a preliminary competition at the Italian Garden of the Washington Arts Club where they walked for six judges and fielded questions about their backgrounds and ambitions. They were evaluated for "real rather than artificial beauty," which disqualified anyone wearing conspicuous makeup. Gorman later said she couldn't recall much about her win; her mind was clouded because she was "madly in love" for the first time. She spent the next week getting squired around the city and attending civic dinners, capped with a visit to the White House, where she met President Warren G. Harding.

Then the real competition began. A few weeks later, Gorman, now sixteen, and seven other contestants from Pennsylvania, Washington, D.C., and New Jersey boarded a train to Atlantic City in advance of a two-day festival called the Fall Frolic, created a year earlier to stretch the summer tourism season into the balmy weeks of early fall. They would compete in the first Inter-City Beauty Contest—the nucleus of the Miss America pageant.

The inaugural 1920 Frolic, the brainchild of a hotelier named H. Conrad Eckholm and organized by Atlantic City's Business Men's League, set the stage for pageants to come. It opened with an hour-long parade featuring marching bands and 350 wheeled wicker "rolling chairs" gliding down Atlantic Avenue, pushed by men, occupied by "beauty maids," and led by a single beauty named Ernestine Cremona, a proto-Miss America in white robes, personifying peace. Later, at the seaside Bathers' Revue, men, women, and babies in swimsuits competed for prizes. That night revelers danced by moonlight at a costume ball on Steel Pier, the ocean roaring beneath their feet.

Banking on the beauty contest drawing bigger crowds to the Frolic in its second year, the Chamber of Commerce hoped to outdo even nearby Asbury Park's supremely successful annual baby parade—where, as it happened, the mothers often attracted more interest than the babies. The pageant committee advertised for contestants through area newspapers, including the *Herald*, asking the staff to choose a winner and fund her wardrobe in exchange for free publicity and a boost in circulation. Breathless press releases spurred interest in the event, promising—falsely—that "thousands of the most beautiful girls in the land, including stage stars and movie queens," would compete. And so their first official beauty competition opened at the second Frolic, now called the Atlantic City Pageant or the Fall Pageant, in 1921.

Known as "Philadelphia's playground," Atlantic City was on its way to becoming a national resort. Situated on a barrier island linked to the mainland by a network of train lines, the city was powered, in the early years of Prohibition, by mobster Enoch ("Nucky") Johnson, who ensured that liquor flowed openly in the city he controlled. It was built on the backs of local African Americans who were banned from enjoying the very beach and hotel culture their labor made possible. In fact, as Bryant Simon writes in *Boardwalk of Dreams: Atlantic City and the Fate of Urban America*, this "public performance of racial dominance" helped make Atlantic City one of the most popular vacation spots in the country. The city's black residents, many of whom had moved north for work at the start of the Great Migration, comprised 25 percent of its population, yet were confined to the cramped Northside neighborhood and restricted to segregated schools, nightclubs, churches, and a single beach.

One of the nation's first twenty-four-hour cities, Atlantic City had evolved, by the turn of the century, into an East Coast Avalon where Victorian decorum could be discarded, men and women could mingle freely in public, and the boardwalk promised amusements from the first Ferris wheel to freak shows, fortune tellers, and baby incubators. It was classier than Coney Island and glitzier than Cape May, but unlike Social Register resort towns like Newport, Rhode Island, it wasn't exclusive. Popular music and Broadway-caliber theater flourished there throughout the 1920s, with Manhattan-bound shows at the Apollo, Globe, and Woods theaters introducing work by the Gershwins and showcasing stars like W. C. Fields and the Marx Brothers.

The boardwalk was the focus, the beach merely the backdrop. Enormous hotels embraced the surging tide of tourists in a seaside architectural mashup: there was the Spanish-Moorish Blenheim (the first to install private baths in every room), the Regency-style Dennis, the English Renaissance Chalfonte-Haddon Hall, and the radically modern Traymore, a $4 million art deco leviathan that housed over 3,000 guests and spanned an entire city block; its deck contained a glass-bottom fish pond that served as a ceiling to a supper club called the Submarine Grill, where strategic lighting sent the silhouettes of marine life drifting lazily around the dance floor.

"Atlantic City is not a treat for the introspective," the critic James Huneker wrote in 1915. "It is hard, glittering, unspeakably cacophonous, and it never sleeps at all . . . From the howling of some hideous talking-machine to the loud, confident blaring of the orchestra of the wooden horses and wooden rabbits in the carousel you can't escape noise." As a resort that offered both family and adult urban entertainment, one of its perennial challenges was squaring pleasure with propriety. The Miss America pageant would be one of its more difficult balancing acts.

From the minute the contestants stepped off the train to meet the hostess committee on September 7, 1921, teeming crowds trailed them nonstop throughout the entire two-day festival, shouting questions, cheering, and demanding that they pose for the cameras. They were escorted to luxurious suites at the oceanfront Alamac Hotel and feted at a banquet where they met the new mayor, Edward L. Bader, freshly hand-picked in an election rigged by Nucky Johnson.

They made their formal debut the next morning, arriving by sea, perched on a barge helmed by King Neptune, a bronzed, bearded patriarch wearing purple robes and a jeweled crown. He was sixty-eight-year-old Hudson Maxim, the cheerless engineer who had invented smokeless gunpowder, contracting, as a result, a pathological sensitivity to smell. ("While I am exceedingly strong and rugged," he told reporters, "if I were placed next to someone smelling to high heaven with perfume, I'd collapse and fall in a heap.") He brandished his trident in his right hand, having lost the other in a lab accident. Deck guns, sirens, train whistles, and church bells heralded the arrival of the sea god and his mermaid court of dancing girls.

Mayor Bader greeted them at the Million Dollar Pier, a complex of theaters, exhibition halls, and a massive ballroom, handing Neptune a silver key to the city before the king and his court boarded a rolling float, escorted, *The Atlantic City Daily Press* observed, by "black slaves garbed in skins"—the only African Americans to participate in Miss America festivities for the next half century. After stepping off at the stately Keith's Theater on the uptown Garden Pier, they chatted informally with the judging panel, chaired by one of the nation's most famous illustrators, Howard Chandler Christy.

An emboldened successor to the statuesque turn-of-the-century "Gibson Girl," the "Christy Girl" was plucky, sporty, a little saucy— and perhaps best remembered from Christy's army recruitment poster: GEE!! I WISH I WERE A MAN. I'D JOIN THE NAVY. She was a fashionable socialite who appeared, in his illustrations between 1898 and 1920, at leisure with boyfriends or classmates, but never at home or at work, because Christy's ideal woman was transitional. She was liberated but limited—no longer the domestic goddess of yesteryear, but not exactly a feminist either. "Charm and a knack for inspiring manly acts are the extent of [her] personal power," writes Martha Banta in *Imaging American Women: Idea and*

Ideals in Cultural History. Christy, who chaired the judging committee for the pageant's first five years, strongly supported educating women—to make them better wives and mothers.

The other judges included, incongruously, the manager of the Ritz-Carlton hotel, the aging actor John Drew (of Barrymore dynasty fame), and two local artists who, with Christy, oversaw a range of sub-competitions, with the most significant division separating amateurs from professionals who'd worked as dancers, actresses, and models. Gorman and Virginia Lee, a stunning silent film actress from New York, were rumored favorites.

That evening, reunited with Neptune, the Inter-City Beauties mounted a waterfront platform to watch a show by a children's vaudeville troupe called Dawson's Dancing Dolls. Seated where the audience could gaze at them as well as at the performers, the women were publicly introduced afterward, and cheers for Gorman could be heard, *The Atlantic City Daily Press* marveled, "from one end of the beach to the other."

The Atlantic City Pageant's central event kicked off the next day with the rolling chair parade, as hundreds of flower-bedecked floats and chairs rumbled, this time, down the boardwalk, the thrumming main artery of the city. The floats advertised businesses, amusements, and civic organizations from the Rotary Club to the Press-Union Company, represented by a nine-foot-long copy of *The Atlantic City Daily Press* bearing a headline announcing the pageant. The neighboring town of Ventnor's procession stretched for an entire block, with the mayor leading, flanked by the police and fire departments. The beauties rolled too, flaunting their assets in the hope of winning one of the many prizes to be awarded at the crowning ceremony that evening. Wearing a gold-spangled dress and bronze-tinted shoes, Gorman bowed and smiled at hooting fans as children threw flowers in her path.

She was already a star, having made a splash that morning in the beachfront Bathers' Revue, where she and the others marched unsteadily along a 1,300-foot swath of sand roped off and marked with flags. Gorman wore a modest taffeta swimsuit with a tiered skirt and dark knee-high stockings, drawing cheers for her "natty beach rig" and earning points as well, since public enthusiasm counted toward contestants' final scores. The others sported one- and two-piece suits, a few with skirts hanging to the knee, and one—Miss Pittsburgh—with pants that ended, shockingly, above mid-thigh.

They wore headbands to secure their hair in the wind, belts or scarves tied at the waist, and laced boots, flats, or low heels, posing for photos with feet splayed or even planted six inches apart, in contrast to the "pretty feet" stance (with one foot slightly forward) prescribed in later years. Likewise, the compulsive smiling that later became a pageant hallmark wasn't yet reflexive. Photos capture the hopefuls looking variously amused, relaxed, bored, impatient, distracted, or downright stern—charmingly human, and more like the children most of them were than the women they were presumed to be.

And yet, something scandalous was happening. *The New York Times* reported that during the Bathers' Revue, "the censor ban on bare knees and skin-tight bathing suits was suspended and thousands of spectators gasped as they applauded the girls, who were judged on their shapeliness and carriage, as well as beauty of face."

The exposure of bare knees wasn't just unusual; it was illegal. The city's 1907 Mackintosh Law prohibited swimwear that ended more than four inches above the knee without stockings rolled up over the thigh to bridge the difference. It was enforced by "beach cops" who trudged around commanding offenders to "Roll 'em up, sister." (Men, too, were required to cover their chests with tank tops.) A few days before the Atlantic City Pageant, a thirty-nine-year-old writer named Louise Rosine was stopped for wearing her stockings rolled down to her ankles on a blazingly hot day, then jailed for delivering a "lusty blow" to the officer who insisted she cover them.

"I most certainly will not 'roll 'em up,'" Rosine declared. "The city has no right to tell me how I shall wear my stockings. It is none of their darn business." She wore her swimsuit in jail—knees exposed—to protest her arrest, and announced, through a formal complaint, that "bare feminine knees" were protected by the Constitution.

Rosine hailed from Los Angeles, where regulations were looser. The question of acceptable beachwear for women was the subject of lively national discussion, and the rules varied regionally. A year earlier, on New York's Rockaway Beach, twenty "sheriffettes" had been sworn in to enforce modesty regulations. In 1921, Hawaii enacted a law stipulating that no one over fourteen could wear a bathing suit without an "outer garment" extending to the knees. The summer before the pageant, one-piece women's suits were banned on Long Island, along with voyeuristic "beach lizards"—"bald-headed men who come to the beach to stare."

Bathing machines—mobile changing rooms wheeled into the surf to drop women in woolen dresses into the ocean unseen—had been retired at the turn of the century, and swimwear had since replaced streetwear at the beach. But there was still no consensus on appropriate fashion for women who now bathed—and increasingly swam—publicly. In 1907, the woman who invented the one-piece swimsuit, champion swimmer Annette Kellerman, had herself been arrested for indecency for wearing it on Revere Beach in Massachusetts. Designed for speed and intended to be paired with stockings instead of bloomers, it was braless, skirtless, and form-fitting—especially when wet, making it that much easier for this Australian powerhouse to break world records, and that much harder for Victorian holdouts to accept its contours.

Historian Blain Roberts notes the dissonance between regulation and celebration of the swimsuit in this period. "As soon as the smaller swimsuit appeared," she writes in *Pageants, Parlors, and Pretty Women*, "beach censors took to the sands to punish women for baring too much skin and the bathing beauty review emerged to reward the very same phenomenon."

The local press published fiery letters to the mayor about the decision to allow the suits at the Bathers' Revue. A doctor defended it with the revelation that swimming with stockings is harder than swimming without them. Two sixteen-year-olds, assuring readers they were "not bold girls," explained that a "good swimmer cannot possibly swim with skirts dangling around her knees." Church stalwarts took up the opposition, along with older members of the newfound League of Women Voters, who passed a resolution supporting knee-length skirts and stockings on the odd logic that relaxing the rules would cause a rift between younger and older "newly enfranchised" women. They worried that "such a division of sentiment . . . might seriously affect [their] political fortunes."

The pageant committee, uncertain about how best to display the newly liberated female body, did what they would do in the face of so many controversies that erupted over the next century: they missed the point entirely. The popular "Annette Kellerman" one-piece—which represented women's new fashion freedom and even encouraged athleticism—would be tolerated, but only for the length of the pageant, to showcase the beauty of the female form. The swimsuit had no practical relevance to women's physical activity from the pageant's inception to the day it was retired in 2018. But women who wore the new suits surely felt a sense of freedom, even exhilaration, in sashaying down the beach freed from the heavy remnants of nineteenth-century fashion. *The New York Times* said as much, reporting that some liked them simply "because they regard them as rather frisky."

The Atlantic City Daily Press weighed in approvingly—and salaciously: "The Bathers' Revue was remarkable for the uncensored costumes. One-piece bathing suits were the rule rather than the exception. Nude limbs were in evidence everywhere—and not a guardian of the law molested the fair sea nymphs who pranced about the sands. Every type of beauty was on exhibition, shown to its advantage in the type of sea togs permitted." But just for one day. The *Daily Press* noted that the spectacle caused the lifeguards, who normally doubled as beach censors, to "blink, gasp—and then remember they were officially blind until midnight."

The beauties weren't the only ones who suited up to compete. There were contests for organizations like the American Red Cross and the Elks, for children and for men. And *everyone* wore a swimsuit, from firemen (in red one-pieces) to policemen (in blue) to sullen King Neptune, who shed his robes and surrendered to the sun atop a makeshift throne.

That night, Steel Pier's ballroom was packed with 2,000 fans awaiting the announcement of the winner. The ceremony ran long, partly because so many prizes were handed out, but mainly because of Margee Gorman. She won both the amateur Bathers' Revue and the Inter-City Beauty Contest, the two most important competitions, sending the crowds into such a frenzy of interruptive cheering, even while other prizes were being presented, that the host was repeatedly forced to walk her out and reintroduce her to quiet her fans.

Gorman was voted the most beautiful girl in America. She took home the Golden Mermaid trophy, a gilded mermaid lounging on a teakwood base lined with seashells, and a two-foot-tall silver "beauty urn" donated by Annette Kellerman herself. Beyond that, she won a vague promise: "Winner of [the] GRAND PRIZE will undoubtedly become nationally famous, as great publicity will be given the winner and her likeness will be used on the Bathing Revue Poster of 1922." There was no crown; this winner was a mermaid, not a queen, and she would be named Miss America later, retroactively. The pageant ended in the wee hours, when King Neptune, having delivered his beauty to the Jersey Shore, returned to the sea. Gorman's entire trip had cost her just thirty-five cents: the price of a collect telegram from a fan that read, "Congratulations. Don't get stuck up."

———

AT FIVE FEET ONE, GORMAN would stand as the smallest Miss America in the pageant's history. She was girlish, with slim hips and ringlets, prompting comparisons to silent movie darling Mary Pickford, "America's Sweetheart." As the historian Kimberly A. Hamlin writes, the judges "were not interested in celebrating the new, emancipated women of the 1920s, but in promoting images of the girls of yesterday: small, childlike, subservient, and malleable."

Indeed, Gorman was less significant, in many ways, for what she was than for what she wasn't. She wasn't an adult, for starters, so the question of how her sexuality informed her beauty complicated the judging. "She was very attractive for a kid," said Harry Godshall, a founding board member. Gorman later described herself as "a little schoolgirl," and newspapers called her "the little Washington beauty" or "little Margaret Gorman." Older, worldlier women competed in the less hyped professional category, while lovable ingénues dominated the pageant proper for years to come. They didn't wear the scarlet lipstick, heavy eyeliner, plucked eyebrows, or boyish bob of the Jazz Age. In fact, for years after Gorman won, even when flapper fashion had landed in the bible of middlebrow apparel—the Sears catalog—newspapers unfailingly noted which contestants wore their hair bobbed. They were never the winners.

Gorman was not quite a woman, and she was decidedly not a "New Woman," by then a popular term for the enfranchised, independent, post-Victorian woman of the modern age. Nor was she a feminist—a term of choice, borrowed from the French *feministe*, for women whose political concerns transcended the single issue of suffrage. She was not a suffragette, though the sash she wore, bearing her city's name, suggested otherwise.

The sashes weren't particular to Miss America (Southern girls had worn state-specific sashes in monument-dedication ceremonies as early as 1908), but they were highly symbolic at that historic moment: suffragettes, for whom pageantry was a powerful vehicle for activism, had worn them in marches beginning with the historic 1913 Woman Suffrage Procession in Washington. ("Through pageantry," wrote Hazel MacKaye, the feminist who pioneered the sashes as a tool of the cause, "we women can set forth our ideals and aspirations more graphically than any other way.") The sashes conveyed solidarity with the National Women's Party through their colors (purple, white, and gold) and their motto, "Votes for Women." By contrast, the beauty pageant sashes expressed local affiliation and individual aspiration. This contest was not about women. It was about Woman.

It was also part of a growing reactionary impulse. In the 1920s, as Susan Faludi explains in *Backlash: The Undeclared War Against American Women*, a counterassault on feminism was already under way: "The media maligned suffragists; magazine writers advised that feminism was 'destructive of woman's happiness'; popular novels attacked 'career women'; clergymen railed against 'the evils of woman's revolt'; scholars charged feminism with fueling divorce and infertility; and doctors claimed that birth control was causing 'an increase in insanity, tuberculosis, Bright's disease, diabetes, and cancer.'" Miss America championed sweet, traditional femininity just when women could see beyond husband-hunting as their only down payment on a future.

Beauty pageants had always reinforced traditional gender roles. In the United States, they dated back to colonial-era adaptations of medieval rituals and May Day celebrations, which endured into the early twentieth century, affirming both women's fertility and community regeneration. Tournaments that included recreations of medieval jousts, where winners chose a queen, were especially popular in the South before the Civil War, using the trope of anointed royalty: she didn't earn her beauty—she was born with it. But the Southern queens were generally married, underscoring the moral and domestic virtues of a mature, experienced ideal womanhood that was, on one level, earned.

P. T. Barnum lowered the bar in 1854 by opening a beauty competition to the masses in what the historian Lois W. Banner has called "the first modern beauty contest." Submitting oneself, in person, to be inspected and evaluated by men was different from being chosen as a beauty by a community—and invited unsavory associations. When Barnum's contest drew entrants "of questionable reputation," he changed the format so that they could avoid appearing in person by sending daguerreotypes from which their portraits would be painted and hung in a gallery, where visitors could vote on them. It was an ingenious repackaging of pop culture as high art.

But the first in-person beauty pageant, as we know it, preceded Miss America by four decades. The 1880 Miss United States contest at Rehoboth Beach, Delaware, was inspired by the same marketing logic that drove Atlantic City businessmen to launch their competition. The judging, based on face, feet, hands, hair, poise, and "costume" (an expensive gown), lasted a week, and the panel consisted of a Delaware Supreme Court judge, a French diplomat, and—go figure—Thomas Edison. The winner, Myrtle Meriwether of Pennsylvania, nearly fainted when she was named "the most beautiful unmarried woman in our nation." She won a gilded plaque and a bridal trousseau. But she was less euphoric the following day, when she faced a conundrum common to so many pageant hopefuls who spend to win: she had to sell her brocade dress to pay for her ticket home, where she was promptly forgotten. The event, the organizers concluded, hadn't been lucrative enough to repeat.

The outstanding success of Atlantic City's first contest hinged on three factors: the terrific growth and class diversity of its resort culture (train travel allowed for day-trippers on a budget, boarding houses served middle-class vacationers, and the wealthy summered in lavish hotels); the relaxation of Victorian fashion restrictions, which led to the acceptance of women's public swimming; and the birth of the "bathing beauty," which filmmaker Mack Sennett popularized in his slapstick comedies beginning in 1915.

As Banner explains, Sennett's Keystone Kops films both exploited the newly visible female body and defused its sexual dangers by presenting it in comical situations. (Police officers at the early Miss America contests even dressed as Keystone Kops.) Sennett claimed to have invented the bathing beauty. So, more legitimately, did Annette Kellerman, who made his films possible by creating the swimsuit in which they cavorted, and whose fame as a swimmer led to a successful vaudeville and silent film career in which her (sometimes fully naked) physique was the focus. Kellerman's celebration of the "supple body, well groomed and well dressed," was consonant with the pageant's; her 1918 book *Physical Beauty: How to*

Keep It offered beauty advice and promoted body-positivity—both for women's own self-esteem and as a means of getting and keeping a husband. (Swimming, she noted, expanded the chest.)

There was also an unspoken motivation for a national beauty competition: eugenics. The momentum of the American eugenics movement of the early twentieth century had inspired Better Baby contests, which applied the principles of evaluating livestock to children and led to Fitter Family contests nationally, the first of which was held at the 1920 Kansas State Fair. Competing clans were graded on their physical and psychological health and—significantly—heredity, in the name of "better breeding" and building larger families as urbanization shrank American farm communities and immigration complexified national idenity. Miss America concentrated the focus: what better way to gauge national fitness than through a contest measuring the quality of the breeders themselves—healthy, young unmarried white women? In the early years, contestants were even introduced with recitations of their genealogical history and "breeding," tracing their pedigree back for generations.

Beauty contests shored up gender difference not just in response to immigration and urbanization, but also to accommodate changing visions of masculinity in the face of women's progress. As historian George Chauncey explains, in the early nineteenth century, adult masculinity was defined in opposition to boys. Late in the century, as women gained power and "the boundaries between men's and women's spheres seemed to blur, many men also tried to reinforce those boundaries by reconstructing their bodies in ways that would heighten their physical differences from women." Bodybuilding and prizefighting, for example, allowed them to flex the muscle they felt they were losing in other aspects of their lives. Pageantry did the opposite, foregrounding femininity and exalting potential wives and mothers.

The introduction of the bathing suit into a beauty contest, however, required a delicate dance of decorum that the Miss America pageant never perfected, though it tried for nearly 100 years. In the 1920s, this meant harnessing the physical freedom of the New Woman while shrouding her in Victorian propriety *and* presenting her as the girl next door. Before bathing beauty contests, the only cultural precedent for the live, public display of semi-nude women was the burlesque show, from which the pageant borrowed its unison formation and (later) its runway—a feature the famous Minsky brothers added to their burlesque performances in the late 1910s so that as the women moved, howling audiences could "look right up their legs." The Minskys also claimed credit for staging the first striptease in 1917.

Florenz Ziegfeld Jr. uplifted burlesque through his Ziegfeld Follies (whose fifteenth season opened in Atlantic City in the summer of 1921) by wrapping his dancers in the European sophistication of the Folies Bergère and ensuring that they titillated without transgressing. Like the Miss America contestants, they were native born, ensuring an ethno-feminine ideal in the wake of the third wave of immigration, which had delivered some 20 million Europeans to American shores before and after the turn of the century.

While women forged ahead in other corners of culture, the pageant held fast to the past, redressing a simmering anxiety about newly empowered women and their impact. Women had worked during World War I, had won the vote, had entered business and politics; by 1921, thirty-three women were serving in state legislatures. The first birth control clinic in the U.S. had opened in Brooklyn in 1916—a huge step for women's self-determination. A year later, women were admitted as medical students at Columbia University. By 1920, female lawyers could practice in every state.

But women weren't just seizing opportunities previously denied them. They were also claiming cultural space historically identified with men: Bessie Coleman, bypassing obstacles preventing women and African Americans from getting pilot's licenses, trained in France and caused a media sensation when she returned with her license to launch a career as a stunt pilot in the 1920s. In 1921, Edith Wharton became the first woman to win a Pulitzer Prize for the Novel—one of five women to claim the award during that decade. Film stars like Clara Bow and Colleen Moore were playing characters who not only enjoyed independence, but also expressed erotic desire, as did blues singers such as Ma Rainey and Bessie Smith. As the film historian Gaylyn Studlar writes, in "actively seeking sexual pleasure, American women of the 1920s were widely believed to be usurping a male prerogative more powerful and precious than the vote." By rewarding girlish women who posed no threat to men, the pageant pushed back.

————

THE TITLE "MISS AMERICA" WASN'T formally used until 1922, when Gorman returned to compete again but could no longer be identified as Miss Washington D.C. That year, newspapers in every Eastern city were invited to send contestants, drawing fifty-eight— ten from New York alone. The 1921 Atlantic City Pageant had been such a success—for the city, the railroad, the hotels, the sponsoring newspapers, and the local merchants—that the budget was nearly doubled in 1922 and the event was extended to three days, with the beauty contest as its centerpiece.

The weekend opened with screaming sirens and booming cannons as Neptune emerged, once again, with his court from the sea, where Gorman met him. He bowed to her as a new crop of mermaids, all Atlantic City locals, shimmied behind him, tossing scentless flowers as he sniffed the air to safeguard against hazardous rogue perfumes. Gorman, designated Queen of the Pageant, wore a flimsy Lady Liberty crown studded with fake pearls, a silver and green gown reflecting the colors of the sea, and a flag as her coronation robe; its stripes rippled in the wind when she extended her arms to her cheering fans.

That year, a bit of showmanship and slapstick crept into the festivities. Four New York City beauties arrived by sea plane, releasing a banner reading HELLOW, ATLANTIC CITY, HERE IS NEW YORK before jumping in the water and swimming ashore. Miss Reading (Pennsylvania) swanned around in a mask, boasting that she had a different one for every outfit she'd brought and claiming no one would see her face until the judging. Miss Indianapolis entered the boardwalk parade in a state-themed rolling chair designed to look like an ear of corn.

The beauty contest now included elimination rounds in which finalists in each section were judged against Gorman. On the pier where the contenders were evaluated in evening gowns and "afternoon dress," *The New York Times* reported, the public "fairly rocked the great structure with its demonstration, in which Gorman appeared to be a favorite." But this year, the popular vote (by cheering) was eliminated, making the judges sole arbiters. Christy had returned, joined now by a graphic designer, a photographer, three other illustrators, and the celebrated artist Norman Rockwell.

Though he had come to appraise the shapely young beauties, Rockwell was battling his own body image problem: he was a lanky six feet tall and just twenty-eight, but his incipient pot belly was a growing source of embarrassment. When he and his fellow judges took a dip in the ocean, the contestants gathered around to heckle and laugh at them in a show of attitude that would be unimaginable today. "You're judging *us*?" they asked. "Look at yourselves. Old crows and bean poles."

Rockwell blushed, sinking into the water to hide his belly, and later that day visited a corset shop where he'd seen a sign reading GENTLEMEN ACCOMMODATED. There he faced further humiliation, eliciting titters from female shoppers as he discussed his purchase with the owner, who answered his hushed questions at theatrical volume: "A *corset*?" "Weeeeel, pink or baby blue?" The artist wore his new corset out of the store and admired his svelte reflection in a shop window, but later, talking to a friend, he saw the man was looking down in astonishment at two pink silk laces that had slipped below the hem of his shirt. "Oh my gosh," Rockwell exclaimed, clasping his stomach and running back to his hotel, where he peeled off the corset and threw it in the trash.

In *Norman Rockwell: My Adventures as an Illustrator*, Rockwell offers a rare look at the contest's free-form early years. The judging was still informal; the women socialized with the judges over lunch as bystanders came and went. (At one point, the world heavyweight boxing champion, Jack Dempsey, on vacation in Atlantic City, strolled in and pulled up a chair.) The artist-judges, many known for their magazine illustrations of elegant women, were enlisted not just to impart their professional wisdom about female beauty, but also to confer class on the spectacle, framing it as a formal aesthetic exercise, just as Barnum had attempted with his 1854 contest. (His recruitment ad, written in expertly coded Barnumese, claimed it would inspire "a more popular taste for the fine arts, stimulate to extra exertion the genius of our Painters, and laudably gratify the public curiosity.")

And so the judges were fed caviar, crepes, and sturgeon, plied with champagne, and assigned chauffeurs. The men, all well-known public figures, brought star power to the event: James Montgomery Flagg had created the Uncle Sam recruitment poster; Coles Phillips, a cover artist for *Life* magazine, was known for his sophisticated fade-away technique. They were given no guidelines for picking a winner. "Just *judge* it," the Chamber of Commerce instructed, so they talked it out and agreed on someone who looked gorgeous in her evening dress. But when they saw her the next day in her bathing suit, they noticed she was knock-kneed.

One of the artists proposed assigning numerical values to facial features—eyes, noses, lips—and body parts—legs, shoulders, necks—then adding up the scores to select a winner. But the point system failed. "A girl might not have anything wrong with her features or figure and so receive a very high score," wrote Rockwell. "But then she might not have anything right either. Individually her features were lovely, but put together they left one cold or bored. We found you can't judge a woman's beauty piecemeal; you have to take the whole woman at once."

They ended up voting on impulse, choosing Mary Katherine Campbell, a hazel-eyed brunette with adorable dimples, barely sixteen years old, from Columbus, Ohio, who was hoisted on the shoulders of the mermaid court and paraded around the ballroom. The decision, said Rockwell, incited the jealous wrath of the other contestants' disappointed mothers, including one who looked "like an enraged lizard," according to one judge. Campbell, the daughter of a CPA, had studied French, played Bianca in a high school production of *The Taming of the Shrew*, enjoyed writing, drawing, tennis, golf, and fishing with her grandfather, and could cook a very fine dish of ham and cabbage. When she'd learned at school she'd been chosen as Miss Columbus because of her figure, she went home and asked, "Mother, what's a figure?"

"That's none of your business," her mother snapped.

Unlike Gorman, Campbell had an athletic build and stood at a more commanding five feet six, weighing 125 pounds. Like Gorman, she wore her hair long and eschewed makeup. In one of her first interviews after winning, battling a cold and holding a thermometer, flanked by her mother and her doctor at the Waldorf Hotel, she announced, "I don't use cosmetics." She explained that she never had, because "I don't need them." It was a political statement. Wholesome girls didn't. (*The New Yorker* magazine drolly reported on her subsequent appearance in a full-page ad for "a certain tonic" and quipped, "If Miss America comes to Atlantic City proclaiming that she never used cosmetics in her life and in future months subscribes her testimonial to a cosmetic ad, be lenient with her, girls. She has but a brief while to gather the berries.")

Hair, too, was a political matter. When the judges noticed that the vast majority of Inter-City Beauties had "natural" (not bobbed) hair, they concluded that the contestants had been chosen with "loaded dice." They certainly didn't resemble the women dancing on the pier at the pageant ball—"piquant jazz babies, who shook the meanest kind of shoulders," according to *The Atlantic City Daily Press*. A *New York Times* editorial agreed, lamenting that "bobbed hair disqualifies or handicaps its wearers. Our enthusiastic feminists . . . ought to have something to say about this obvious attempt to restore the double standard."

Bobbed hair and makeup were two emblems of women's new liberty, which the emerging hairdressing and cosmetics industries enabled. For women who danced, who swam, who played sports and rode bikes, who studied, who worked as nurses or cooks, who zipped around in automobiles with wind in their hair, bobbing was a practical choice. For women who wore the new streamlined fashions, with clean lines and drop waists, it made more aesthetic sense than billowing tresses. The celebrity soprano and actress Mary

Garden, who bobbed her hair in 1921 at age forty-seven, called long hair "one of the many little shackles that women have cast aside in their passage to freedom."

The contest's bias toward tradition was not just a default embrace of the familiar; it was also key to the paradoxical essence of the exercise: exploiting women's bodies while suppressing their sexual and physical power, a double standard best dramatized when a contestant was arrested on the beach for wearing the swimsuit she'd competed in the day before.

Campbell competed again the following year and won, beating more than seventy girls and women and becoming the only queen ever to be crowned twice. By 1924, the pageant was a national event, running for five frenetic days and drawing entrants from cities west of the Mississippi. Governors, mayors, and a senator attended. Even President Harding, a notorious womanizer, vacationing with his wife in Atlantic City, had formally greeted Gorman and—creepily—held her hand for a meaningful moment. But some Christian and women's groups were already intent on axing it. The New Jersey State Federation of Women's Clubs condemned beauty pageants as "detrimental to the morality and modesty of our young women," inviting seventy-five organizations in nearby states to do the same. "The girls are exposed to grave dangers from unscrupulous persons," their statement read, "and the shocking costumes which such contests encourage certainly call for protests."

Ratifying the view that the pageant filled contestants' heads with "vicious ideas," the eighty-four beauties who competed in 1924 were slicker in their self-presentation, especially the four New Yorkers, who, *The New York Times* said, "seemed to have been well primed for the long series of poses and parades" they appeared in that week. Miss St. Louis, a crowd-pleaser that year as well as the previous one, had her dimples insured by Lloyd's of London for $100,000 and distributed fans bearing her photo, identifying her as the "Popular Favorite."

Because the 1923 Miss Brooklyn had turned out to be Mrs. Everett Barnes, the wife of a professional baseball player, a new rule now forbade married women from entering, but Miss Boston had missed the memo and, faced with disqualification, cried in her hotel room with her seven-month-old son while her husband, a lawyer, threatened a lawsuit, and the rule was relaxed.

The need for clearer guidelines was further highlighted when Helmar Liederman, Miss Alaska, a vivacious favorite in white—swimsuit, stockings, and jazzy tam—was exposed as a married New Yorker who had immigrated from Sweden a year earlier and spent all of three days in Juneau. One newspaper reported that she'd "made the long journey from her native town by dog sledding, hiking and automobiling." Known as the "Arctic Venus," she and her grifter husband had posed as a brother-sister team at other beauty contests.

Liederman made national headlines by filing a $150,000 lawsuit against the pageant for barring her from it, spelling out the damages in exquisite detail: "My worth in future beauty contests was reduced tremendously thereby. For you can deplore the fact all you wish, but marriage certainly hurts a girl who wishes to appear before the public . . . To the American public there is no romance, no zest, no mystery to the married woman. Her eyes are opened; her case is decided. She is as flat as a blown out tire, as tame as a dish of rice and milk. She is like a story read several times, all discovered and finished." Which was exactly why married women were forbidden from competing in the first place.

The 1924 parade included thirty bands, a cohort of weary Civil War vets in faded blue uniforms, and floats propelled by great sums of money—but not, evidently, enough for eighteen-year-old Ruth

Malcomson, Miss Philadelphia, who balked at the shabby—though mammoth—contraption she was expected to ride, dressed as Betsy Ross, with a court of honor packed with girls costumed as Quakers. She surveyed the fake fireplace and spinning wheel installed on a flatbed truck and broke down in hysterics, crying until a doctor was called to calm her into compliance.

Once aboard, Malcomson was hugely popular both for her looks and as a Philadelphia candidate—second only to Atlantic City nominees in whipping up local enthusiasm. She handily took three preliminary awards, but the Miss America title was harder won. The judges mulled over the five finalists for four hours on a night so hot that four women fainted. Philadelphia's mayor lost patience and took off for a theater across the boardwalk, asking to be alerted if his girl prevailed. Finally, Campbell, a return competitor and finalist, was asked to step forward and stood quaking at the prospect of a third victory. She was stilled when a thunderous voice announced Philadelphia was the winner, and the band broke into the national anthem. Wearing a knee-length tunic and gladiator sandals, Neptune crowned Malcomson, and Campbell kissed her, whispering, "You have been my choice."

Malcomson was five feet six, with delicate lips, melancholy blue eyes, and auburn hair, worn natural—a strategic choice, considering the previous year she'd sported a bob and lost. One reporter described her as "a startling combination of athletic prowess and femininity." She was a sprinter, gymnast, swimmer, and baseball player who, the boys in her neighborhood said, could throw a ball "as straight as a bullet and play any position on the team." She was *sort of* interested in a film career but considered herself a "home girl" who loved singing in her church choir and wanted to keep playing ball with her friends, who knew her as Rufus. She'd shrewdly worked the pageant to her own advantage—growing out her hair to win and grandstanding over the hokey float—but her ambition, it seemed, ended with the title.

Frank Deford, who wrote a 1971 history of the pageant, *There She Is: The Life and Times of Miss America*, deemed Malcomson, Campbell, and Gorman early prototypes of one enduring kind of winner, "generally a shy woman, with no sustaining interest in pageants or any other form of publicity; but for this one incidental burst of fame, she is never again in the public eye." Gorman had gone home to be feted in D.C., then forgotten; Campbell worked in theater for eight months, went to college, then dropped out to care for her father after her mother's death. Malcomson did a bit of modeling but rejected stage and movie offers; she visited hospitals and church bazaars in Philadelphia during her reign, then married and largely faded into obscurity.

But on one subject, she was no wallflower: the following year she refused to return to crown Miss America 1925 because of the influx of professional beauties using the pageant as a career stepping stone. "What chance has an ordinary girl," she asked, "untrained, to win a contest in which girls who have been trained to make the most of their beauty are competing?" She was especially irked by two New York showgirls, one of whose employers was a pageant judge.

Confirming Malcomson's allegations, the 1925 contestants were asked to sign a contract promising that if they won, they would appear in a film produced by Famous Players-Lasky Corporation (later Paramount Pictures). Shortly before the contest, Miss Pittsburgh backed out, declaring, "This whole thing reeks of commercialism." But the others had no objection, least of all the winner, Fay Lanphier, Miss California, who landed a leading role in a comedy-romance called *The American Venus*. In a case of art imitating life, Lanphier played an aspiring beauty queen.

Though she was toasted by Will Rogers and Rudolph Valentino

and appeared in a Laurel and Hardy film, Lanphier's acting career never lifted off. By 1927 she was running a beauty parlor, and in 1934 she described herself as a housewife. Deford dubbed her a second Miss America prototype: the Hollywood dreamer—whose dreams were almost always dashed. More losers, it seemed, made it in Hollywood in the 1920s than winners: Georgia Hale (Miss Chicago 1922) costarred in Charlie Chaplin's *The Gold Rush*; Adrienne Dore (Miss Los Angeles 1925, second runner-up to Lanphier) signed a five-year contract with Universal Pictures; Joan Blondell (Miss Dallas 1926) starred in films with James Cagney.

Lanphier, nineteen, was the first winner to represent a state, the first from the West, the first to appear in a feature film, the first whose win was broadcast on live radio, and the first to wear a bob. She was also the first to be crowned with something that looked more like metal than cardboard, as the crown evolved from a headband evoking Lady Liberty to a coronet connoting royalty. A secretary from Oakland, she had lost ten pounds since placing third in 1924 and was yet the heaviest of the bunch, at 130. But her crown was quickly tarnished; later that year, in an extraordinary lapse of judgment as the one veteran pageant judge, Christy unveiled a nude sculpture called "Miss America 1925," eliciting whispers that she had posed naked for it, which she hadn't. That fall, tabloid rumors swirled that the pageant was fixed and Famous Players-Lasky had chosen Lanphier as their star before the competition began.

Film contracts were just one element of the creeping commercialism of 1925. Miss Chicago scandalized the crowd by posting an ad for a powder puff on her rolling chair, prompting onlookers to yell, "How much are you getting for that?" Ads for a railroad and a telegraph company also appeared. "It had never been done just that way in previous years," *The New York Times* explained, "but there had been rumors that the contestants weren't all that altruistic." In fact, they'd never been altruistic at all: they competed to win prizes, careers, recognition, or husbands.

Recognizing that the contest was corroding Atlantic City's image (already damaged because of open gambling in its pool halls, along with the heroic volume of alcohol it was bootlegging—nearly 40 percent of the entire nation's supply), Mayor Bader supported terminating it. But instead of giving in to the opposition, the committee tried to bring the pageant to heel. New rules for 1926 said the beauties couldn't be married, divorced, or widowed; couldn't be professionals (including stage and screen performers and artists' models); must be over sixteen and under twenty-five; and couldn't have competed previously. Seventy-three women entered, fifteen judges were recruited, and still everything went wrong.

When the "Beauty Train" arrived from Philadelphia with its cargo of contestants, the bands played, the crowds cheered, and the welcoming party hoisted the flag, but the rope broke and Old Glory went crashing to the ground. Stormy weather prevented King Neptune (now played by comic actor DeWolf Hopper) from arriving by sea. Returning champion Lanphier suffered "a slight nervous breakdown" after the introductory formalities at City Hall, repeatedly bursting into tears at the luncheon in her honor. A *New York Times* headline offered an apt metaphor for the troubled mermaid pageant: RULER OF THE SEA FINDS WATER TOO UNRULY.

The judges again wrestled with their decision. (*The New Yorker* cracked, "It's becoming hard now to find a beauty queen, which may or may not be a comment on the types of pulchritude at hand.") The vote went to Norma Smallwood, Miss Tulsa, an eighteen-year-old who was part Cherokee, an oversight of yet another unspoken pageant rule that would later be formalized: contestants had to be white. In fact, the previous year, in response to Miss America's blatant segregation, a black beauty pageant had materialized. Sponsored by the African American press and modeled on Miss America (sans swimsuits), the National Golden Brown Beauty Contest was also held in Atlantic City, where thirty-two state nominees received diamond rings and the winner, Josephine Leggett of Louisiana, was awarded a new car. The founder, Madame Mamie Hightower of the Golden Brown Chemical Company, purveyor of cosmetics for black women, appeared to be a pioneer in the spirit of Madam C. J. Walker and claimed to be promoting racial pride through her pageant. But there was something rotten at its core: Golden Brown sold skin bleach, the winners were mostly light-skinned, and Hightower turned out to be a fictional character created by the white owner of the company.

Smallwood's Cherokee heritage wasn't mentioned, but in a spasm of recognition that Native Americans might bear some relevance to American beauty (and with a nod, perhaps, to the 1924 Indian Citizenship Act), the pageant committee installed Okanogan beauty queen Jessie Jim in Neptune's coronation court as a "guest of honor." Wearing family heirloom buckskin and beads, she functioned as an ethnic analogue to the royalty on display—or merely added a note of novelty. Earlier that month, nineteen-year-old Jim had been crowned Princess America II at the second annual National Indian Congress in Spokane, Washington. Her father, Long Jim, a chief forced to leave his ancestral land on Lake Chelan in Washington for a reservation, was still fighting for his family's return.

Back then, contestants cried with disappointment, not joy. After losing 7–8 in a face-off with Smallwood, Miss Washington D.C. wept backstage while fans cheered the winner in the ballroom. "Tears trembled on her lashes," reported the United Press, and "her mouth jerked with the effort to smile and take the blow standing." Smallwood, who had graduated from high school at a precocious sixteen, was a student at Oklahoma State College for Women, where she studied art. She rode horses, played hockey, swam, loved painting and music, and wanted to be an artist. She was chosen for "her beauty, intelligence and personality," but newspaper reporters didn't concern themselves with much beyond her marriageability and her measurements, which one syndicated article described in demented detail, from "her well molded throat, which is 12 inches in circumference," to her "normal 33-inch bust."

"What kind of man would suit her?" she was asked. She ventured a description, then added, poignantly, "But it's silly to talk about. I'm a day dreamer—most girls are. But dreams hardly even come true. I guess in our hearts we know they won't."

While she lounged in her presidential suite at the Traymore Hotel after the crowning, Smallwood received three fraternity pins, stage and film contracts, an offer of a cook stove, and a marriage proposal from a college professor who had seen her photo in the paper. She accepted the cook stove on the logic that "cook stoves are sometimes essential." A husband, by contrast, was "not absolutely essential just now." She had other ideas, and they didn't involve domesticity.

Smallwood was the first college student to win and the first to go out on a full sponsorship year as a spokesperson. Her crowning may have been a victory for traditional womanhood (she wore her hair neatly braided in buns at her ears, and the United Press called her "a type entirely apart from the bobbed haired, boyish flapper"), but she was set on getting paid in money, not marriage, and shrewdly parlayed her banquet appearances and product endorsements into a reported $60,000, which, if true, meant she earned more than Babe Ruth that year. And that wasn't all. The next year, when she returned to crown her successor, she demanded $1,200 for her services. When her fee was rejected, she grabbed her mother and left town in a huff.

That year, the pageant committee had invited another Princess America from Spokane, Alice Garry, who substituted for Smallwood during the formalities. Raised on the Coeur D'Alene reservation, Garry had won her title in 1925. She was the great-granddaughter of Chief Spokane Garry, and sister of Joseph R. Garry, who became the first Native American state senator in Idaho. Garry carried a beaded bag, one reporter noted, "that would be the envy of any flapper," and laughed when she was told some of the beauties didn't swim. "What for, then," she asked, "are they bathing beauties?" She arrived on the Beauty Train with the others and led the parade in place of Smallwood, saying she was "thrilled to the eyebrows" to serve as the guest of honor. But her role was purely ceremonial, subservient, and likely subsidiary. After the pageant, she went to Washington for more important business: meeting President Coolidge, commerce secretary Herbert Hoover, and the Commissioner of Indian Affairs.

By now, the judges were wary of setting off another firecracker like Smallwood. So in 1927, after eliminating the women wearing bobs, makeup, gold teeth, and plucked eyebrows (and measuring the contestants themselves), they settled on Lois Delander, Miss Illinois, a demure sixteen-year-old blue-eyed blonde who had won a medal for reciting Bible verses. Delander assured reporters she didn't smoke, drink tea or coffee, or, for that matter, eat pickles. Like Smallwood, she was set on becoming an artist. She said she had no interest in performing and would not accept professional contracts because "I want to become a great artist. I want to draw, to make a name for myself, to be somebody in this world." (The statement is remarkable in light of the few women artists who actually *were* "somebody in this world." Around this time, the pioneering abstract expressionist Lee Krasner had resorted to sneaking into a classroom at the National Academy of Design reserved for men.)

A few weeks later, the United Press ran a photo spread called "Miss America is 'a Great Help About the House,'" showing her back home in Joliet, Illinois, with her mother, "handling household weapons" like a dust rag and a vacuum cleaner. That fall, Delander hit the vaudeville circuit and performed with the young Bob Hope, but she didn't like it, so she returned to high school, became a sales-girl, married, then vanished from public life. Hers was a classic case of pageant whiplash: she was pushed by her ballet teacher to compete, dumbfounded that she won, and confused when, at sixteen, she was expected to enter vaudeville merely because she was pretty.

Even before Delander took the crown, the Atlantic City Hotel Men's Association was debating ending or suspending the lavishly produced pageant. Careerism was one concern: "There has been an epidemic recently," one member explained, "of women who seek personal aggrandizement and publicity by participating in various stunts throughout the world, and the hotelmen feel that in recent years that type of women [sic] has been attracted to the pageant in ever-increasing numbers." Another grumbled, "Many of the girls who come here turn out bad later and though it may happen in other cities, it reflects on Atlantic City."

More significantly, the pageant attracted a low-class "Coney Island crowd" and exploited women. The latter charge was echoed by an unexpected critic: the legendary actress Mae West, whose first published play, *Sex*, had landed her in prison in 1927 for "corrupting the morals of youth." That fall, her drama *The Wicked Age* opened in Manhattan with a live jazz band. It was, she wrote, "an exposé of the bathing beauty contests of the 1920s—the Miss Americas, crooked contests, and fixed winners."

West starred as a flapper named Babe who pulls strings to get the pageant rigged for her. When she wins, she develops a huge ego and a devastating coke habit. The play not only blasts the corrupt national pageant industry and the businessmen who ran it but also mocks the women who submitted to it—presumably without West's sexual self-awareness or business smarts. Lobbying for launching a seaside New Jersey beauty contest, one character declares, "The basis of any industry that needs immediate attention of the public for success today is based on the exploitation of the female form ... everything is an excuse for a horde of almost naked women to parade up and down the stage."

And so Miss America got shelved before anyone had ever really defined what she signified. What was American beauty in a nation of immigrants, and how did it benefit the women who won? Throughout the pageant's history, people—specifically men—made vacuous pronouncements about it. In 1922, Samuel Gompers, the conservative head of the American Federation of Labor, proclaimed, ridiculously, that tiny, elfin, seventeen-year-old Margaret Gorman "represents the type of womanhood America needs—strong, red-blooded, able to shoulder the responsibilities of home-making and motherhood. It is in her type that the hope of the country resides."

William G. Kreighoff, a 1926 pageant judge, imagined Miss America as "a girl of balance and mentality, who has ambitions to marry and have a flock of kids." Illustrator Haskell Coffin, who painted Lanphier after her win, believed the queen should be a "dainty girl of temperament, delicacy, and charm—a home-loving, modest, effeminate, but healthy girl."

Character, beauty, body type, ambition—they all figured in the equation. But what was being calculated? Was Miss America merely the prettiest woman in America or a symbol of American womanhood? And by what measure was she, or could she be, symbolic?

Despite the pageant's patriotic trappings, from Gorman's Lady Liberty crown to Malcomson's Betsy Ross float, Miss America symbolized nothing beyond a few dozen men's fantasies about women's roles in post-suffrage society. The pageant was a marketing opportunity in need of a bigger purpose, which required articulating a national ideal against which young women could be gauged—something that proved challenging in this period of transition, which was saturated with ambivalence about women's progress. The coin of conventional beauty, the winners learned, was women's greatest currency; it purchased romance, often a husband, a short career, or a flicker of fame—but even that was brief. Gorman returned to watch the pageant just a few years after her win and moved through the crowds unrecognized. The best-case scenario for winners was the kind of fast fortune Smallwood squeezed out of it.

As Banner observes, although beauty contests "offered the possibility of social mobility to a few working class women, their primary purpose . . . was social discipline and not social advance." Though some of the early Miss Americas returned to great acclaim in their hometowns (Malcomson was late to her own wedding because of swarming crowds), the title was never professionally transformative, and not all savored it. Decades after her win, Campbell said, "I got so tired of the publicity, I didn't ever want to hear about Miss America again." Malcomson had no regrets but much later said winning the title "never affected my life." In 1980, Gorman, then a D.C. socialite who said life had been "extremely kind" to her, confessed, "I never cared to be Miss America. It wasn't my idea. I am so bored by it all. I really want to forget the whole thing."

But the contest wouldn't be dormant for long. When it was revived in 1935, the city officials who thought it had attracted insufficiently docile women could have no idea what new insurgencies lay ahead. Likewise, little Margaret Gorman, shooting marbles in the dirt that sultry summer day in 1921, couldn't have dreamed that the quest to define American womanhood, first played out on her body, would continue for nearly a century.

TWO

Dreamers

BEAUTIFUL FAY LANPHIER WAS SEATED in the lunch-
room of Paramount Pictures talking about the five years
since she'd been crowned Miss America 1925. She had not
become a star. She had married and divorced a millionaire. She
had opened and closed a beauty parlor. Now twenty-four, she was
working as a stenographer in the very studio that had signed her
after the pageant. And she had something extraordinary to say: she
was happy.

"Those days when I was 'Miss America'—they were nice in one
way, but I was never happy. Something was always bothering me,
causing me to worry," she told the reporter profiling her for *The
New Movie Magazine*, a popular gossip monthly. In fact, it was everything: her looks, her weight, her talent, her right to be in the
spotlight, her fear of letting people down, and her very worth as a

public figure. The studio hadn't wanted *her* for *The American Venus*; they had wanted Miss America.

"I wonder if you know what it means to be wanted not for yourself?" she asked. "How it feels to know that people are interested in you not because you are you, but because you are something?" It was a misgiving any celebrity might share, but she sharpened the point and aimed it at the very heart of the pageant. "Perhaps if that something is a real accomplishment on your part you can take pride in it and so feel all right. But I couldn't."

Crowned for her non-achievement, Lanphier felt unworthy of the attention. "*I* did not build myself," she explained. "I just happened to be like I am." Or *was*. She had since quit wearing makeup and had gained almost thirty pounds. "I suppose that a person dying of thirst would overdrink when he first got a tank full of water," she noted without remorse. "You'll never catch me getting the same ailments some of the girls who win beauty contests work themselves into. Fifteen pounds overweight is better than ten pounds underweight. So that is that."

Lanphier's frank allusion to pageant-inspired eating disorders was unusual in the early twentieth century. The problem became obvious in the fitness-crazed 1980s and '90s, when Miss Americas proudly described their starvation diets and kamikaze exercise regimens as if they were commendable, not crazy. Later, one honest ex, Kate Shindle (1998), affirmed that the pageant preparation had left her with both an eating disorder and a "massively unhealthy" exercise compulsion.

Thinness had defined the first wave of Miss Americas, who competed in a period when the corset was in decline and disciplining the body through dieting was on the rise. The Victorian paradigm of fleshy beauty had shifted as women became more physically active and fashion became less restrictive. In 1918, the first popular weight loss book, *Diet and Health, with Key to the Calories*, was published by Lulu Hunt Peters, a formerly fat doctor who offered a scientific method for slimming down: counting calories. She assured aspiring dieters that "fat individuals have always been considered a joke, but you are a joke no longer" and entreated women to ignore husbands who claimed they preferred zaftig women. The book was a bestseller from 1923 to 1927.

Like so many former beauty queens who gain weight, Lanphier was fat-shamed. She'd heard the whispers behind her back at work, but she didn't care, because with the pounds came relief from the pressure. "The prize," the reporter concluded, "was not worth the game." He added that she was still very pretty, and "a great part of that attractiveness was her perfect ease of manner," which set her apart from the flutteringly self-conscious women—even a few stars—he had spotted lunching on the Paramount lot that day.

The oldest of six children whose father died before the last was born, Lanphier entered her first beauty contest in Oakland, California, in an effort to improve her life as a secretary. She placed second, which didn't qualify her to compete statewide for Atlantic City, so she raced to San Francisco the next day to try there. But as she stood in the wings waiting to walk out and be judged, she was paralyzed with fear and plagued with self-doubt. She couldn't budge. The pageant host gave her a shove and told her to smile and keep moving. "Don't stand still out there. SMILE! Do you hear?"

She smiled and she won, qualifying for Miss America, which she lost in 1924, and to which she returned—thinner—to win in 1925. All that was fun. But then came the fashion shows and sponsorships and a sixteen-week stint demonstrating Underwood typewriters as Miss America and the inkling that she wasn't really the most beautiful girl in the United States, which was true—*no one* was. Soon after her *New Movie Magazine* interview, she married her childhood sweetheart, had two kids, and rarely made news again, except in articles about failed pageant winners.

Already, the media had launched a lasting practice of shooting down beauty queens, Miss Americas among them. Swimsuit pageants had sprung up all over the country, from copycat regional contests to Miss NRA. A 1924 article titled "Cursed by Their Fatal Gift of Beauty" ran down the "tragic misfortunes" high-profile winners had suffered. A 1931 piece announced, "Tragedy or Obscurity Comes to Beauty Queens; Disaster Follows Scores of Winners; None Has Made Good as Actress." Miss America winners were dismissed directly in a 1934 article that asked, "What Has Befallen the 6 Beauties Who Won the Title 'Miss America'?" It took three columns to explain: not much. Except, perhaps, Norma Smallwood, whose marriage to an oil millionaire ended with a fantastically sordid public divorce in which she lost custody of her daughter. Smallwood's husband alleged that she'd allowed their toddler to drink whiskey, had entertained men while he was away (earning her the media moniker "Mistress America"), and had taken a lover who not only slept in the couple's bed and hung his clothes in their closet, but also—the ultimate indignity—wore the oilman's pajamas.

It was this sort of press that had caused the pageant to disband in 1928. The city still hoped to reboot it, since the 1927 event had been a genuine financial success, and an epic $15 million convention center, covering seven acres—big enough to swallow Madison Square Garden in one bite—was slated to open by the end of the decade, promising whole new orders of extravagance. But the Depression delayed it until 1933, when the revamped pageant not only failed to restore order, command respect, make money, attract decent crowds, or even secure the support of the Hotel Men's Association, but actively plunged it deeper into disrepute, causing Miss

America 1933 to be snubbed for decades while pageant officials dis-avowed the rogue event.

She was Miss Connecticut, fifteen-year-old Marion Bergeron, a platinum blonde with a sheepish smile and an hourglass figure reflecting the fleshier ideal of the Depression era, as the reedy look of the flapper disappeared. Her typical day began at 6:00 a.m. when she milked ten cows. The daughter of a policeman, she'd won her first beauty pageant just weeks earlier after entering on a lark. Few of the thirty Miss America contestants that year were selected through newspaper nominations; most were sponsored by carni-vals and amusement parks, attracting a rougher and more desper-ate range of beauties, some of whom cried openly when they were bested during the elimination judging. Neptune did not sail forth from the sea; rather, the hopefuls debuted at something called the Evening Dinner Party on the arms of uniformed Morris Guards—volunteer militia members who squired the women around the room for the benefit of onlookers. This was the first mistake—no one likes a beauty queen with a man attached.

The Bathers' Revue moved from the beach indoors, opening with a parade led by twenty women in white swimsuits who rode bicycles ahead of the contestants, one of whom, as she passed the judges for inspection, keeled over and writhed around on the floor in pain from an abscessed tooth. The rolling chair parade also came indoors—the new Convention Hall and its $5,000 pipe or-gan had to be put to good use, though it broke down ten bars into the "Star-Spangled Banner," forcing the mailmen's band to step in. The finalists were trundled in on wicker rolling chairs and pushed around the aisles in what seemed more like bingo night in a retire-ment community than a beachside beauty contest. The contestants' ranks were thinning at an alarming rate: one dropped out to get an emergency appendectomy, three were disqualified for lying about their home states, one was outed as married, and one quit before the final judging, claiming the pageant was fixed. At fifteen, Bergeron *should* have been disqualified, but she hadn't mentioned her age, and no one asked.

The ten all-new judges included *New Yorker* illustrator Peter Arno, whose trailblazing one-panel cartoons skewered New York society, reserving special contempt for women, and *Life* illustrator Russell Patterson, whose leggy sophisticates had defined flapper fashion before it yielded, in the 1930s, to curvier silhouettes. They were joined by the Bronx-born Ziegfeld girl and Broadway actress Gladys Glad, herself the winner of a *Daily News* beauty contest. Her husband, theater columnist Mark Hellinger, covered the pageant, writing that "a funnier looking set of monkeys I never gazed upon in all my life. There are two or three cute ones among the group, but the rest are all depression Miss Americas." Seven had arrived exhausted after touring all summer, unpaid, in a vaudeville show called *The Pageant Beauties*, on the promise of new clothes and job offers in Atlantic City. "They have been conned before they start," wrote Hellinger, amazed that they'd signed contracts agreeing to work for free.

One day in their hotel lobby, Patterson and Arno were buttonholed by thugs sent by Nucky Johnson, who told them Nucky had chosen Miss New York to win. The men were outraged. "Look, that's the way we run the contest down here," one said, patting his chest where a pistol might be holstered.

"Or else?" Arno replied, pushing past them.

"Hey," Patterson suggested as the two men walked away, "let's cross them up altogether and pick a girl from out of left field. How about the little blonde from Connecticut?" He meant Bergeron.

Gladys Glad was already smitten with someone else, Miss Ohio; they'd even posed together for photos, and it seemed most of the judges preferred other contestants to Bergeron. But once it emerged that Nucky had bullied other judges as well, they all teamed up to fight corruption, agreeing to vote for Bergeron. Patterson claimed that many of the early Miss Americas were Nucky's picks; a City Hall employee had even told him Bergeron was the first honestly chosen winner he'd ever seen, which, if true, would make an illegally entered, underage Miss America the only legitimately crowned one thus far.

But the audience had been rooting for Miss Ohio, a nineteen-year-old nanny who'd flouted protocol by appearing at one of the official events in a white evening gown instead of the pageant-approved sportswear, endearing her to fans. The rowdy crowd hissed when Bergeron's victory was announced, and angry shouts rang out from the box seats reserved for city officials, presumably in Nucky's pocket as well. (According to Nelson Johnson's book *Boardwalk Empire*, by the mid-1920s, every Atlantic City employee top to bottom was beholden to Nucky.) Bergeron was backstage with no idea she'd won until she was told to pull a dress on over her swimsuit, slapped with a Miss America sash, and hustled out to take the crown, flanked by two runners-up who looked on with unhappy smiles. As the flashbulbs popped, said Bergeron, "I felt like I'd been hit with a stun gun."

Afterward, Hellinger interviewed Bergeron backstage as other reporters vied for her attention. "She is a nice kid, natural and unaffected," he wrote. "She probably doesn't know that this mantle she has inherited has never brought more than momentary happiness to any girl in the past." He asked about her ambitions; she told him she wanted to be a singer. In fact, she'd been singing blues on a local radio station since she was twelve.

"Be careful, honey," he told her. "You're in a tough racket now. Be wise in everything you do."

"Don't worry about me, Mr. Hellinger," Bergeron said with a dismissive wave. "I know what you mean. You're thinking of what has happened to other beauty winners. But don't worry about me. I'm—I'm different."

Bergeron won a lavish array of mostly age-inappropriate gifts: a Ford she was too young to drive, a diamond-studded watch, a trip to Bermuda, a piece of property on the Jersey Shore, and a fur coat. A screen-test offer vaporized when her age was revealed, but it was all good: unlike Lanphier, she got exactly what she wanted as Miss America. She began performing live when she turned sixteen, signed a record deal at seventeen, and was soon sailing through a career crooning with bandleaders Rudy Vallee, Guy Lombardo, and Gene Krupa.

Hellinger was entirely wrong about Bergeron. "If I hadn't been Miss America," she later told a reporter, "I would never have had a contract with CBS." And she liked carrying the title ("You're just a little bit special all the time," she said), even if her crown was stolen from her hotel room that night and her Catholic school kicked her out when she returned home, but especially after the organization finally rallied—in 1965—to reclaim their Depression queen, the most talented and successful in Miss America's short history.

———

NOT SURPRISINGLY, THE PAGEANT TOOK a powder in 1934. But the concept was pirated elsewhere, first in Madison Square Garden's "Queen of American Beauty" competition that year, then again in early 1935, when the San Diego Exposition staged a beauty contest in Balboa Park next to two midget attractions, naming a professional nudist, Florence Cubitt, "Miss America of the Midway." (When journalist Joseph Mitchell interviewed Cubitt a year later in a New York hotel room, she greeted him in her standard publicity attire: naked but for a blue G-string.) Nearby Wildwood, New Jersey, had even poached the title while it was dormant in 1932, throwing an "American Beauty Contest" and crowning the winner Miss America.

This wouldn't do; the brand had to be reclaimed. An Atlantic City publicist who still saw profit in the pageant persuaded his boss to strike a deal with the Variety Club of Philadelphia, a local chapter of a national charitable organization, to recast it in 1935 as the Showman's Variety Jubilee, drawing candidates through other Club sponsors nationally. This third rebirth involved a mastermind of a midwife: twenty-nine-year-old Lenora Slaughter, the only female beauty pageant director in the country. Slaughter had overseen the successful Festival of States Parade in St. Petersburg, Florida, an early spring event created to entice snowbirds to remain south a bit longer.

Slaughter was hired away on a temporary assignment with the blessing of her boss at the St. Petersburg Chamber of Commerce, who told her she should "go up there and show those Yankees how to do a *real* job with a pageant." So she did, and the following January, back in Florida, after her bid to become the Festival of States Parade chair was rejected, she quit, then headed to New Jersey for good. Slaughter spent the next thirty-one years in New Jersey, engineering the Miss America pageant, for the most part, as it survives today. She added a talent section, formal entry requirements, a coronation ceremony with evening gowns instead of bathing suits, a Miss Congeniality prize, and—most significantly—the scholarship program that endures as the pageant's greatest point of pride. "I didn't like having nothing but swimsuits," she said. "I had to get Atlantic City to understand that it couldn't just be a beauty contest."

Forceful, efficient, controlling, outspoken, censorious, sometimes terrifying, and often affectionate with her "girls," Slaughter was a tangle of contradictions. She pushed the women to make money while grooming them for matrimony (in 1970, she was still telling them "the most important thing in your lives will be your marriage"); she was socially conservative but kept her surname professionally after her own wedding in 1948; she was a Southern Baptist laboring to save the very leg show the Southern Baptist Convention, along with other religious groups, had condemned in the 1920s. Perhaps the one biographical fact that meshed with her mission was that, for lack of money, she had never finished college.

"She was extremely articulate and persuasive, and very determined," said lifelong board member Adrian Phillips. "She had an innate sense of diplomacy. But there was another side to Lenora. She could be really rough and tough if the situation called for it." Her polarities were perfectly calibrated: she could rumble with the big boys of Atlantic City, and if any women's clubbers were still exercised about seeing a bathing beauty pageant in their town, a proper Southern lady had come to reform it.

She began with the recruiting process. Slaughter learned that the pageant director, a huckster named George Tyson, was tapping women from amusement parks and fairs and making state contestants loiter in swimsuits outside the contest venues like prostitutes. "It was awful," she said. "I wanted to throw out all the cheap promotions. I said I believe I can get civic organizations to run the [feeder] pageants and we can get a better class of girl." That class explicitly excluded women of color. Sometime in the 1940s, after Slaughter had become executive director, the notorious Rule Seven surfaced, stating that contestants must be "in good health and of the white race." It stood until the 1950s.

In *Ain't I a Beauty Queen? Black Women, Beauty and the Politics of Race*, Maxine Leeds Craig traces black beauty pageants back to the 1890s, explaining that they served as "non-confrontational ways of expressing racial pride." There was no sustained push to integrate white contests, she says, until after World War II, with a watershed moment in 1948 when a black Brooklyn College student named Thelma Porter was named Miss Subways and her smiling face appeared on 9,000 subway posters throughout New York City. After that, black women competed in formerly white contests in the North, and sometimes even in the Deep South and Midwest. But neither that, nor the *Brown v. Board of Education* decision of 1954, nor the gale-force wind of the Black Power movement of the 1960s could move the Miss America pageant to integrate—until 1970.

Slaughter's racism targeted black women directly. In 1948, when the South Dakota Black Hills Indian Council pressed the issue by writing her to question the whites-only rule, she responded that they were welcome to compete, explaining, "We have eliminated the Negro from this contest due to the fact that it is absolutely impossible to judge fairly the beauty of the Negro race in comparison with the white race." Her claim that this was a matter of categorical fairness was a perfect inversion of the truth. Miss America's ideal was hierarchical, built on classifications of class and race that put black women at the bottom, drawing on centuries of prejudice that presumed they were ungroomed, unfashionable, socially unrefined, hypersexual, and, with declining segregation, a threat to white supremacy. Unlike newly arrived European immigrants or fully subordinated Native Americans, they were, in Slaughter's eyes, uniquely unassimilable. In fact, the pageant's first full Native American contestant, Mifaunwy Shunatona, an Otoe-Pawnee-Wyandot of Oklahoma, had broken the race barrier in 1941, before Rule Seven was added. (A year earlier, Ada Woods, a part Choctaw Oklahoman, had placed sixth.) Asians and Latinas were accepted before the rule was retired—in 1948, Chinese

American Yun Tau Chee, Miss Hawaii, competed, as did Miss Puerto Rico Irma Nydia Vázquez, upgrading Puerto Rico from "official guest" to contestant.

The 1935 pageant, now part of the Showman's Variety Jubilee's weeklong festival of sports, circus, fashion, and entertainment events, featured one of Slaughter's first adjustments: talent was now an option, though, thankfully, it wasn't judged. Slaughter believed a winner shouldn't just be pretty but admitted that "at least half of the girls would get out there on the Steel Pier and sing or dance or do something—badly." It would take a few years to perfect the format (three women sang the same song in 1938) and attract and reward more decorous contestants. Through the late 1930s, she used a whack-a-mole approach to controlling the obstreperous beauties, laying down new rules for each new infraction. And there were plenty: a new naked sculpture model; a pissed-off contestant, disqualified for wearing mascara, who held a press conference dubbing herself "The People's Choice" Miss America and set off on her own tour using the title; and the one who—literally—got away: Bette Cooper, the 1937 Miss America who wasn't.

A private high school junior from Hackettstown, New Jersey, Cooper had won an amusement park pageant that led her to Miss America. Though her parents were reluctant to let her compete in Atlantic City, they decided it would make a good vacation. Cooper didn't expect to win; more to the point, she didn't want to. She caught a cold and was sick all week in Atlantic City, her father said, from dieting and drinking only orange juice, and she was disappointed to discover that Miss America fans were "a couple of ticket-takers on a roller coaster, a barker or two, and a few hot dog vendors." One of the contestants was a stripper. That summer, Atlantic City was making national headlines because of a crackdown on prostitution.

There was one bright spot: Cooper's twenty-one-year-old pageant-appointed chauffeur was all class. The handsome, urbane son of a hotelman with his own cabin cruiser, Louis Off provided comfort as Cooper's anxiety about getting mixed up in the pageant mounted. They fell in love. The night she was crowned, she called him at 2:00 a.m. from her hotel room, desperate to get out of it. Off rushed over to find her—and her parents—crying. With their approval, he smuggled her out through a side door and the two sped away in his boat, leaving baffled pageant officials looking for her the next morning on Steel Pier, where she was expected for a photo shoot. By then Off had taken her home, where the blinds were drawn and the phone was unplugged. The most surreal pageant photo in Miss America history shows Cooper's runners-up posing gamely next to an empty throne draped with an ermine robe, the crown on its seat. It raced around front pages across the country.

Everyone had a position on Cooper's reason for quitting. Her father told reporters that not all that glitters is gold, referencing the Persian lamb coat she'd been promised, which turned out to be an offer to buy the coat at a discount. Plus, he said, "She's so young and we feel it's not proper to shove a kid into vaudeville."

Slaughter, spinning it just right, suggested love had made her girl bolt. In 1981, Off said he'd told her the day before she was crowned, "You realize, Bette, that if you become Miss America, I'm not going to be your Mister America. I'm not going to follow you around on your coattails."

Cooper cheerily told the press she just wanted to finish high school and wasn't ready for vaudeville, though she still considered herself Miss America and even directed a reporter to call her "queen." She said she was happy to have been chosen but didn't think it was sensible "to sacrifice my home life, my education, and all my girlfriends for it."

After much deliberation about whether to crown her runner-up, the pageant board let her keep the title. She modeled a bit and even made some appearances as Miss America, including with her successors, Marilyn Meseke and Patricia Donnelly, at the 1939 World's Fair. But she declined offers to join the Miss America alumnae "sorority" reunion at subsequent pageants, then renounced her affiliation altogether. She went to college, worked in public relations, and married, after which, until her death in 2017, she refused to discuss "the incident," meaning the pageant, ever again. When a journalist called to request an interview in 2000, she said, "There is no Miss America here."

The Cooper mutiny left Slaughter at an entrepreneurial impasse. She was just the kind of polished contestant the pageant wanted. (Off described her as "a very dignified person," who "couldn't stand cheapness. Even that little bit of leg that the pageant demanded at the time was not for her.") Slaughter needed to attract this kind of refinement, crown it, and keep it leashed. The solution: more rules. She set the minimum age at eighteen. Female chaperones were assigned to shadow contestants nonstop, day and night, to keep them out of trouble and protect them from exploitative "talent agents" who might try to rope them into shady deals. Even the chaperones had a chaperone: their manager was a well-known Quaker socialite married to the mayor, whom Slaughter described as "the Quakerest of the Quakers." ("Why, one time I went to see her," she said, "I was so scared I took off all my nail polish and lipstick.")

Then the rules got weirder. 1937: Contestants were banned from bars and nightclubs and couldn't be seen talking to any men all week—even their fathers (because how else to shield them from menacing men short of asking the dads to wear name tags?). 1938: Contestants had to be single, childless, and never married. Chastity became a lasting mandate for this perennial "Miss"; even today, she must be childless and unmarried. The restrictions simultaneously tamped down the erotic implications of women vamping in swimwear and sustained the impression that they were sexually available. It was as American as apple pie: cranking up interest in female sexuality while punishing women who acted on it.

Once the talent section was boosted to one third of the total score in 1938, the live show got better and the women's careers flew higher. That year, in a stroke of media savvy, Slaughter persuaded fashion features director Vyvyan Donner, one of the few successful female Hollywood directors, to do a short film highlighting the swimsuits, the parade, and the crowning of Marilyn Meseke, Miss Ohio. It ran on Movietone, a news service shown in theaters before feature films, reaching millions of people and pushing Miss America into the national consciousness. Donner would return as a judge in the 1940s.

By 1940, the pageant stood on solid financial footing, rebuilt with the support of civic groups and local businesses, refueled by endorsement deals, registered as a nonprofit corporation with a large board and bylaws, and officially named the Miss America pageant. Most of the contestants now represented states, as opposed to sometimes obscure regions. (Cooper had competed as Miss Bertrand Island, prompting her predecessor to ask, as she crowned her, where it was.) "We are past the time," Atlantic City mayor Charles D. White had declared—no doubt praying this was true—"when beauty parades are in the nature of floor shows. This is a cultural event seeking a high type of beauty."

In 1941, after butting heads with the board over a harebrained plan to stage the pageant on ice, Tyson stepped down and Slaughter was named executive director. Thus, the real queen ascended, carefully coiffed and manicured, to steer the pageant out of the dire straits of the Depression toward a bright future of decorum and substance. A week later, the Japanese bombed Pearl Harbor.

Atlantic City resort culture was utterly transformed during World War II. Nearly fifty resort hotels were converted to barracks and hospitals. The town was hit hard by labor shortages and rationing. Soldiers simulated attacks up and down the shoreline and snipers trained on rooftops, unnerving pedestrians below. In *The Last Good Time: Skinny D'Amato, the Notorious 500 Club, and the Rise and Fall of Atlantic City*, journalist Jonathan Van Meter describes what "The World's Playground" looked like by spring of 1942: "Because of its location between Delaware Bay and the New York Harbor, New Jersey had more commercial ships targeted by German U-boats off its coast than any other state along the shore. The beaches were awash in tarlike slicks of oil, and pieces of sunken ships began to wash up on the shore. The coast guard patrolled the boardwalk, and armed, mounted troops with dogs covered the beaches, on the lookout for spies attempting to come ashore from the U-boats." For the entire month of March, when Nazi submarines were feared to be prowling offshore, the city went dark: streetlights were snuffed, and the riot of electric signs on the boardwalk were unplugged.

But though the war strained the pageant's finances, it strengthened its patriotic underpinnings. After talk of suspending the event until peacetime, Slaughter persuaded city officials that it was "emblematic of the spirit of America" and should continue, even if that meant moving to the Warner Theater from 1942 to 1945, while Convention Hall, repurposed as "Camp Boardwalk," served the Army Air Forces.

The war presented not just a new way for the pageant to channel its patriotic aspirations, but also a fresh reason for showcasing

American beauty. As women entered factories and shipyards to fill servicemen's jobs—supplying 57 percent of the workforce by war's end—new assurances about American femininity were marshaled to allay fears about their unladylike new roles. The beauty industry expressed this through advertising; Miss America reified it through pageantry.

"This conundrum of glamour and grime, of Miss America and Rosie the Riveter, defines the America of 1941–45," writes the scholar Mary Anne Schofield. She cites a 1943 lipstick ad in *Ladies' Home Journal* as its crystallization: "For the first time in history," it read, "woman-power is a factor in war . . . It's a reflection of the free democratic way of life that you have succeeded in keeping your femininity—even though you are doing a man's work! . . . No lipstick—ours or anyone else's—will win the war. But it symbolizes one of the reasons why we are fighting . . . the precious right of women to be feminine and lovely—under any circumstances."

While Miss America was busy embodying the feminine and the lovely, she was also evolving into a boots-on-the-ground war worker, traveling with the United Service Organization (USO), which delivered entertainment to servicemen, and visiting hospitals and Red Cross canteens. In 1943, when the Chalfonte-Haddon Hall and the Traymore became Thomas M. England General Hospital, the largest amputee hospital in the world, contestants visited troops there. The soap manufacturer Lever Brothers Co. offered the pageant $5,000 and 1943 winner Jean Bartel $2,500 if she would go on a national tour with Slaughter selling war bonds to finance military operations. The War Finance Department approved it, and Bartel sold $2.5 million in bonds. One headline chirped, "Miss America Arrives to Smash Hearts, Banks" above an article listing Bartel's measurements from bust, waist, hips, and thigh to calf, ankle, neck, and arms. But 80 percent of her sales were made to women, cultivating a hefty new fan base.

Bartel was a terrifically popular, successful, and hardworking (though poorly paid) winner—the first to star in a Broadway musical, and one who helped dispel women's misgivings about beauty queens. "The fact that I approached them as their contemporary helped," she told Frank Deford. She's routinely misidentified as the first college student to win the title (that was Smallwood), but she *was* the first coed, and she faced the unhappy task of coping with relentless public surprise at the discovery that beautiful women could indeed be intelligent.

Bartel's successor, Venus Ramey, doubled her record, selling $5 million in bonds in 1944 and receiving a citation from the Treasury Department. She also inadvertently made Miss America a pinup. When a GI based in Foggia, Italy, wrote her asking for a signed photo, she complied; it was scaled up and painted on the nosecone of a B-17 that flew sixty-eight missions by men who named Ramey "the girl we'd most like to bail out with over a deserted Pacific isle."

Ramey, who became the first Miss America to run for office when she campaigned as a Democrat in the Kentucky House of Representatives in 1951, was no Miss America booster. She felt the pageant abandoned her after her win, when she was exploited by one of the dreaded talent agents Slaughter had hoped to deter through chaperones; he took Ramey to New York and deflected all her phone calls, including one from the prestigious William Morris Agency when it called to offer her a contract. She was still holding a grudge at seventy-nine, when she said, "They try to keep us hidden from the public when they get old and wrinkled like me." But she also wrote an unpublished article attesting to the power of the Miss America image during the war: "It wasn't Venus Ramey

that excited those boys, it was Miss America: a symbol of home ...
a reminder of decency, goodness, mercy, freedom, sanity from the
world where they were, gone mad."

Slaughter reflected on the pageant's achievements in her 1944
Board Report, saying that "if the war had not interfered, I am confident that we would have one of the smoothest running civic events
in America." Two major challenges remained. The first was finding
better regional hosts and sponsors. Despite having contacted every
Chamber of Commerce in the country (Slaughter was *that* thorough), the committee had been forced to approach skating rinks and
hotel ballrooms. She spelled out nine reasons her pitches to better
venues had been rejected. Most related to the war: a manpower
shortage, low interest because of wartime activities, and a dearth of
"girls" because they had enlisted, were doing defense work, or had
become war brides—wedded hastily before a serviceman's deploy-
ment or during his furlough. Changing mass media also weakened
PR interest; movie theaters were so packed they didn't need outside promotions, and newspaper advertising was shifting to radio,
thereby reducing available airtime for pageant ads.

Then there was reason number six: "Do not approve of beauty
pageants." Slaughter had a solution for that. The Jaycees (Junior
Chamber of Commerce) were a socially and politically conservative
national young men's leadership training organization. They could
convince local families that the pageant was an upstanding civic
exercise and sponsor it locally. "What better," Slaughter told Deford, "than to have the ideal men of America run a pageant for the
ideal women?" She'd already worked with a few of them to attract
Miss North Carolina and Miss Texas, with positive results. The
women had arrived "properly wardrobed," had "good talent," and
sent thank-you notes afterward. Their mothers were agreeable and
supported the contest. The Jaycees were based in rural and suburban

areas that would become—as postwar migration pulled middle-class families out of major cities—pageant country.

The second challenge, Slaughter explained in her report, was "Better Disposition of Miss America." By that she meant rewarding the winners well enough to make the title both desirable and respectable. It was too late to stop Ramey, who would call the pageant an "entrée into oblivion" and work a number called "So What" into her post-reign nightclub junkets (being Miss America had made her life "très gai," she sang. "Now if I could only find a way to eat three times a day"). But she could offer others more.

Slaughter had taken the pulse of the nation while touring with Bartel, polling people informally about their views of Miss America, and she had thoughts. "There is no need to elaborate on the favorable reactions," she wrote. Her focus was the holdouts she wanted to convert, whose response (which she quoted in language that prefigured Ramey's novelty song by a year) amounted to "Miss America—So What?" They wanted to know what happened after Miss America won, whether she contributed anything worthwhile to society, and if she enjoyed sustained success.

Likewise, reluctant contestants asked, "Why should I want to be Miss America?" "Is the title one I can proudly claim throughout my life?" "Can the title Miss America help me attain my ambitions?" "What kind of girl seeks the title Miss America?"

Slaughter was confident that most of her recent queens would vouch for the pageant as "the most educational experience of their lives" and had letters to prove it. But (she felt so strongly about this she broke into all caps) "WE HAVE GOT TO PROVE OUR INTENTIONS TO THE DOUBTING PUBLIC WITH FACTS." A $5,000 scholarship for the winners, she wrote, was the way to do it.

"In five years, think what a reputation a Miss America pag-

eant could build in the schools in this country? Girls would no longer look upon the pageant as a beauty contest, but would respect
the title for its genuine value to them and its rating in the nation."
She even allowed, presciently, that the educational mandate might
eclipse the beauty piece of the pageant altogether. With a scholarship, she predicted, "The Miss America title will offer a constructive inducement to all types of girls." (Well, all except black girls.)

The question of who brainstormed the idea of scholarships has
never been resolved—whether Slaughter, Bartel, or a student they
met on tour at the University of Minnesota who told them that "no
college girl would enter a contest that afforded as few opportunities as the Atlantic City Pageant." Regardless of its provenance, the
idea resonated deeply with Slaughter. "I wanted to go to college
more than anything in the world, but I didn't have the money,"
she said. "Now I wanted my girls to have a scholarship, something
constructive. I knew the shine of a girl's hair wasn't going to make
her a success in life, and I knew good and well that the prizes Miss
America had been getting were a joke . . . a fur coat that couldn't
have been worth more than two hundred dollars, the Hollywood
contract that they got for fifty dollars a week—why, they couldn't
even live on that in California."

She also knew that not all winners wanted a Hollywood career in the first place; scholarships would open other options. She
believed the pageant could produce doctors and lawyers, which
seemed laughable at the time, but which, in time, it did.

Her proposal was well timed. During the life of the pageant
thus far, women's college enrollment had declined steadily since a
then-historic peak in 1920, when they represented 47 percent of
students. In the 1930s, a cultural backlash against the feminist
gains of the progressive era and the sexual freedom of the Jazz Age
nudged women back toward marriage and motherhood and away

from college. Hastened by the Depression, enrollment numbers fell to 40 percent in the 1940s, then continued downward, first as women dropped out to take defense jobs, and postwar, when many swapped their studies for domesticity once their veteran husbands rejoined the workforce.

Government-sponsored newsreels promoted domesticity as their duty. A 1942 *Ladies' Home Journal* article titled "What is Your Dream Girl Like?" included a "blueprint" based on a survey of military men that said, "A college education isn't necessary, and most young men would prefer not to have their wives work after marriage." The 1944 federal GI Bill also bit into their numbers: its scholarships overwhelmingly served white men at the expense of women (who represented less than 3 percent of veterans) and black men (who were largely denied their benefits). Slaughter may have set her sights on an opportunity she personally wished she'd had, but it was also one of national importance.

Because many of Slaughter's board members preferred to cultivate movie stars, the scholarship was only grudgingly approved, and to her astonishment, she alone was expected to raise the $5,000 to fund it. She merely flinched, then sat down and hand-wrote letters to 230 companies who sold products a beauty queen might endorse, landing $1,000 contracts with Bancroft & Sons, a textile manufacturer; Fitch Shampoo Company; Harvel Watches; and Catalina Swim Suits, which had been designing swimwear since 1912, inspired initially by Annette Kellerman. With giants Jantzen and Cole, Catalina had been dictating affordable beach fashion for decades. Now its suits would become Miss America's crowning uniform.

Weeks before the 1945 pageant, however, a fifth sponsor had yet to materialize. Desperate, Slaughter put up her own money. Then, a week before the pageant, she got a call from Sandy Valley

Grocery Company, a wholesaler in the South whose owner had a knack for publicity, a taste for philanthropy—and, until that year, AWOL Miss America Bette Cooper on its payroll as marketing director. They wanted in.

With funding secured, Slaughter recruited the executive director of the Association of American Colleges and Universities to head the scholarship program and spread the word to colleges. And so, in 1945, the pageant began its evolution from leg show to Honors Club. The inaugural scholarship was awarded to the first—and, to this day, the only—Jewish Miss America. Bess Myerson was one of the most gorgeous, talented, ambitious, uncompromising, and socially significant winners ever. She was also, in the end, the most bewilderingly disappointing.

THREE

Seekers

ITH BROAD CHEEKS, DAZZLING BROWN eyes, and an exuberant, toothy smile, five-foot-ten Bess Myerson routinely stopped traffic and turned heads on the streets of the Bronx, where she grew up. But beauty wasn't important to Myerson's Russian Jewish parents and their three daughters, who lived in a one-bedroom apartment in the Sholem Aleichem housing co-op. "Nobody [there] cared about looks," a childhood family friend told *The New York Times*. "They cared about books and brains."

The co-op was a workers' housing project built in the 1920s to preserve secular Yiddish culture, named for the author of the stories that inspired *Fiddler on the Roof.* Snuggled between Jerome Park Reservoir and Van Cortlandt Park, it served as a haven for Jewish families who left the crowded Lower East Side for the greener pastures of the Bronx at the dawn of its urban growth. Its fifteen

Tudor-style buildings contained a nursery school, an auditorium, three art studios, and two schools—one for communists, another for socialists, leaving members of the resident anarchist group to make their choice. Landscaped with gardens that snaked between the buildings, its inner courtyards nurtured a communitarian spirit, though skipping across the rooftops was sometimes the quickest route to a friend's place.

"It seemed to me that almost every child in the building took piano or violin," Myerson said in Susan Dworkin's *Miss America, 1945: Bess Myerson and the Year that Changed Our Lives.* "The place resounded with music. There was an unwritten rule that you could not practice after 9 o'clock at night because the tenants—truckers, butchers, garment workers, blue collar people—rose early and needed their sleep."

Because Myerson's demanding mother wanted her girls to be music teachers, she made them practice for hours every day and drummed into them that they should be prepared to make their own living, just in case. Myerson, who played both flute and piano, paid for her music degree from Hunter College by giving piano lessons. She graduated with honors in 1945. Though she wanted to attend graduate school to train to become a conductor, she couldn't afford it. But her older sister Sylvia had a plan. When Myerson was in college, a photographer friend had taken modeling photos of her; she'd slathered on the makeup and hammed it up in pinup poses, imitating Betty Grable and Rita Hayworth. In the summer of 1945, while she was working as a music counselor at a New England summer camp, she learned that Sylvia and their friend had used the photos to enter her in a beauty contest. She'd been picked from 1,200 applicants to compete for the Miss New York title at the Ritz Theater. Bess was reluctant to go, but Sylvia persuaded her, arguing that a victory could win her money to buy a piano or start a music school.

"I remember walking onto the stage," Myerson told Dworkin, "looking around at the other girls, feeling like I was out of another mold. They were very blond and cover-girlish . . . I was tall and dark and had no hips . . . I thought surely one of them would be chosen." She was also intensely uncomfortable appearing in a bathing suit. But she felt more confident once she changed into a gown to perform Grieg on piano and Gershwin on flute. She made the final fifteen.

When she returned for the finals on Wednesday, August 15, the city was teeming with euphoric New Yorkers. The previous day, half a million people in Times Square had looked up to see the news rolling across the ticker: OFFICIAL—TRUMAN ANNOUNCES JAPANESE SURRENDER. For the next two days, millions of people flooded into midtown Manhattan to cheer and cry under showers of streamers and confetti. "Buildings ablaze with parties," Myerson wrote in her diary. "Finals tomorrow."

The next afternoon, following rehearsals for the evening finals, she met Lenora Slaughter, who, Zelig-like, managed to attend regional contests across the country when she wasn't jousting with her board, smooth-talking Atlantic City businessmen, masterminding the fall pageant, or managing the latest winner. She struck Myerson as "a bright woman who knew exactly what she wanted" but who "scared most of us because she was so self-assured and flamboyant." Slaughter, impressed with Myerson's statuesque beauty and fine musical talent, invited her to chat.

Sitting in the empty third row of the theater, they talked about the history of the pageant, the scholarship, and Myerson's dreams of graduate school. Myerson was just the type of cultured, sensibly ambitious candidate Slaughter wanted to see at Miss America. But there was a problem: the name. "Bess Myerson is just not a very attractive name for a career in show business," she told her, though that wasn't exactly Myerson's stated ambition, nor was it consonant with Slaughter's new vision for the pageant.

"What would you suggest?" Myerson asked.

"'Betty,' or whatever, 'Merrick' or something," Slaughter ventured.

Myerson knew this was about more than a stage name. In the first of many tussles she would have with Slaughter, she put her foot down. She recalled her father, a house painter who had survived a pogrom as a child in Russia, telling her to remember who she was— meaning a Jew—and refused. "I cannot change my name," she said. "I live in a building with two hundred and fifty Jewish families . . . If I should win, I want everybody to know that I'm the daughter of Louie and Bella Myerson."

Slaughter later said she was merely concerned that Myerson's chances would be hurt when she encountered anti-Semitism in Atlantic City. "I figured that if I could get her name changed it would help her because she didn't look Jewish or anything like that," she told the writer Jennifer Preston. She claimed the Quakers who ran the pageant didn't like Jews, and that there weren't many hotels for Jews there. In fact, there were (along with about a dozen synagogues), though they were largely segregated, built in response to discriminatory "Gentiles Only" hotel policies, as was the Jewish country club.

When Slaughter pressed the point, Myerson dug in. She was already losing her sense of who she was. "I was in a masquerade, marching across stages in bathing suits," she told Dworkin. "Whatever was left of myself in this game, I had to keep, I sensed that."

Myerson's sheltered life changed irrevocably that week. The day after she was crowned Miss New York, her diary read, "Had champagne! Met Spanish playboys. Chauffeur drove us home at 6 a.m.!" She had just turned twenty-one. Her photo appeared in the city papers, showing her seated, legs extended, on a deeply unglamorous tar beach rooftop, tanned from summer camp and wearing a white two-piece swimsuit with lacing down the hips. Her parents weren't happy about it—until she told them winning Miss America could mean graduate school and a baby grand piano. But her sudden celebrity had a downside: a steady stream of obscene letters and phone calls that continued even after she was crowned Miss America. She was mortified when her father discovered a used condom hanging from the apartment doorknob.

Myerson found herself being whisked around to lunches, cocktail parties, radio interviews, and photo shoots. When she met mayor Fiorello LaGuardia, founder of her alma mater, the High School of Music & Art, he wanted to know why a LaGuardia graduate would stoop to such a thing. "He asked me if the Miss America Pageant was merely another fanny-shaking contest where I'd have to compete with a lot of empty headed females who show their legs," her diary read. "Made me promise to stick to my music and write and tell him what school I was going to attend." LaGuardia, who killed New York City burlesque by shutting down all six Minsky's theaters in 1937, may be the only elected official in the pageant's history who was immune to the glamour of a beauty queen.

Despite lingering prejudices against it (and, in big cities, general indifference to it), the pageant was poised to enter a new era. The scholarship was in place. With the war over, Slaughter hoped to make her baby "the first major national event of the peacetime era." Nucky Johnson had finally retired as mobster-in-chief after spending four years in prison, which, combined with the wartime military presence in Atlantic City, had tamped down racketeering and softened the city's public image. Many soldiers who'd spent time there liked it so much they wanted to return with their families. In 1944, a popular film called *Atlantic City* was released. Set in 1915, it centered on a fictionalized Miss America pageant as it dramatized the making of the ritzy resort town, luxuriating in flashy nightclub sequences with performances by Louis Armstrong and Dorothy Dandridge.

Myerson and the other contestants registered at the pageant headquarters on Monday, September 3, receiving their Catalina suits with instructions to call them swimsuits, not bathing suits, because Catalina's founder had decreed that bathing was for the tub. Myerson paused, pen in hand, where the pageant questionnaire asked about the contestants' favorite foods. As the only Jew among them—the only minority contestant, period—she thought better of listing knishes and herring and lied, citing Southern fried chicken instead. Having packed her clothes in shopping bags, leaving her Yiddish-speaking mother at home (sister Sylvia came in her place), she also fudged her ancestry, boldly declaring that her family went back four generations in the United States. And for good measure, she shaved an inch off her height. But she was honest about her commitment to music and her interest in getting a graduate degree. Myerson so valued her education that she'd submitted a photo for the pageant program taken, of all things, in her cap and gown. Her portrait, placed at the center of her program page, showed her beaming in her commencement regalia, cap tipped, surrounded by full-body shots of bathing beauties in swimsuits, including one in short shorts, heels, and a feather headdress.

On Tuesday, the women stood in long rows on low bleachers, modeling their swimsuits for the panorama photo that was by then a pageant staple. Slaughter didn't like the format; it had a homogenizing effect, presenting the girls interchangeably, like "horseflesh," she said. She also disliked the continued inclusion of male illustrators on the coed judging panel; unlike the film and modeling industry people who could not only appraise contestants' talents but also might employ them, all the illustrators saw, she said, "was legs."

Slaughter was bristling at a media dynamic that wouldn't be fully articulated for another thirty years: the male gaze. In 1975, British film theorist Laura Mulvey published the influential essay "Visual Pleasure and Narrative Cinema," identifying the ways a heterosexual male perspective was coded into the language of film. "In a world ordered by sexual imbalance," Mulvey wrote, "pleasure in looking has been split between active/male and passive/female. The determining male gaze projects its fantasy on the female figure, which is styled accordingly." The concept, now a keystone of feminist theory, critiques a practice that reduces women to the wiggling rear, the bouncing breasts, or, in Miss America's case, the tanned, shaved, endless legs. Slaughter, always playing both sides, wanted to have her cheesecake and eat it too.

Meanwhile, her brittle affability was driving everyone nuts. The women found her officious and insincere, smiling relentlessly as she hustled them around. "She had a Holy Roller way of reeling out the encouragement," Myerson said, "like Jimmy Swaggart or Oral Roberts, exhorting us in this high-pitched southern voice."

"You are the living symbols of American womanhood!" Slaughter trilled, addressing the women as states. "Out of my way, New Hampshire, I'm coming through!"

She also alarmed them by enumerating all the ways they could be disqualified: drinking, fraternizing with men, padding their bras, lying about their age. Worst of all, they could make a mistake and get axed without being told. "They would just let you go on through the whole week, performing your talent, parading in your swimsuit, trying to impress the judges," said Myerson. "Meanwhile, however, you would be out of the running and wouldn't even know it!"

Many of the week's events involved veterans. (Myerson later quipped that the beauties were "the cheesecake that followed the flag.") She won a preview pageant staged for air force vets and attended a victory ball, cosponsored by the navy and the coast guard, where the forty contestants were assigned escorts, all former POWs. Myerson's date, a sergeant from Brooklyn, gushed, "From a prison camp to this—please don't wake me up." A swimsuit parade was staged for wounded and amputee vets still recovering in the Thomas M. England General Hospital, many of whom watched from stretchers or wheelchairs. Some of the women made excuses not to go; others fought back tears when they did. Miss Florida, Jeni Freeland, told Dworkin about having her picture taken with a man who was a quadruple amputee; as she walked away to get in a convertible, an officer told her, "Turn around and smile at him and don't you dare cry." The exercise was tasteless at best, cruel at worst, but two of the most seriously disabled later said they found it thrilling and even traveled to New York to see Myerson at a March of Dimes event during her reign year.

Myerson was winning preliminaries and attracting lots of media love. Still, she worried about her too-tall body and too-small swimsuit, which Sylvia, who was heavier, slept in the night before the swimsuit competition to stretch it out. Her frosty chaperone unnerved her, and she felt out of place with the other women with their manicures and suitcase sets and hovering mothers. She didn't know that some of her rivals had also struggled with the financial demands the pageant presented, or that she struck them as vastly more urbane and independent than they were.

But it turned out more concerted forces were working against her. A reporter told her, "Watch yourself, Bess. There are people involved here who don't want a Jewish winner." A pageant official was overheard saying there had never been a Jewish Miss America and never should be. The judges weren't supposed to discuss their preferences during the week, but they always did, and when it became clear that Myerson was a front-runner after winning both the talent and the swimsuit portions, some of the judges got anonymous phones call indicating that they wouldn't be invited back if they cast their final votes for her.

If her Jewishness inflamed anti-Semites, it was attracting Jewish fans, who were buying tickets to the 1945 pageant in unprecedented numbers. The full impact of the Holocaust hadn't yet been documented—that November, the debut issue of the Jewish cultural magazine *Commentary* put the numbers at 4,750,000. But the first eyewitness account of a newly liberated concentration camp, Buchenwald, had been broadcast on CBS radio in April, and that year American Jews raised $45 million in aid to European Jews— then the largest NGO philanthropic fundraising project in history. Though the extent of the savagery had yet to be measured, its severity, and the desperate state of starved survivors, many of whom would linger in displaced persons camps for years, was coming into terrifying focus.

A Jewish couple approached Myerson one day and asked, in Yiddish, if she was Jewish. When she answered yes, they hugged her and told her they lived nearby and had come to the pageant for the first time because of her. "You've got to win, for all of us," they said. After that, others did the same, telling her, "You have to show the world that we are not ugly." Suddenly the swimsuit and the hair care and the wardrobe changes and Slaughter's ridiculous rules didn't seem so frivolous if it meant seizing this victory.

"Beauty with brains—that's Miss America of 1945!" a Paramount News announcer exclaimed when Myerson was crowned that Saturday. As she walked the runway in her swimsuit, scepter in hand, her crimson robe trailing behind, shouts of "Mazel tov!" rang out from the audience. She saw Jews looking not at her, but turning to hug each other, reveling in the discovery that although they were still the victims of all manner of discrimination, barred from jobs and even blamed for America's involvement in the war, one of their own had taken the crown.

Myerson's win was not only a nod to Jewish assimilation, but also a justification for U.S. troops sent overseas—and, on some level, an admission of the racism that had plagued the pageant from the start. A Jew was now America's model woman, albeit one who "didn't look Jewish or anything like that," as Slaughter had put it. For decades to come, the pageant would make baby steps toward inclusion by accepting minority women who best approximated a white ideal. Asian Americans, African Americans, Native Americans, and Latinas all held local pageants, each with its own nuanced histories and postwar purposes beyond boosting community pride—and, in the case of some immigrant populations, demonstrating cultural assimilation.

For example, as historian Shirley Jennifer Lim explains in *A Feeling of Belonging: Asian American Women's Public Culture, 1930–1960*, Japanese American pageants like the Nisei Week queens in L.A.'s Little Tokyo celebrated these Americans' reclaimed citizenship after internment had stripped them of their civil rights. During the Cold War, Chinese American pageants, notably San Francisco's Miss Chinatown (originally held on the fourth of July, now called Miss Chinatown USA), exalted democratic capitalism in the face of the "red threat." Its winners flouted the plain look of the proletariat worker and, after the Cultural Revolution in the 1960s, fortified China's endangered cultural heritage through traditional dress and practices.

As a pop culture phenomenon, Myerson was swimming in the

current that carried the serial radio comedy and later TV show *The Goldbergs* to commercial success from the 1930s to the '50s. It featured a first-generation Jewish family from the Bronx struggling to resolve old world values with new world challenges. Though the plots touched on some real-life issues—a 1939 episode invoked Kristallnacht, and others, during World War II, referenced Jews trying to escape the Holocaust—most addressed themes any working-class family could relate to, paving the way for sitcoms like *The Honeymooners* and *All in the Family.* The show's star and creator, writer and producer Gertrude Berg, was one of the first American women to strike gold as a renowned and prolific radio and TV writer. She won an Emmy in 1950. Like Myerson, she was a Jew who'd managed to grab a piece of the American dream.

But for Myerson, the dream wouldn't hold. She had committed to a four-week vaudeville tour called American Beauty Review, where she and her runners-up performed four shows a day on a bill with chorus girls, ventriloquists, and animal acts for drunken audiences who demanded to see her rocking a swimsuit instead of playing a flute concerto in an evening gown. It was a far cry from the dainty lunches and prim chaperones of pageant week. (Decades later, Slaughter called the tour "a colossal failure," saying, "In my heart I knew it wasn't the right thing.") It was also lonely for Myerson, who traveled solo; the others brought their mothers along. When she finally shook free, she switched gears, visiting hospitals, appearing in a Fitch shampoo ad, and modeling Everglaze fabrics for Bancroft & Sons. But though the work was better, the pay was worse, and the other pageant sponsors showed no interest in using her as a spokesperson.

Once her travels took her to the South, where she saw NO JEWS signs, she began to grasp why. One day, wearing her crown and gown, poised to enter a country club where she was scheduled to promote the pageant, she overheard the hostess saying, "Well, you didn't tell us she was Jewish ... We do not have Jews, and we don't have Negroes."

That was it; she was done. She packed her things, took a train home in tears, and pondered her options. "I realized this title was mine forever, that I didn't really lose it at the end of the year. I just didn't want to be remembered as a beautiful but dumb broad." Soon after, when she was invited to meet the leaders of the Anti-Defamation League of B'nai B'rith, founded in 1913 to battle anti-Semitism, she found a more meaningful way to use her title—and channel her rage. She finished out her year on a six-month lecture tour called "You Can't Be Beautiful and Hate," savoring her appearances at schools and community centers where no one introduced her by her measurements or so much as mentioned a swimsuit. Slaughter scolded her, saying she was betraying the pageant by using it for political ends. Myerson considered this a huge failure of imagination. "They could have said, 'You speak well; let's find something good and useful for you to speak about,'" which was visionary, considering that more than forty years later, the pageant would do just that, requiring contestants to choose a social issue to campaign for on the road.

One of the paradoxes of combining scholarship money with a sponsorship tour was that the year of travel often derailed women from whatever their ambition was in the first place. In the early decades, most winners who wanted a career were focused on acting, singing, or modeling, and the sponsor events propelled them in that direction by boosting their public profile. With the addition of the scholarship, their options widened, but winners with interests beyond entertainment were locked into a year of unrelated though increasingly profitable promotional appearances, a prerequisite to getting the scholarship money. Though some held steady (Rebecca

King [1974] became a lawyer; Deidre Downs [2005] is a doctor), many others drifted away from their avowed goal. Yolande Betbeze (1951) wanted to be a professional opera singer but performed little during her reign and infrequently after, partly because she couldn't train while on tour; Elizabeth Ward (1982) hoped to become a lawyer but ended up studying acting; Gretchen Carlson (1989) had her eye on Harvard Law School before winning and said she wanted "to do some kind of hosting on TV" after.

The one skill they all carry beyond the pageant is public speaking. Myerson, who later concluded she didn't have the talent to become a conductor, used her skills first as a spokesperson for the Anti-Defamation League, then as a TV quiz show personality, then as New York City's first commissioner of consumer affairs, pushing through some of the nation's most progressive consumer protection laws, a few of which, like unit pricing and freshness dating, were adopted nationally. She was campaign chair to New York City mayor Ed Koch in 1977 and later served on commissions under three presidents, addressing issues from crime and violence to mental health and world hunger. After losing the Democratic nomination for Senate in 1980, she was named New York City's commissioner of cultural affairs.

A clip of a riveting anti-war Mother's Day speech she gave in 1972 offers a glimpse of Myerson's fierce oratorial powers—and evidence that she shook off her Bronx accent somewhere along the way. "Our security, defined by the Pentagon, lies in adding to their inventory of insanity," she says, delivering one harrowing fact after another, without so much as blinking when she stops to let the audience applaud, and expressing the merest flicker of a smile as she finishes, flashing a peace sign and turning to leave the podium.

Myerson might have made history as the twentieth century's brightest star in the Miss America galaxy, but for men. She married at twenty-two, a month after her reign ended, surprising even Slaughter, who muted her disappointment that this would sink Myerson's plan to get a master's degree—which it did, though she used the scholarship money to take courses at Columbia University and buy the fabled piano.

"We were never taught as women or as girls that we could make it on our own," Myerson said. "You had to get married and the man you married would take care of you." After tasting independence during her reign, she'd returned to her parents' apartment and saw no option to live away from them as a single woman—she said it wasn't part of her culture. She also felt she needed protection from men who stalked her as Miss America, including a GI who repeatedly turned up at the entrance of her building after traveling from Iowa to see her.

But her relationships were disastrous. Her first marriage, to an alcoholic, was plagued with violence; the second (and third, to the same man) imploded in an ugly high-profile custody battle for her daughter. But it was her affair with a married, mobbed-up sewer contractor named Carl Capasso, born the day after she became Miss America, that toppled her crown. In 1987, Myerson was indicted in an alleged attempt to bribe a judge to lower Capasso's alimony payments to his soon-to-be ex-wife. She was acquitted in 1988, but the investigation concluded that she was involved in serious misconduct, and the scandal, known as the "Bess Mess," transformed her celebrity into infamy. A shoplifting conviction the following year sealed the disgrace.

She was also, according to her only child, Barra Grant, a negligent, narcissistic mother. "She was very, very busy. She had an agenda and I didn't figure into it," Grant told the *Hollywood Reporter* in 2018, after staging a play about their difficult relationship called *Miss America's Ugly Daughter*. "And there were always men.

She was always on a quest to get a new guy, a better guy, a more wealthy guy."

Her personal failings aside, Myerson blew open the possibilities of the Miss America title even as she compromised for men and struggled, for decades, to surmount the stigma of her beauty queen past in pursuit of a future. As Dworkin writes, her reign stood "between the ascendance of Rosie the Riveter and the Happy Homemaker, a perfect time for a well-educated, professional Miss America to flower." Her marriage/work conflict echoed that of strong movie heroines of the 1930s and early '40s, whose breezy intelligence animated films like *His Girl Friday* (1940), in which a star journalist (Rosalind Russell) imagines, after divorcing the workaholic editor who hired her (Cary Grant), that she'll realize her true womanhood by marrying an insurance salesman and retiring to the suburbs. Her ex proves her wrong by tricking her into reporting one last story, thereby rekindling her passion for work—and for him.

Like Myerson, Russell's character expresses, in the words of film critic Molly Haskell, "[the] anomaly of the woman professional and the bewildering state in which she is torn between the impulse ... to relate to men sexually and defer to their authority, and the contrary impulse to assert herself and forfeit her rights as a woman." Russell invokes both when she tells her ex, "You are no longer my husband and no longer my boss." (Myerson's first husband was rankled by the fact that she made more money than he; her second routinely berated her, sometimes publicly, for infractions like setting the table incorrectly for dinner parties, a domestic felony that literally ended their marriage.) The film also touches on the role beauty plays in the success of many career women. When Grant tells Russell she was "a doll-faced hick" from a college journalism program when he hired her, she snaps, "Well, you wouldn't have taken me if I hadn't been doll-faced." Myerson, too, might never have risen to the professional level she did if not for her beauty—and the recognition it, through the pageant, engendered.

If the public was charmed by powerhouse characters like Russell's in *His Girl Friday* and ambitious women like Myerson in the 1940s, the forces of history were working against them. In the first two years after the war, as men returned to work and as women (those who could afford it) were pushed back into domestic roles, 2 million women lost their jobs, and many who remained employed were demoted—women of color being the first to go.

Women's magazines idealized the devoted homemaker and demonized careerism. In 1946, *Ladies' Home Journal*, which had put a female combat pilot on its cover during the war, published an article titled "Are You Too Educated to Be a Mother?" and offered a zero-sum conclusion: "We must learn that we are not too educated to be parents; we must learn that we are too educated *not* to be." Even Wonder Woman, who had debuted in 1941 as the first female superhero to get her own comic, was hustled toward the altar; a 1949 cover showed her swept off her feet by her boyfriend, with the caption, "Only a sudden call for help could prevent Wonder Woman from marrying Steve Trevor!"

The emerging field of pop psychology pathologized working women in a 1947 book called *Modern Woman: The Lost Sex*, written by a sociologist, Ferdinand Lundberg, and a psychoanalyst, Marynia Farnham, who called feminism "a deep illness." It charged that modern women were miserable, and that urban, educated working women were the most miserable of all. Among other things, they suffered from a "sexual disorder" resulting from too much recreational (as opposed to reproductive) sex, which was shrinking American families. A promotional newsreel undercut this message by showing Farnham in a lab coat in her New York office, explaining her theories while an attentive female journalist took notes. An early review closed by saying, "Physician, heal thyself." It became a bestseller.

In 1946, the pageant was still buoyed by the success of its re-branding and the promise of scholarships. Slaughter had miraculously increased the fund fivefold, so runners-up and ten finalists could also receive money in decreasing amounts from the $5,000 top prize. A contractual proviso allowed the awards to be used for performing arts training instead of college. (One of the finalists, Miss Chicago Cloris Leachman, later of *The Mary Tyler Moore Show* fame, used it for singing and acting lessons and went on to win eight Emmys, though in 2016 she told a reporter that dropping out of Northwestern University to compete in pageants "seemed rather stupid" in retrospect.)

That year, the pageant staged a press event on the boardwalk in front of a giant diploma-themed backdrop bearing the scholarship amount and sponsors' names, where Myerson and Slaughter handed out certificates in a mock commencement ceremony. But the muddled visuals confirmed the pageant's ever-conflicted identity. Miss America received hers in a swimsuit; the others wore street clothes.

Media interest in the pageant had cooled a bit since the 1920s and '30s as weightier wartime news superseded it. Myerson's historic win landed her on page forty-four of *The New York Times*, sans photo, even though she was a New York native. The night she passed the sash to Marilyn Buferd, Miss California, the story was kicked to page three of *The Los Angeles Times*. Other publications chortled at the pageant's new leanings. *Life* magazine jeered, "Having carefully publicized itself this year as the most refined, cultural and downright intellectual pageant ever held, [it] once again ground to a smashing close as the best leg show of the year." And though the talent had fanned out to include oil painting and a lecture on education, along with the usual singing and dancing, the article implied it was Buferd's performance in a swimsuit, not as a thespian, that clinched her win.

So much for women's education. Buferd didn't give a damn about college anyway. She set off on an acting career interrupted by high-profile engagements, marriages, and rapid-fire divorces; a contract with Italian director Roberto Rossellini led to an affair and work as his translator, partly because Slaughter persuaded her to take Berlitz language courses if she wasn't going to attend college, for God's sake. The next year, winner Barbara Jo Walker, a Sunday school teacher who was engaged when she competed, stated her priorities up front. "I'm only interested in one contract: the marriage contract." She didn't even care to reap the growing harvest of endorsement opportunities, though she wore a Bancroft & Sons Everglaze cotton wedding gown when she was married during the summer of her reign.

In 1948, Slaughter arranged for the winner to be crowned in an evening gown instead of a swimsuit, prompting a temporary walk-out by the incredulous press. The move capped a series of changes designed to dignify the pageant. Along with the scholarships, she'd added a new judging category called "personality." She'd restricted the contest to high school graduates, installed a paid pageant tour chaperone, and revised the winner's contract, granting the pageant exclusive agenting rights. That covered what Miss America *did*, but not what she *said*. When 1948 winner Beatrice ("BeBe") Shopp's father offered to help manage Shopp's schedule, Slaughter agreed, and he extended BeBe's tour to Europe, where she was feted and, at the legendary Folies Bergère, invited onstage so Josephine Baker could hand her flowers. But when she sounded off in the press on topics like the scandalous size of French bikinis, Slaughter threatened to bring her home. "BeBe is too young to have opinions," she pronounced.

A self-described "naïve" Minnesotan farm girl, Shopp was unprepared for the media mugging she got in Europe, but sometimes gave as good as she got. At 140 pounds, she was the heaviest Miss America yet, a subject of abiding public interest. (The *Minneapolis Star Tribune* even polled readers about whether she needed to diet.) When a British reporter asked her what she planned to do about her "surplus fat," she said, "What fat? I think I'm just right."

The winners were all—within the pageant's narrow demographic—so varied, from Myerson, an urban intellectual, to Buferd, a Hollywood dreamer, to Shopp, a rural Midwesterner whose easygoing good cheer was still in evidence at an autograph signing at the 2018 competition she attended at age eighty-eight. Who *was* Miss America? Who was she *supposed* to be after winning? Gleaning these women's identities from newspaper articles about the pageant is dicey. For one thing, they were written by men who too often had it both ways, leering at them on the page while patronizing them for wanting much beyond the leering. Only the writer who profiled Fay Lanphier for *The New Movie Magazine* had taken the time to draw her out, unpacking both her backstory and the true impact of the pageant on her young life. But in 1949, a female journalist set out to chronicle the pageant from the perspective of an active contestant, rendering it with deeper nuance in a long article called "Symbol of All We Possess."

Lillian Ross (who had graduated, coincidentally, two years ahead of Myerson at Hunter College) began her reporting by traveling to the Bronx to meet Wanda Nalepa, Miss New York State, and her family, then driving with her to Atlantic City to witness the full bounty of pageant week. Her story opened with who *wouldn't* compete: anyone was eligible, she explained, "if they were high-school graduates, were not and had never been married, and were not Negroes." Her editor wanted to cut the sentence, thinking it best not to "inject the race problem" into the piece since she didn't return to it later. But Ross insisted. "I was repelled by the discrimination in the Miss America business, and I felt strongly that I should emphasize it," she said.

Ross presented the hitherto neglected perspective of the Miss America loser—the girl who didn't get the Nash sedan and the Everglaze wardrobe and the raft of marriage proposals from strangers. Nalepa was a twenty-two-year-old nurse, just five feet three, with flaxen hair and green eyes, whose friends had pushed her to compete. She worked long days and had had to quit for the month or more it took to prepare for the pageant, borrowing money to pay for competition clothes and a course in modeling. But she didn't have a talent.

"Her act, as she planned it, was going to consist of getting up in her nurse's uniform and making a little speech about her nursing experience," Ross wrote. After the others performed—dramatic readings, songs including "I'm in the Mood for Love" (played on electric guitar), and astoundingly, a 4-H demonstration involving a cow, Nalepa, clad in a powder-blue evening gown, gave a talk on nursing.

"She spoke without any expression at all," Ross reported, "as though she were reciting something she had memorized with difficulty . . . Miss New York State said she had decided to become a nurse when she visited a friend who was a patient in a veterans' hospital during the war. She had been shocked by the men's helplessness. She would now show a film of herself going about her usual duties. While the film was being run, she made flat, realistic comments on it. She was pictured in the children's ward, in the maternity ward, and assisting a surgeon at an operation. At the end of the picture, the audience applauded halfheartedly."

Tedious as the lecture evidently was (and for sheer drama that year, no one could hold a candle to Miss Montana's palomino horse getting spooked and crapping on the stage, rearing back into its mess, and nearly slipping into the orchestra pit), it aimed for something the talent portion should encourage but rarely has: the performance of knowledge. Nalepa took pride in her work and wanted to show it, unlike contestants who frantically practiced a random song or dance for the talent segment. In 2015, the Nalepa scenario was repeated by another nurse, only this one did it well. Dressed in her scrubs, Kelley Johnson, Miss Colorado, delivered a moving monologue about working with Alzheimer's patients. "Every nurse has a patient that reminds them why they became a nurse in the first place," her story began. "Mine was Joe." The next week, the women on the TV show *The View* mocked her for overstepping the bounds of a beauty contest.

Using the eyewitness technique that made her a pioneer of New Journalism (rendering stories in narrated scenes), Ross presented a range of situations and characters that Nalepa faced as a contestant. She described Slaughter ("extravagantly cheerful"); small talk among the chaperones ("Some years you get a better-looking crop of girls than others"); the formal breakfast with judges where the ring of a bell signaled their rotation from table to table; veteran BeBe Shopp motivating the hopefuls ("She smiled and told them to keep smiling from the moment they woke up every morning to the moment they fell asleep"); and rivals like the one who told Ross she liked Nalepa ("*She* doesn't giggle, the way some of the others do").

And without so much as raising an eyebrow, Ross portrayed the belittling assessment of the women. "The MC asked the judges to examine the girls' figures carefully for any flaws. For example, he asked, did the thighs and the calves meet at the right place." In one passage, a scout from RKO Pictures watched the talent and groaned, "Those poor, poor kids. Look at them. They look as though they had been knocking around Broadway for fifteen years."

In rehearsals, Bob Russell, who hosted the pageant from 1940 to 1954, directed the contestants in a parade around the stage and down the runway, where the baby-faced Shopp was stationed, wearing a thirty-pound gown appliquéd with the official flowers of the forty-eight states. Russell serenaded her, "the Sweetheart of the U.S.A.," with the pageant theme song. It was a toast: "To the one, to the one / Who's the symbol of all we possess."

Nalepa stood at the center of Ross's narrative, doubtful (because of her height and lack of a talent) but hopeful. She just wanted to make more money than nursing allowed. When Miss Arizona won, a fellow reporter turned to Ross and said, "She's going to spend the rest of her life looking for something. They *all* are." Ross and Nalepa walked back to the dressing room together to find the first runner-up in tears. Nalepa didn't cry, she told Ross, "because when you don't expect very much, you're never disappointed." The daughter of a factory worker, she'd earned nothing but a few gowns and a luggage set after winning Miss New York State, and had lost time and money competing in Miss America. But she knew what she'd signed up for.

Fifty years later, Ross would write about another losing Miss New York, Brandi Burkhardt, in a piece that echoed many of the themes of 1949, from the incessant smiling to the hope for transformation (which at least in Burkhardt's case paid off in solid theater and film work). Her goal in covering the pageants, Ross said, was to show, "without moralizing, that the beauty contest is—now as it was in the past—the same desperate path to finding 'more.'"

It would have been fascinating to learn what she thought about the 1948ers seeking a shortcut to success—or merely trying to get an economic leg up—as a young professional who'd found her place in a male-dominated profession without needing beauty to do so. *The New Yorker* had hired Ross in 1944 after much of its male staff went to war; she stayed for sixty years, becoming a celebrated journalist known for profiles of American icons from Ernest Hemingway to Lassie.

What Ross didn't know, in foregrounding Nalepa that year, was that the contest had spawned an entirely new breed of contender: the full-blown pageant professional. Winner Jacque Mercer, Miss Arizona, hadn't been pushed into it by friends, hadn't been told her whole life she was beautiful, hadn't hoped for a lucky win; she'd *willed* herself into becoming "the symbol of all we possess" with ferocious planning. "I had all this doped out," she said. "It was a lot like creating an advertising presentation."

A perky, petite, slim-hipped eighteen-year-old who'd decided at fifteen she wanted the crown, Mercer studied newspaper articles about the pageant and persuaded her parents to divert her college tuition to four different coaches in the months before it. She researched the judges' tastes and selected her dramatic reading (*Romeo and Juliet*) accordingly; lied on her entry form, saying she was headed to Stanford instead of on leave from community college; wore clothes that made her look more imposing than her five foot three frame allowed; avoided appearing in public beside taller or prettier rivals; sleuthed out what the others were planning to wear each night, then chose ensembles that made her pop against them; and coordinated with Miss Arkansas, who was positioned next to her in alphabetical formations, to seem lively and chatty for the judges by mouthing "ABC" then "DEF" back and forth through the alphabet for as long as anyone was watching.

And she smiled. "I'll be glad when this is over and I can frown at people if I feel like it," she told Ross, laughing, when the journalist ran into her in her hotel. "I sometimes feel as though my face is going to crack. But I keep that bi-ig smile on my face." That very year, the French philosopher Simone de Beauvoir published *The Second Sex*, the groundbreaking feminist study of women's subordinate status throughout history in which she wrote, "One is not born, but rather becomes, a woman," laying the groundwork for the idea of gender as a social formulation. Though it wasn't translated into English until 1953, Mercer was a textbook example of it. She had done well in school and believed that "if you could learn to be a brain, you could learn to be a woman."

She later codified her system in a book called *How to Win a Beauty Contest*, offering beauty tips, practice and performance pointers, and a philosophy: the ideal queen was not as flashy as an actress or as gaunt as a model—a turnoff for judges—but rather "the kind of girl you hope your son will marry; the kind of girl of whom you say, 'Isn't she nice?' rather than 'Isn't she beautiful?'" She recommended tanning, wearing gloves with gowns during the competition (always matched to the dress, never with trim beyond buttons), and keeping mum about an engagement or boyfriend. She prescribed practice for laughing "correctly" and recommended "smiling at lamp posts or at every mailbox you see" as training.

Mercer's formula of self-editing and self-improvement, of cut-throat ambition and laser-focused determination (she advised staring straight at hecklers and singing louder), of faux modesty and toxic cunning ("Oh no, not her," the others gasped when she won), would warp anyone's ego. Evidently, it nearly destroyed her. "I don't think Jackie [sic] herself knows how close she came at times to a complete nervous breakdown," someone who'd witnessed all this in action told Frank Deford. "She wasn't just a high strung kid. She looked like she was ready to jump off a building."

And for what purpose? She won. For Mercer, the win seemed to be an end in itself—a popularity contest, not an avenue to something bigger. She certainly had the flamboyance to be a public figure, arriving at her first post-pageant press conference in New York wearing a slim-fit Western ensemble paired with a Stetson and red boots. But she didn't meet fame with the same fortitude that drove her to win Miss America. One paper reported that after the pageant she was offered a starring role with Burt Lancaster, but she couldn't make up her mind about taking it and only knew for sure that marriage was her dearest dream. Three months into her reign, she entered the first of her four marriages—one to a pro football player, another lasting eleven days—and drifted away from acting and into writing ad copy for her husband's firm.

Whatever she gained in becoming Miss America, including good money, she'd lost in scraping away the Jacque who'd driven her farmer father's tractor to earn enough money to see her first play and studied to become the eighth-grade valedictorian. "That year is so drastically superficial," she told Deford in 1971, reflecting on the pageant, "that jelling takes five years afterwards. You learn things that work, you practice them, but eventually you start to go stale ... You just know that things are not working anymore ... You don't know why, but *you* are not working anymore."

When she died of leukemia in 1982, at fifty-one, she was an alcoholic, following failed attempts at rehab. Her stepmother suggested Miss America had been the cause of most of her troubles. "You just don't come down off of it," she said. But it seems more likely she couldn't get back up to it. Her first husband, a lifelong friend, said, "She never quite recaptured the excitement of the Miss

America achievement . . . there's not a heckuva lot else for a former Miss America. Jacque never found that something else."

It turned out that the reporter who'd told Ross that Miss America 1949 was going to spend the rest of her life looking for something was right.

FOUR

Achievers

W HEN JACQUE MERCER STEPPED BEHIND her
seated, regal, raven-haired successor, placed the spar-
kling tiara on her head, and bent down to bestow the
traditional annunciatory kiss, she unleashed a demon.

"There was nothing but trouble from the minute that crown
touched my head," Yolande Betbeze later said. Tellingly, as Mercer
stepped back, the tiara fell to the ground, sending the new queen's
subjects scrambling—and setting the tone for Betbeze's subversive
reign.

Betbeze and Mercer couldn't have been more unalike. One did
everything she could to win the crown, the other did nothing—
beyond capitalizing on her smoldering beauty and well-trained
voice—and seized it almost effortlessly. Betbeze was an opera
singer of French Basque ancestry from Mobile, Alabama, weeks
out of braces when she stepped off the train in Atlantic City to

meet Slaughter and her new husband, who were stunned at what they saw.

"She was the sexiest, most glamorous thing I ever laid my eyes on," Slaughter said.

Back home, in 1949, Betbeze had been a runner-up in the Cotton Queen contest and took the Spring Hill College Miss Torch title, but she had no intention of pursuing other beauty contests until a critic at the *Birmingham News* who'd seen her sing with the Mobile Opera Guild suggested she try for Miss Alabama. She said she did it in hopes of getting voice lessons in New York. The only child of a widow, she had spent twelve years in convent school and countless spare hours reading Hegel and Hume, Sartre and Schopenhauer in the public library. With six years of voice and ballet training behind her, she'd appeared in a production of *Angel Street* by a Mobile theater group. And she was studying Italian, French, and German. Beauty with brains, she *was*.

On the night of the finals, Betbeze sang a coloratura aria from Verdi's *Rigoletto* and was applauded through two encores, backed by a pianist she'd practiced with for twenty minutes after losing patience with the pageant orchestra during the preliminaries and recruiting her own accompanist. In those days, winners were given the good news backstage, then escorted back out for a public announcement. Sitting at her dressing room table, Betbeze took it in calmly, nodded, picked up an eyelash curler, did one set of lashes and then the other, stood, and said "Let's go" before gliding out to claim her crown, unfazed, in her eggshell satin gown.

She returned afterward to find the words HAIRY SITS HERE scrawled in lipstick on the mirror where she'd been seen earlier plucking her eyebrows. "All those little girls were really tough," she later said. "Everyone wanted to win so badly I thought one of them would take a wallop at me. I was too much of an intellectual to mix with them very well, and they were sort of suspicious of me because I was different." When she spotted a matron rushing over to remove the graffiti, she said, "Don't you dare. Don't anyone dare rub that off my mirror." Then she thanked everyone, flashed her devastating smile, and turned on her heel to meet the press.

Pelted with the usual inane questions (Acting? Hobbies? Cooking?), she answered impishly. (Men? "I haven't anything against men. I think they are here to stay.") In response to a compliment on her Southern drawl, she said she'd need better diction for stage work, then felt Slaughter's elbow in her side and added, "I'm crazy about the southern accent and I wouldn't advise anyone to lose it."

She was an instant media darling with an endless supply of quotable sass. But her most famous comment, dropped like a bomb the morning after her coronation at a breakfast where she was told she would tour the country modeling Catalina swimsuits, was a simple "no" that changed not just the course of Miss America, but the landscape of American beauty pageants, period. "I'm a singer, not a pinup," she declared.

Conveniently, she had failed to sign the binding contract, so the pageant backed her decision and Catalina was out of luck. Infuriated, they pulled their sponsorship. Months later, when Jacque Mercer was still modeling for them, Catalina president E. B. Stewart griped to her about the Miss America contest, which he felt focused too much on talent and not enough on the Catalina curves. To Slaughter's enduring dismay, Mercer replied, "Why don't you start your own pageant?" Thus Miss Universe was born, along with its own feeder pageants, Miss USA and later Miss Teen USA, all of which now run parallel to Miss America, and which Donald Trump owned from 1996 to 2015. In March 1951, *Business Week* reported that Catalina's rival contest would focus "strictly on the body."

To this day, Miss USA and Miss America are conflated in the

public mind, though the former has historically been the lowbrow cousin to the latter—more voluptuous, less wholesome, and only belatedly adopting the high-minded girl-power rhetoric that Miss America has been pushing since the 1940s. (When I tell people the topic of this book, 90 percent respond by saying it's timely because of Trump, who has boasted about barging in on underage Miss Teen USA contestants in their dressing room and famously fat-shamed a Miss Universe for gaining weight after her win. They think this was all Miss America scandal.) YouTube reels of beauty pageant gaffes—always good for a malicious laugh—feature far fewer Miss Americas than Miss USAs, yet journalists routinely confuse the two pageants and razz them equally.

"They were funny old men," Betbeze (by then Betbeze Fox) later said of the Catalina people, "and I knew how to make them march."

To be fair, Slaughter's original beauty with brains, Jean Bartel, had already pushed back on the swimsuit requirements, minimizing the number of appearances she made on tour in 1943, but that was before Catalina came on board. Now the pageant was down a sponsor, but Slaughter worked her magic and found more, and Betbeze saw her fees shoot up as a result of her insurrection. ("My mother was smart enough to know that if she caused that big a ruckus she was gonna be famous," says her daughter, Yolande Dolly Fox. But "she did something she really believed in and she didn't give a damn if it got her good or bad publicity.")

Like Norma Smallwood in 1926, Betbeze milked it. Most queens returned home for a delicious dip in local celebrity before hitting the road for a year, and the warm wash of community adulation was usually reward enough for their time. Betbeze not only charged for these events, but also demanded gifts of clothing and jewelry from local businesses, then auctioned off what she didn't like in her backyard, as Deford put it, "with the style of a local rug merchant."

"I was the only one who ever looked at it strictly from a business sense," she told him. "The Pageant uses its Miss Americas, and most of them don't even know they're being taken. They come into Toledo or Pocatello and see their picture in the paper and think how wonderful it is. Five miles outside of Toledo, nobody knows Miss America is alive. So you work the sticks, and you receive no recognition. You might as well try to get some money out of it."

That year, the pageant began postdating the title by three months, so although Betbeze was crowned in 1950, she became Miss America 1951, leaving a gap in the title timeline. Her tour log shows a packed travel schedule starting the day after she won, with each place and event neatly enumerated next to the payment amount, and little sick faces appearing for three- and four-day stretches most months, presumably when she had her period. She traveled to forty-eight states and abroad and made almost 200 radio and TV appearances. She pitched for Nash Motors and Bancroft fabrics, dedicated supermarkets and furniture stores, met mayors and governors, advised on local pageants, and awarded a trophy to a horse. On a goodwill journey to France, where she wore her wrinkle-resistant Bancroft Everglaze fabric wardrobe, she was asked to carry a vial of Hudson River water to be poured into the Seine as a sign of friendship, but it leaked out in her suitcase so she refilled it from the hotel tap when she arrived.

By March 1951, Slaughter had reframed Betbeze's swimsuit rebellion as the pageant's own. "We no longer permit our Miss America to go traipsing around the country in a bathing suit," she said. There was even talk of scrapping the swimsuit altogether, but by August Slaughter had shelved this idea.

Betbeze said all the right things but did largely what she wanted, including tacking vacation days on to her pageant stops. (Other "formers" describe a year-long forced march of appearances six days a week, through brutal weather, homesickness, and 102-degree fevers.) The night she won, she announced she wasn't a smoker, but over a meal of corned beef and cheesecake with a reporter in Miami that year, she bummed a cigarette and confided that when high school assemblies asked if she smoked, she told them, "Well, I didn't smoke in high school." She received piles of marriage proposals during her reign—163, if you must know—and suggested her mail-order suitors see their local psychiatrists. Though handsome bachelors were whistled in to escort her to formal events wherever she traveled, she claimed she had no time for romance, and anyway, she was more interested in the type of simple man who wouldn't have the nerve to ask a Miss America out.

Slaughter liked her, calling her, in a letter written to her shortly after her reign ended, "the sweetest kid I ever knew" and "the nicest Miss America in our history," signing off, "with much love." In letters to Betbeze over the next few years, she thanked her for managing an unspecified assault on the pageant, gossiped about office politics, and discussed the latest winners' earnings ("That old Miss America title pays off these days to my children, and the more they make the better I like it"). But she was also keen on the opportunities men might offer, cheering Betbeze on through various liaisons (including with an unnamed prince), encouraging her to "enjoy the little boys" and, in a vaguely pimpy moment, telling her to make sure any millionaires she dated "pay for the pleasure of knowing Betbeze." Of course, Slaughter had her limits. When Betbeze traveled to Cuba, she advised her not to get involved "with any Cubans or foreigners—just stick with Good Old American Money."

After her reign, Betbeze declined numerous movie offers because (depending on where you're reading) signing meant the studios controlled you, she simply wasn't interested ("I just didn't want to be an actress," she said, "but back then no one could believe that"), or a 20th Century Fox executive who came calling had offended her by patting her backside and telling her it was too big. Also, says Dolly, "There was a very private part of her." When a Columbia Pictures rep told her she could be the new Rita Hayworth, she said, "I think I'll stay the old Yolande Betbeze."

She toured with the Mobile Opera Guild in 1951–52, then moved to New York to study philosophy at the New School for Social Research over the next two years. Though she'd taken some voice lessons during her reign, there had been little time to practice, and between that and the fact that "people expect you to be a raving idiot" as Miss America, it was difficult to parlay her talent into a career. Plus, she said, the title "brings all the wrong types around and the good people stay away."

In 1955, Betbeze was studying acting with Stella Adler in a class with Marlon Brando. That year, she renovated the old Minsky's burlesque theater on East Houston Street to launch an Off-Broadway venue called the Rooftop Theater, and began coproducing plays there, both classics and new work, though she said she wasn't ready to act in them herself. In 1955, she considered casting three New York-based Miss Americas as the witches in *Macbeth*, then reconsidered, because "people that are interested in Shakespeare aren't interested in beauty winners." *The New York Times* ran reviews of Rooftop productions (including a much-lauded *Ulysses*, starring Zero Mostel) through 1958.

But from the minute she arrived in New York, Betbeze was drawn irresistibly to activism. She volunteered for the NAACP and CORE (Congress of Racial Equality), and her consciousness-raising drove her to question the meaning and merits of Miss America as an institution. In 1952, she, Myerson, and Shopp publicly decried a South Dakota State College rule against Native American contestants in their pageant. "It is a humiliation to every girl who enters the contest to feel that others just as pretty but of a different race are not free to compete with her," Betbeze said.

In a 1953 *Look* magazine article about her Miss America tour of duty, she wrote, "There was (and still is) something baffling about the public's enthusiasm about someone caught suddenly—and briefly—in the limelight of publicity. Why are temperance clubs asking me to come out publicly against drinking and smoking for women? Why are boys' clubs interested in having me speak about civics?" Like Myerson, she saw there were good uses for this kind of platform. She demonstrated outside Sing Sing Prison when Julius and Ethel Rosenberg were executed as accused communist spies in 1953, and in 1960 she joined a group of Broadway actors (many from the cast of *A Raisin in the Sun*) to picket a Manhattan Woolworth store in protest of Woolworth's segregated seating in the South. "I'm a southern girl, but I'm a thinking girl," she told *The New York Times*. "Every southerner in New York I know is in favor of the Congress of Racial Equality." ("That was against her dignity," Slaughter later sniffed.)

In the coming years, Betbeze would drift away from the pageant, calling out its racism in the 1960s and sexism in the '70s, then softening in the '80s after it became more diverse. She had returned to judge twice in the 1950s and appeared in an onstage reunion in 1960, but declined later invitations, saying, according to Dolly, "Why would I want to do that? You're not Miss America, y'all are Miss White Christian. When you include all ethnicities and religions, races, creeds, then you're Miss America, and then I'm back."

Its provincialism also drew her disdain. In a 1969 profile in *The Washington Post Magazine* called "Miss America Was a Rebel (and

Still Is)," where she appeared in leather boots and mod sunglasses, she was asked if she attended the pageant each September and replied, "Good Lord, no. I love to watch it on TV though. It's great to see the essence of mediocrity chalked up on a point system . . . Usually they don't have a talent at all and they have two weeks in which to learn how to do something, a cultural thing, you know . . . [like] some Southern belle reads Shakespeare with an incredible accent. Oh, it's the greatest show on earth. I wouldn't miss it."

Betbeze ran her private life as she had her pageant life—very intentionally, with her hand firmly on the tiller. In 1954, she married Matthew Fox, a film and TV executive, who Slaughter was no doubt happy to learn was a multimillionaire, albeit a short, balding, 200-pound one. He was nearly twice her age, smart and charming and forward-thinking (he bought the first substantial commercial film archive for television and acquired a pay-as-you-watch TV station). They lived a jet-set life, with houses on two coasts and jaunts to Europe. But eight years in, with no luck getting pregnant, they had a problem, and Betbeze Fox found a solution. She had a brief affair with an Italian actor and director, Joseph "Pepi" Lenzi, and—voilá—her daughter was born on Betbeze Fox's own birthday.

"It was a means to an end," says Dolly, who took a DNA test to confirm Lenzi's paternity. "There were no surrogates. She was always ahead of her time and she was always going to get what she wanted." Matthew Fox died of a heart attack when Dolly was a toddler, and when she was in kindergarten, Betbeze Fox told her who her father was. She never met him. Later, when Dolly asked her mother if her biological father had known about Lenzi, she responded in her buttery drawl, "Everything's *aaaallll* right."

To pursue her political passions, Betbeze Fox moved with Dolly to Georgetown, where she managed to compound her glamour and

general fabulousness beyond the scope of any Miss America before or since. She bought Jackie Kennedy's former house, became
a Democratic fundraiser, and started a lifelong romance with the
resistance fighter Cherif Guellal, Algeria's first ambassador to the
United States after it gained independence from France.

"For more than a year now," *The Washington Post* gushed, "it has
been the true life romance Broadway producers wanted to make
into a musical . . . Random House thought to turn it into a best
seller with six figure movie rights. Magazines such as *Esquire* sent
top talent like Gay Talese to Washington to chronicle its develop-
ments." Guellal served as a loving stepfather to Dolly, though the
couple never married. When Dolly, like her mother, lost her husband at a young age, Betbeze Fox helped raise her granddaughter.

She was "very ERA, anti-nuke, anti-Vietnam, very liberal, [a]
raging Democrat, and put a lot of energy into that, which is why she
moved to Washington," says Dolly. Betbeze Fox knew five presidents and hobnobbed with luminaries from journalists Ben Bradlee
and Sally Quinn (her neighbors) to Andy Warhol, Liz Taylor, and
birth control pioneer Margaret Sanger. She was friends with Bobby
Kennedy (and possibly more, if his monogrammed pajamas, which
Betbeze Fox owned, are any indication). "She was the first Miss
America that had true opinions of her own," says Dolly. "She just
didn't know any other way to live. If somebody was going to make a
racial slur or omit somebody because they were of a certain race, she
wasn't going to be quiet; she was gonna say, 'Well, that's just wrong.'
Or 'I'm not coming.' Or '*In your hat.*'"

Betbeze Fox didn't become a career singer, didn't run for office
(though she considered it), didn't even complete her degree. So what
did she represent as Miss America? She wasn't a typical American
girl—a self-described loner and bookworm before she competed,
a New Left activist afterward, albeit one dripping in diamonds.

She certainly didn't fulfill Slaughter's prissy Protestant ideal. She was a Catholic who married a Jew, lived "in sin" with a Muslim, and bore a child out of wedlock. (Also, she wore flats.) She was, perhaps, more like a first lady than a Miss America, connected to a dashing and influential Washington diplomat, but her causes and affiliations were her own, and she arrived in D.C. independently. If the pageant's claim to patriotism carried any weight, her political engagement reflected it most admirably, especially in a conservative decade before Miss Americas dared to express their political views. Had she not won the crown, she said in her seventies, "I would probably be in Mobile still, active in historic preservation and pouring a lot of tea."

———

WHATEVER PATRIOTIC CHORD THE PAGEANT still hoped to strike in the early 1950s, the U.S. military was playing against it. In 1952, two years into the U.S. involvement in the Korean War, the Department of Defense released a ten-minute recruitment film pointedly titled *The Real Miss America*. Actor Henry Fonda narrated as the film showed perfectly average-looking women at work as air traffic controllers, photographers, mapmakers, and biochemists laboring alongside men. It was a different tack from a World War II recruitment film called *Glamour Girls of 1943*.

Conversely, glamour was outpacing patriotism in the Miss America pageant. In 1952, the pageant brass decided that instead of appointing one of the usual city fathers to be grand marshal in the boardwalk parade, Hollywood celebrities would be invited—a risky decision, considering their power to outshine the beauties on display. Odder yet, given Slaughter's commitment to downplaying the flesh factor, was the choice of Marilyn Monroe, already known as much for her plunging necklines as her rising star after the release of *Asphalt Jungle* in 1950. Scheduled to be in Atlantic City for the premiere of *Monkey Business*, she also worked the pageant, riding atop an open convertible, smiling and waving to 150,000 cheering fans, wearing a halter dress cut treacherously in a V to the waist, and leaving the contestants to play, as the Associated Press put it, "wallflower roles to the bosomy, blonde screen star."

"It was rather embarrassing for the Pageant at the time," said that year's winner, Neva Langley, the first to triple-ace the swimsuit, evening gown, and talent segments. "I actually think she was rather *exposed* several times."

Albert Marks, a newly arrived pageant volunteer who later became its CEO, recalled that Monroe's dress was so tight he'd had to give her "a push by the derriere" to get her up onto her seat. Though her publicist claimed that "she murdered those poor little Miss Americas," Monroe was intimidated by them. "Surrounded by all those fresh, young, incredibly beautiful girls," she said, "I was terribly nervous, very unsure of myself." They were each photographed with her after the parade, but none, she said, would talk with her; most likely they too were intimidated. Back in town as a pageant judge, Betbeze stepped in and chatted with her to put her at ease. "She took it on herself to make that time bearable to me," said Monroe.

The next year, a photo of Monroe leading the parade landed on the cover of the revolutionary new men's magazine *Playboy*, which also contained nude shots taken of her four years earlier, packaged as the debut *Playboy* centerfold. Hugh Hefner's wildly successful magazine signaled the first stirrings of the sexual revolution, coming on the heels of the bestselling Kinsey Reports, published in 1948 and 1953, which candidly documented Americans' sexual appetites and practices, including premarital, extramarital, and gay sex. *Play-*

boy offered soft porn along with fashion, food, and wine advice for middle-class men at leisure in a world of postwar plenty; Hefner said it was for worldly men like him who wore loafers, owned hi-fis, and enjoyed jazz, foreign films, and dining out.

The bunnies disporting themselves in *Playboy*'s pages, however, were decidedly *not* sophisticated. Hefner described the Playmate of the Month as "a young, healthy, simple girl—the girl next door . . . we are not interested in the mysterious, difficult woman, the *femme fatale*, who wears elegant underwear, with lace . . . The *Playboy* girl . . . is naked, well-washed with soap and water. And she is happy."

She sounded a lot like Miss America, undressed. ("Girls, show this great city that you're happy American girls, happy to be in Atlantic City, the city of beautiful girls!" BeBe Shopp had entreated the class of 1949.) The playmates were introduced with their measurements, just like the contestants profiled in the pageant program each year. They too delivered cheesecake with a side of culture— or culture with a side of cheesecake. They too, Hef claimed, came from "respectable families" and earned both money and "a passport to TV and the movies, generally" by posing. They too embodied a wholesome white ideal, though *Playboy* would put a black woman on its cover nearly two decades before Miss America crowned a black winner. As David Halberstam wrote in *The Fifties*, the bunnies "seemed to have stopped off to do a Playboy photo shoot on their way to cheerleading practice or to the sorority house."

To be sure, the beauty queens had to do more than sizzle in their swimsuits to win their titles. Colleen Hutchins (1952) had a master's degree before she even competed. Evelyn Ay (1954) was the first Ivy League winner. But the emphasis on "beauty of face and figure," the pageant's axiom, dovetailed uncomfortably with Hefner's more salacious celebrations of feminine pulchritude. "Miss

America is not a beauty contest," Slaughter kept insisting, by which she meant it wasn't a skin show. When the Vatican City newspaper reached across the ocean to call it "a cattle market-like display," she countered, "There must be nothing to create a feeling of emphasis on the body. The swimsuits must just show a natural, healthy girl." Slaughter might tell one newspaper they were necessary to show fitness, and another that they made sense in a beach town like Atlantic City. But her justifications didn't resolve other fine points of illogic, like the fact that after the Betbeze rebellion, winners were required to wear a swimsuit in the competition but forbidden to do so on tour. At least the *Playboy* centerfolds had a purity of purpose.

The two worlds collided in 1992, when 1982 Miss America Elizabeth (Ward) Gracen stripped down for *Playboy*; but for the moment, the pageant held the line unwaveringly. Betbeze's successors were scandal-free, low-profile winners—one was even a Mormon. And in 1954, Miss America reached a glorious apotheosis by crowning Lee Ann Meriwether, who had the movie star looks and solid talent to launch a lasting acting career, along with something that would put wind in Miss America's sails for decades: television.

At first, Slaughter was reluctant to agree to a pageant telecast because it could hurt ticket sales, but when ABC ponied up $10,000 for rights and Philco, an electronics manufacturer, stepped in as a sponsor, the deal was on, and it paid off handsomely. Twenty-seven million people watched Meriwether's crowning—about 39 percent of TV viewers that night. Bess Myerson, by then a well-known TV personality, coanchored, staying on for fourteen years. (And a future royal, actress Grace Kelly, judged.) The timing was perfect. TVs were being purchased at a rate of 20,000 a day that year; by 1959, nine in ten households would own one. Miss America became one of the longest-running TV broadcasts in American history.

Meriwether hadn't set out to compete. A drama student at City College of San Francisco, she'd been unwittingly entered in the Miss San Francisco contest by a fraternity to represent her sorority, then went on to win Miss California. "I had no knowledge of the pageant really at all," she said in the 2002 PBS documentary *Miss America*. "I knew there was a Miss America pageant, but I thought it was a 'bathing beauty' contest, and as such I would never have entered. And then my father passed away and . . . my life sort of stopped right there. And my mother said the money is no longer here, Daddy's gone, and if you want to continue on with school . . . go to Atlantic City."

One of the most successful Miss Americas—she was nominated for two Golden Globe Awards and an Emmy—Meriwether appeared in the first *Batman* film as a sultry Catwoman in a glittering, skintight catsuit; played long-running roles on *Barnaby Jones* and *All My Children*; and guest-starred on *The Fugitive*, *Star Trek*, and *Mission Impossible*. A 1954 Associated Press photo shows her flanked by Yolande Betbeze and Jean Bartel during a rehearsal for her first starring role, in a Philco-sponsored teleplay called *Run, Girl, Run* that ignited her career. "Yolande and Jean were there to support me," says Meriwether, and the three became good friends.

In 1955, the pageant saw another historic first: the arrival of Bert Parks, the emcee who became synonymous, for viewers of a certain age, with Miss America for more than a quarter of a century. A former actor and radio and TV host, Parks was sometimes called "Mr. Miss America."

"He wasn't a celebrity flown in on a Saturday night," said Atlantic City historian Vicki Gold Levi (also a former pageant judge) in PBS's *Miss America*. "He was there all week getting to know them. They trusted him. He loved what he was doing, and he really was one of the defining factors that made . . . television households love Miss America." Well, he *usually* loved it; his first year, when the number of women doing dramatic presentations hit a high in the wake of Meriwether's success with a J. M. Synge monologue, he tore backstage and exclaimed, "No, no more, I can't stand any more Bobby-sox Bernhardts!"

Parks was smooth, accommodating, genuinely excited onstage as he crowned queen after queen, and reassuring to the most tentative and terrified contestants as they were blindsided by random questions he pulled from a fishbowl, such as "When you raise a family, give us your reasons for raising a large or small family." He inaugurated the pageant's signature song, "There She Is, Miss America," which had been written in under an hour by composer Bernie Wayne (who also wrote "Blue Velvet"), a man who'd never attended a beauty contest. Parks sang it with a swoony, slightly tragic glissando, launching the winners down the runway with his serenade. As historian Kathy Peiss has observed, it evoked a wedding or a debutante ball, with Parks, then forty, giving away the bride.

> There she is, Miss America
> There she is, your ideal
> The dream of a million girls who are more than pretty
> Can come true in Atlantic City
> For she may turn out to be
> The queen of femininity
>
> There she is, Miss America
> There she is, your ideal
> With so many beauties she'll take the town by storm
> With her all-American face and form

And there she is
Walking on air, she is
Fairest of the fair, she is
There she is—Miss America

For all Slaughter's protestations that the pageant wasn't just about beauty (to prove it, she had even tactlessly remarked that Miss America 1952 was not the prettiest contestant), the song ballyhooed nothing but. Then there was the phrase "your ideal." Whose ideal? In her memoir *Negroland*, the Pulitzer Prize–winning writer Margo Jefferson recalls coming home with her sister after "a rapturous night" watching the pageant at her grandmother's house in Chicago in the 1950s. "Mama, you could be a Miss America!" they exclaim, and, Jefferson writes, "Their mother's laugh deflects them, as does her grandmother's smile. (*These children know so little about the world* . . .) The two of them know exactly who is beautiful, who is pretty, and who is *attractive* by the national beauty standard . . . Mother considers herself attractive. She and Grandma believe that most Negro women are considered, at best, attractive."

This double standard had consequences beyond beauty contests. After the 1954 *Brown v. Board of Education* decision banning separate schools for blacks and whites, similar inequities were challenged in housing, on public transportation—famously by Rosa Parks in 1955—and in the workplace, where in some female-specific jobs, race-based discrimination was entangled with looks-based bias. In 1956, for example, when a black woman named Dorothy Franklin was rejected after applying to be a stewardess with TWA, she filed a lawsuit against the airline, which claimed it was her appearance, not her race, that cost her the job. "These men regarded beauty as a fact upon which all reasonable men could agree," Maxine Leeds Craig writes in *Ain't I a Beauty Queen?*

"They discussed race as if it had nothing to do with appearance and beauty—as if beauty had never been racialized."

Ever since Thelma Porter was named Miss Subways in New York City in 1948, black women had pressured white beauty contests to integrate, often with the support of the NAACP. They occasionally succeeded. (Sometimes, however, the racism *followed* the victory; when Dora Martin Berry made national news as the first black Miss State University of Iowa in 1955, the university refused to acknowledge her win and canceled events normally scheduled for the campus queen.) Though African American pageants initially prized a light-skinned ideal, they evolved to include a broader range of black beauty. Even so, segregated contests came to seem marginalizing, as Craig notes, like "mere imitations." Why *shouldn't* black women assume center stage, especially when Miss America delivered the biggest jackpot? Why couldn't *they* represent America?

A remarkable case of separate-but-supposedly-equal was happening within the pageant as well. Though Mifaunwy Shunatona had competed in 1941, the pageant wouldn't see another Native American contestant for thirty years. But astonishingly, noncompeting Native American "guests" were serving again as cultural ambassadors in the 1950s. Princess America was no more, but the Miss Indian America pageant, modeled on Miss America, ran from 1953 to 1989 as part of the All American Indian Days festival in Wyoming and later North Dakota. The Native American queens crowned from 1953 to 1957 embarked on a goodwill tour east, typically culminating in a visit to Washington, D.C., with a stop at the Miss America Pageant. The winners didn't compete, however, because their competition wasn't part of a pageant franchise like the Jaycees that fed Atlantic City.

The Miss Indian Americas weren't included as members of American culture, but rather as emissaries from another culture altogether. The 1954 titleholder, a Standing Rock Sioux named Mary Louise Defender, who later became a 1999 NEA National Heritage Fellowship honoree, rode in the parade and gave a three-minute talk at the pageant for "the easterners," as *The Bismarck Tribune* noted, "many of whom still have fantastic ideas of North Dakota, its wild western ways, and the Indian situation." She wore a hand-sewn deer sinew dress, a belt of silver disks, and a carved deer bone necklace. Her successor, Rita Ann McLaughlin of the Crow Nation in Montana, was a dental technician who spoke sardonically about her journey east in 1955: "I'm afraid I may disappoint some people . . . It may disillusion them when they find out that I can speak English and that I don't live in a tepee."

It's hard to imagine a bigger cultural mashup in pageant history than the medley of characters in attendance the year the last Miss Indian America appeared, in 1957. A Navajo named Delores Jean Shorty was the honorary guest; Yolande Betbeze Fox served as one of eleven judges along with TV personality Kitty Carlisle, composer Deems Taylor, theater producer Theodore Mann, and the chairwoman of the National Panhellenic Conference of national sororities; Bess Myerson was still coanchoring; and novelist-to-be Philip Roth was covering the event for *The New Republic*. The pageant was either finding its cultural bearings or had no idea what in God's name it was doing.

"The first few moments under the crown," Roth wrote of winner Marilyn Van Derbur, Miss Colorado, "must be perilous ones for a new Miss America; not only must the young lady extricate herself from the gleeful ooze secreted by the Master of Ceremonies, Bert Parks, but she must not falter under the pandemonium of music, flashbulbs, and applause." (She did not.)

Roth had fun cracking on the talent: "Some of the . . . girls did the Charleston while smiling, played the accordion while smiling, and sang while smiling. More ambitious talents were displayed by Miss Oklahoma, who recited Edna St. Vincent Millay with gestures . . ." Van Derbur played a song (the only one she knew) on the organ (while smiling). When Parks plucked a question out of the fishbowl and asked Miss Oklahoma what her ambition was—for her firstborn—she said, "to be normal . . . and exactly like my brothers and my daddy." It sounded like something out of *Deliverance*.

In an aside, Roth confessed that he was trying to figure out why he watched the pageant every year and could only point to the rather unremarkable fact that his boyhood barber always had a picture of the latest winner on his scissor tray. He imagined the old man would be disappointed to learn, had he lived to watch it on TV, that the contestants nattered on about "their brothers and their daddies." But he went on to think about it much more after that, because the character Dawn in his Pulitzer-winning novel *American Pastoral* (1997) was a disaffected beauty queen.

The strangest moment of the 1957 pageant passed entirely without notice. Roth noted that after Parks sang "There She Is" and before twenty-year-old Van Derbur was taken backstage to receive a Philco television, her family was invited onstage. This was a first. The pageant wanted to spotlight the perfect American family: Marilyn, an athletic Denver debutante with straight As; her three sisters, all pretty University of Colorado alums; and their classy, attractive parents. It was, after all, the 1950s, when a mythical ideal of suburban family bliss was in ascent on TV shows like *Ozzie and Harriet*. But they couldn't have picked a worse family to showcase. Van Derbur's father had sexually abused her from age five until she was eighteen.

"People were saying, 'Here she is, Miss Colorado,' and my subconscious was saying, if they really knew you, you would not be here," says Van Derbur, now in her eighties, who still works as an incest survivor advocate. In her memoir, *Miss America By Day* (the title references the daytime identity she split off from her nighttime self), she writes, "People commented on my Miss America posture. How regal I was. I wasn't regal, I was rigid. My physical rigidity, brought on by locking up my body so no one could get in, has been one of the most difficult and unrelenting long-term effects of incest. But my rigid, erect body was perfect for 'the Miss America look.'" Many of her achievements leading up to the pageant, from joining the college choir and a sorority to being a debutante and winning Miss Colorado, grew out of a pursuit of perfection to offset her decimated self-image.

Van Derbur repressed her memories until she was twenty-four, had a breakdown at forty (when her daughter reached the age she was when the abuse began), and struggled with anxiety, panic attacks, and spells of paralysis. When her story went public in 1991, she became an early media test case of public responses to the concept of repressed memories: her story was questioned—until her sister revealed she too had been abused. She helped puncture the myth that abuse didn't happen in "good" families—her father was a millionaire philanthropist and the president of the Denver Area Boy Scout Council.

Like many Miss Americas after her, Van Derbur became a motivational speaker. The pageant, she says, was excellent training for the job, but it was a terrifying baptism by fire. Winners were given no coaching or preparation for what lay ahead. The day after her crowning, she and Slaughter rode in a limousine to New York, where Van Derbur would appear on *The Steve Allen Show*. They arrived at the Waldorf Astoria, with police escorts amid screaming sirens, three hours before the show. As they headed to their rooms to change, Slaughter said, "Hurry, dear, they're waiting."

"Who is waiting?"

"The National Mayor's Convention. You're going to address them."

"What should I say?" Van Derbur asked, flooded with anxiety. It was the first she'd heard of this.

"Anything you want to, dear."

Van Derbur sees this not as a failure of the system, but as a vote of confidence—"a gift," as she puts it. "It forced me to develop my own ideas," she says, "to say the things I felt strongly about—not too many in that era, but she just knew that I could do it." Van Derbur gave as many as fifteen talks a day (sometimes in the midst of an anxiety attack), including one following Vice President Richard Nixon at a Green Bay Packers game.

Still, her reign was, she says in her memoir, "a year of incredible loneliness, and extreme stress, which were exacerbated by not having anyone with whom to share my feelings." She hadn't made friends at the pageant because while the others were out shopping and swimming, she spent her spare time in her hotel room trying to center herself, visualizing the confidence she needed to project her public persona. Difficult as it was, she doesn't regret it—first, because the money she made left her financially independent at twenty-one (the pageant took no cut of the winners' earnings), which was huge at a time when banks could refuse women credit cards without a husband's signature; second, because she honed the skills she would use professionally as an advertising spokesperson and as the first female guest lecturer for General Motors; and finally, because the title "gave me the entrée for the rest of my life. The reason I was on the cover of *People* magazine was not because I was an incest survivor but because I was a Miss America incest survivor."

Van Derbur's transformation from her post–Miss America years, when she gave exhaustingly peppy talks on airy topics like "Goals and Dreams," to her decades as a speaker of searing intensity about incest, is profound. (In a 2018 lecture, she mentions feeling like she'd had "an ax embedded in my body.") Playwright Eve Ensler called her 2004 memoir "the finest book ever written on this subject." And several female journalists told her, before or after interviewing her about it, "Me too."

It's no surprise that the swimsuit portion of the pageant was miserable for her, but her objection to it—and she has *always* objected to it—concerns viewers, not contestants. To the women who said, when the swimsuit was eliminated from the pageant in 2018, that they were proud to show their bodies and wanted it back, Van Derbur says, "This isn't really about us. This is about the message we give to young women throughout America . . . that we need certain measurements to be worthy of competition. And I think it's the *wrong* message to send."

Though her relationship with Slaughter would end with disappointment, Van Derbur is helpful in illuminating what made so many winners devoted to her, despite, in some cases, their ambivalence about her. Betbeze Fox was fond of her, despite her racism, because she'd believed in her educational mission. Myerson said, "I learned a lot from Lenora. I was always impressed by her ability to sell . . . I watched her feed her 'dreams and ideals' pitch to hundreds and hundreds of people and make them believe it as I believed it. Truthfully, I never stopped believing it."

Van Derbur sharpens the point: "She was a powerful woman, and I was brought up in what I think was a normal home in the 1940s [where] the man had the power and the woman did what she was told to do. That's certainly what happened in our family. My mother had no power at all. So, to meet a woman so powerful . . ."

Slaughter didn't disguise her power or hide it behind men, including her husband. When she married Brad Frapart, a suave Tennessee businessman, the wedding was in Atlantic City, and she got him a job with the pageant—first as a parade director, then as business manager. She continued to use her own surname professionally, and she was never coy about asserting her authority, which included banning a *Life* reporter from the 1958 contest because she didn't like a story he had written about it the year before. In 1954, when a woman claiming to be Miss Connecticut took the Connecticut badge during registration, wouldn't return it, and picketed the pageant outside in a rolling chair for three hours after the real Miss Connecticut was identified, Slaughter waltzed out and interceded. "I run the pageant, dear. I'd like my badge returned. You are not Miss Connecticut."

But too often and for too long, her intolerance poisoned her proto-feminism. When Van Derbur was invited to appear on Edward R. Murrow's *Person to Person* celebrity TV show on the same episode with Nat King Cole, Slaughter tried, unsuccessfully, to prevent it because she didn't want Miss America on a show with a black man. And in the 1990s, soon after Van Derbur's incest story was public, she visited Slaughter in retirement in Scottsdale, and they discussed her coming out with it.

"She let me know that talking about sexual abuse was not OK," says Van Derbur. "I got in my car [to leave] and thought, you know, we're working for the same thing. What was most important to Lenora was that her girls had a college education. And I wanted to help young women overcome their shame at having been raped." After she left, Van Derbur wrote Slaughter a letter saying, "I was ashamed of myself for 53 years. I have great pride in myself, and I have chosen not to be in the company of anyone who feels shame for me. So, I will not be in touch with you again. But please know that I will always love and respect you."

She never heard from Slaughter again.

WITH ITS BOUNTY OF POLISHED, media-ready winners, the 1950s, generally considered Miss America's golden age, closed with one of the pageant's brightest stars: Mary Ann Mobley. She was a spunky singer from small-town Mississippi who went on to success as an actress, earning a 1965 Golden Globe Award as Most Promising Newcomer and appearing in films with Elvis Presley and Jerry Lewis, as well as on dozens of television shows. The 1958 pageant crystallized the mood and format of the ritual for years to come, with its combination of glamour and kitsch, small-town women quivering in the national spotlight, and Christian values rewarded with the fruit of atomic age capitalism; that year, Philco even launched a new series of Miss America brand television sets.

The gowns followed Christian Dior's New Look, launched in 1947, with nipped waists and billowing bell skirts that had announced the end of wartime rationing—and curtailed the ease of movement that had been so well suited to women's postwar independence. Ceil Chapman, an American designer who adapted the Dior look in more affordable dresses, used Bancroft fabrics in creating the official gowns throughout the decade. Until the mid-1960s, most of the women wore virginal white. The ever-evolving crown had finally jelled in a four-point model. And the talent (performed on air by the ten semifinalists) was dominated by ballet, opera, and classical piano—perennial pageant staples, bolstering its high culture bona fides against the pop music youthquake that artists like Elvis, Chuck Berry, and the Coasters had triggered.

Mobley's routine acknowledged the high/low tensions of the competition. Dressed in a white gown with a tiered lace skirt, she sang an aria against spare, tasteful piano chords, then stopped midway to announce, "I'm tired of being proper and cultured . . . I want to sing and dance to something that's solid and hot." She peeled the lower half of her dress away to reveal a tight knee-length pencil skirt and sang a vaudevillian rendition of the popular jazz standard "There'll Be Some Changes Made," unhitching her skirt before the final verse and dancing in a camisole just a bit longer than the swimsuit she'd appeared in earlier that evening. She was also wearing, as she did throughout the pageant, a charm bracelet bearing a Bible quotation—a gift from her Sunday school teacher.

Sanitized as it was by its campy-cute execution, the performance both reclaimed the burlesque baggage the pageant had worked so hard to discard and hinted at the liberatory impulses that would draw Mobley's generation to rock and Motown music in the 1960s. Slaughter said it was terrific but promptly added stripping to the running list of pageant prohibitions.

The on-stage interview questions—mostly about dating, men, and parenting—underscored Miss America's role as a compliant, virginal, family-focused belle—one whose winning scholarship might lead her to a husband, not a career. "How do you get a young man to say goodnight without calling your father?" "When you raise your children, will you be a strict parent, or a permissive parent, and why?" "What would you say is the most conspicuous fault of American men today?" (Miss Iowa broke the string of platitudinous answers by announcing that she and Miss California had just discovered they'd been dating the same cadet. "He has two very lovely ex-girlfriends," she laughed.)

Asked "What is your favorite topic when with a young man for opening the conversation?" Mobley paused, gathered her energy, and answered forcefully. "Well, I've read different articles that tell you how to get along with the opposite sex, and the first thing that they say is get him to talk about himself. So the first thing I ask is,

'Do you play football?' or 'What sport are you interested in?' Then if he doesn't say anything, you say, 'Well what are your hobbies?' And then you go down the line from there, and if you can't get him to answer you on any of those, then you're just quiet for the rest of the evening." The audience roared with approval.

That year, Miss Oklahoma, Anita Bryant, a singer who would record four Top 40 hits and become a notorious evangelical homophobe, fumbled badly when she was lobbed a current events question: "Do you think our education of today is preparing us for the space age?" She answered, "I think because of the emphasis that has been put on space, uh, the space age in education nowadays, that they *are* putting more emphasis in the education to uh, to take care of the problems that arise, that uh . . . yes, I do." As she realized she was bombing, she shot Parks a desperate glance that would be echoed, through the years, when other contestants fielded questions at once impossibly vague (education at what level?) and confoundingly specific (how should *she* know what schools were teaching?). Then, as now, answering "I don't know" was simply not an option.

The pageant had formalized the return of ex-queens, reintegrating them into the event by inviting them to be parade grand marshals, network commentators, or honored guests. With natural charm and an easy smile, Lee Meriwether coanchored the broadcast, now on CBS, beside Douglas Edwards, CBS's first evening news program anchor, who ran down the women's "vital statistics" like they were matters of grave national significance and called Meriwether "honey" as they bantered. The broadcast, expanded from ninety minutes to two hours, captivated nearly two-thirds of TV viewers that night: 60 million people.

Meriwether was later summoned onstage with five other formers, including Patricia Donnelly (1939), a singer and later a travel writer who betrayed none of the canned effervescence of a beauty queen, answering Parks's questions with polite, declarative indifference. Van Derbur, exhausted, delivered her farewell speech, poised and perfect and ready to pass the sash. Slaughter, too, was introduced and stood behind the five seated finalists, anxiously holding the ermine robe at the ready for the winner.

Since 1954, when the live audience was miffed to discover they'd missed seeing the finalists learning backstage, in front of TV cameras, that they were in the homestretch, winners stood on-stage for the announcement after an elimination process that pre-saged reality show competitions of the twenty-first century. In the final moments, Mobley and Miss Iowa, Joan Lucille MacDonald, were the lone survivors. It seemed a bit cruel to MacDonald when Parks announced, in one breath, that she was the first runner-up and Mobley was the winner, but she took it gamely, standing to exit in defeat and bowing to congratulate Mobley before she left. But Mobley had covered her face with her gloved hands and missed it. Slaughter draped the robe across her shoulders and walked the new queen over to Parks and Van Derbur, where she took a knee and received her crown.

No longer the mermaids of King Neptune's day, nor the citizen-scholars of the Jean Bartel and Bess Myerson era, the bathing beauties were now make-believe monarchs with a fully codified royal annunciation ("The Cinderella hour is approaching," Edwards an-nounced at the start of the broadcast). Parks, a mid-century King Neptune in a tailcoat and Brylcreem, took Mobley's hand and ad-dressed her solemnly: "Miss America, I ask you to rise. Go down and meet your subjects as I now sing you your song." And she did, stopping at the end of the runway to cry and blow kisses to the cam-era, then returning to join her family onstage. It was her mother, asked to comment, who injected a belated note of patriotism into the evening by saying that "with the placing of that crown on her head, she represents the best people in the world." As it happened, Mobley hailed from the state with the highest number of lynchings in the nation, including, three years earlier, that of fourteen-year-old Emmett Till. For better or worse, Miss America was indeed "the symbol of all we possess."

FIVE

Resisters

B
Y 1960, THE MISS AMERICA pageant was both a national institution and a template for niche competitions popping up all over, from the fleeting Miss Rural Electrification pageant in Texas to the swimsuit-free Miss Navajo Nation, which continues today, rewarding fluency in the Navajo language and knowledge of tribal history and traditional skills, including butchering sheep.

The men's bodybuilding competition Mr. America, founded in 1939, followed Miss America's lead, championing contestants for their moral and physical fitness; it also struggled for decades in its shadow, aspiring, according to historian John D. Fair, to become more than a body spectacle as Miss America had, and failing as steroids ultimately reduced it to a show of sheer vein-popping hulk. And from its inception in 1938, the *Mrs.* America contest haunted the pageant like the Ghost of Christmas Future, with married beauties doing expert baking, cleaning, ironing, diaper-changing, and bed-making. Winners received cash—no scholarships—and though the contest recognized homemakers' invisible labor, it mainly promoted a dreary aspirational domesticity.

The scholarships set Miss America apart from its imitators and sealed its brand. Even runners-up benefited from smaller winnings, tallied annually in the pageant yearbooks. But when contestants returned to college, their pageant pasts could backfire. Jacque Mercer said that professors at Arizona State University assumed she was stupid and students took her for a snob and snubbed her. Nancy Fleming, Miss America 1961, recalled, "I felt like a freak at MSU [Michigan State University]. I had just been on television three days before and I entered with a lot of fanfare. There was a lot of weirdness and rudeness. I was pointed out and stared at. It was really creepy."

After Miss New York State Miriam Russell competed against Mobley in 1958, she returned to college and was called to the dean's office to explain why she wanted "this leg show" on her resumé, she says in her memoir. She told him she'd won a $500 scholarship and had been proud to represent New York in Atlantic City. But she stopped listing the pageant on her resumés thereafter. Now a retired professor, she writes that though the scholarship helped her get her degree, "world events and the feminist movement made the Miss America pageant something that no longer spoke to what I was becoming or cared about." She quit watching it.

Like other educated women, some winners saw their career plans upended, after graduation, by social pressure to marry early and have children—something the pageant couldn't protect them from. But the board sent conflicting messages, both highlighting the scholarship in its yearbooks and profiling past winners according to their marital status and number of children, adding their professional history as an afterthought, if at all. Marilyn Buferd's film work was excised in a bio that read like a scold: "Marilyn Buferd is twice divorced. She and her eight-year-old son Nicky live in Hollywood." BeBe Shopp's degree from the Manhattan School of Music and subsequent work as a vibraphonist counted for nothing. She was married with three children. End of story. And during the 1963 pageant, three state winners dressed as cheerleaders did a dance number that seemed to miss the point of women's education altogether. "T-E-A-M, Yay . . . football!" they cheered in a duet with Parks, who sang, "What good is college without the football game?"

In the early 1960s, American culture was changing in ways the pageant couldn't reconcile with its vision of Miss America as "our Cinderella queen." The arrival of the Pill in 1960 was a giant step toward sexual agency. Women began to question the double standard that assumed, as Parks's fishbowl questions had, that it was a woman's job to thwart a date's advances when in truth she might share his desire. In her bestselling 1962 book *Sex and the Single Girl*, Helen Gurley Brown (later *Cosmopolitan* magazine's editor) exhorted readers to enjoy sex and put off or even forgo marriage while they racked up lovers—and burnished their own careers. The single woman, she announced, "far from being a creature to be pitied and patronized, is emerging as the new glamour girl of our times." Brown's maniacal focus on men and how to attract them through soul-sucking self-improvement regimens would become the bane of *Cosmo* (beauty was something to be achieved, sometimes through illusion, always for men, often at great expense). But her message of fulfillment *with* a man, instead of through one, was progressive.

One could argue that for women, the 1960s as we know them—a decade that would transform American culture, overtake the pageant, and trample the genteel womanhood Slaughter held dear and worked to preserve—began in 1963. The Equal Pay Act outlawed gender-based pay discrimination at a time when white women were paid 60 percent of what men earned in comparable jobs, and black women just 42 percent. Betty Friedan's landmark book *The Feminine Mystique* documented middle-class homemakers' roiling dissatisfaction with domestic life and, for those who'd been to college, the waste of their degrees on it. Its tremendous popularity spurred women to organize. In 1966, when the pathbreaking African American lawyer Pauli Murray proposed, in a meeting with Friedan, the creation of an NAACP for women, the National Organization for Women was born.

In early 1963, weeks after poet Sylvia Plath committed suicide, her novel about a young working woman in New York, *The Bell Jar*, was published. It voiced a scorching cynicism and despair through an autobiographical character struggling with the smothering social constraints on women—especially ambitious women like Plath herself. The same year, pop culture began to churn with women's restlessness and rebellion. In the comedy *Sunday in New York*, Jane Fonda played a music critic who fears she's the only twenty-two-year-old virgin in New York City and sets out to change that by pouncing on a virtual stranger. She grapples with the budding sexual freedoms of the period and questions the double standard that allows her brother to sleep with anyone he wants while admonishing her to remain a virgin.

With their ratted bouffants and rivers of eyeliner, the Ronettes sang "Be My Baby," and Martha Reeves and the Vandellas dropped the simmering, sexy "(Love is Like a) Heat Wave," sending a thrill up the spines of American girls by voicing a frank erotic hunger. These urban glam goddesses were a hell of a lot more exciting than the mousy Cinderellas puttering around the pageant stage in ball gowns. And when Lesley Gore's proto-feminist "You Don't Own

Me" hit number 2 on the Billboard chart after the Beatles' "I Wanna Hold Your Hand," it was a declaration of independence.

The female body, which the pageant simultaneously paraded and policed, was coming undressed in the art world by women who claimed it as a visual medium after centuries of serving as muses and models for men. That year, Carolee Schneemann appeared naked in her photo series *Eye Body: 36 Transformative Actions*, the first of many body art–themed pieces she would create on paper and in live shows as a feminist performance art pioneer. (The next year, in *Cut Piece*, Yoko Ono allowed people to snip away her clothing—a comment on the passive female form in visual art and the viewer's complicity in exploiting it.) Even Jacqueline Kennedy, the fashionable and refined first lady Frank Sinatra dubbed "America's Queen," used her body in an act of resistance by refusing to remove her blood-stained suit on the day of JFK's murder, including during Lyndon B. Johnson's swearing-in. "I want them to see what they have done to Jack," she told Lady Bird Johnson, who noticed her right glove was caked with blood. It was a year when women's public truth-telling began to puncture a legacy of stifling politesse. And it was a year of dawning possibility. Even Barbie, that other embodiment of perfect plastic (white) womanhood, now four years old, was on the move: Mattel introduced "Career Girl" Barbie in 1963.

As the decade marched on, the pageant dug in, steadying itself against the currents of change, anchored by bigger sponsors—Pepsi and Oldsmobile—and sanctified by illustrious older judges—George Balanchine, Arthur Fiedler, Joan Crawford, Vincent Price. The stage shows became showier and better produced for television, sidestepping any concession to the erupting youth culture of the moment, which was on fire for bad girls with attitude like the Shangri-Las, or in awe of the chart-topping women of Motown—the Supremes and the Marvelettes, Mary Wells and Tammi Terrell.

Even after the 1964 Civil Rights Act banned race-based discrimination, Miss America merrily carried on without a single black contestant. At a 1965 press conference with winner Deborah Bryant, a reporter asked why. Slaughter stepped in and shut it down. "She shouldn't have to answer a question about a national problem. She's not the president," she snapped before piloting Bryant out of the room, adding that "there is no bar whatsoever" to black entrants.

On the one hand, it was true that the judges had only the largely segregated state contests' picks to choose from; they were fed by organizations like the Jaycees, whose membership was 3 percent African American. (As Frank Deford snarked, "Miss America merely deals in the same processes that also keep blacks, and other minorities in some instances, from the best schools, houses, jobs and suburbs.") On the other hand, when Slaughter had disliked the lowlife fairground girls turning up in Atlantic City in the 1930s, she overhauled the national feeder system. Diversity, in fact, was down: by 1965, only states could compete, which cut Puerto Rico out of the running altogether.

Latinas were likewise unofficially excluded. In *Something to Declare: Essays*, Dominican American author Julia Alvarez wrote about watching the pageant with her immigrant family as a teen in the 1960s: "There they stood, fifty puzzle pieces forming the pretty face of America, so we thought, though most of the color had been left out . . ." She and her sisters complained about "how short we were, about how our hair frizzed, how our figures didn't curve like those of the bathing beauties we'd seen on TV." But the pageant also opened a window of possibility, she noted, by celebrating college women as role models. "Everything in our native culture had instructed us otherwise: girls were to have no aspirations beyond being good wives and mothers."

———

WITH THE TELEVISION BROADCAST TARGETING a demographic sweet spot of middle-American viewers (the pageant claimed the highest ratings five times during the 1960s), the winners got blander and smoother, more rural and suburban, hailing overwhelmingly from the Southern and Plains states. (In the decade following the Brown v. Board of Education ruling, half the winners were Southern white women.) Gone were the saucypots like Betbeze and the careerists like Myerson. Vonda Kay Van Dyke (1965) brandished a Bible throughout the competition. Days after her crowning, she was on her knees, praying with Billy Graham.

And something strange was happening. The pageant Slaughter had rebuilt as a road to college was becoming an expressway to evangelism. In her 1966 memoir, *That Girl in Your Mirror*, Van Dyke wrote, "I wanted to be Miss America for one reason—I wanted to tell people about the Christ I love and try to serve." Miss America 1968 Debra Barnes (now Snodgrass), a music professor at Missouri Southern State University, told me that her win was a springboard for her teaching career, but more significantly, though she didn't find God until 1970, it positioned her to share that "the greatest thing in my life is that I know Jesus Christ is my savior." Months after her win, Phyllis George (1971) was testifying at a Billy Graham stadium crusade. From the early 1960s, when Christianity crept into the ceremony itself (the song "May God Keep you in the Palm of His Hand" preceded the 1964 coronation), to the '80s and '90s, when more than half the contestants were born again, Convention Hall did double duty as an evangelical launchpad.

Squaring the swimsuit with scripture required deft semantic gymnastics. Some reasoned it was their duty to use their looks to spread the good news, even if that meant first clomping around in heels and little more than lingerie on national television. Others linked physical beauty with God's beauty—a gift to be celebrated through pageantry. A Christian miracle was all Cheryl Prewitt needed to justify competing in 1980, years after a car accident that left one leg two inches shorter than the other. She was healed, she said, by a Pentecostal minister whose touch sent her to a faraway place where she met Jesus and her leg instantly sprang back to its full length.

As the judges sized her up during the swimsuit competition, she thought, "Anyone who's had any doubts about my story, just look at these legs. Look at them! They're great. They're perfect. They are living proof that God, in his love and power, can take the most crippled legs and transform them into something beautiful." Unlike the women who merely endured the swimsuit portion—or worse, sweated, shook, or vomited in anticipation of it—Prewitt was jazzed about it. "I felt fabulous," she wrote in her memoir.

The swimsuit itself had seen a sea change since the Inter-City Beauties first hit the sand in the 1920s. What began as a celebration of fashion emancipation had become a hidebound allegiance to the past as popular styles skipped beyond the pageant-approved standard. Until its mutiny in 1951, Catalina had kept things current by dictating the annual model (including, just once, a magnificent two-piece with its signature flying fish soaring across the skirt). From the trimmer two-pieces of the 1940s, to the structured maillots of the '50s, with low-cut molded bras and corset-like bodices, to the bikini, which landed on American shores in the 1960s, swimwear covered less and less and showcased more and more. (The 1960 novelty hit "Itsy Bitsy Teenie Weenie Yellow Polkadot Bikini" described a girl turning blue in the water for fear of coming out in her skimpy new suit.) But until 1970, the pageant insisted on one-pieces with modesty panels—lengths of fabric that stretched straight across the lower crotch like vanishingly short pubic skirts. They were so dated, the contestants had trouble finding them in stores; likewise, the knee-length skirts Slaughter required because she thought mini-skirts were the devil's own handiwork. Once *Sports Illustrated* rolled out its first swimsuit edition in 1964, however, anyone hankering for a culturally sanctioned all-American flesh fest could enjoy spicier displays in the privacy of their own home.

As the pageant crowned small-towners throughout the decade (the one exception, Vonda Kay Van Dyke, hailed from Phoenix), the realities of the reign year often came as a mind-snapping surprise, especially to women who'd entered their first pageants just a month or two before. Some had never been on a plane; most had never lived away from their families. "I'd never worked before . . . most of the contestants haven't," said Lynda Lee Mead (1960). "I'd never even inquired what a Miss America does. All of a sudden, I was getting up at six every morning and spending all day in the limelight."

Jane Jayroe (1967) detailed this whiplash effect in her 2006 memoir *More Grace than Glamour: My Life as Miss America and Beyond*. From the post-crowning moment when she was hounded by photographers backstage, separated from her parents, and mobbed by fans screaming her name and trying to touch her gown, to her first night as Miss America, which she spent crying in her hotel room while a disgusted pageant hostess glowered at her, she felt isolated and ill-equipped for the title as a shy teen from rural Oklahoma. A six-page letter from Slaughter spelling out her responsibilities was her only road map. Months earlier, after being crowned Miss Oklahoma City, she'd blown an opportunity to meet with Miss America Deborah Bryant because she was so nervous she couldn't bring herself to park her car and go to the scheduled meeting.

"I was so immature and unprepared for such a role," she writes.

"I was nineteen and wanted to be with my friends and audition for summer theater . . . I had agreed not to date for a year, to be told what to wear, where to go, and what to say. I did not want to travel every day and continuously be with strangers who would sit and stare at me for hours." She was forbidden from smoking or drinking in public, chewing gum, appearing with any soft drink except Pepsi, and expressing her opinion unless she was knowledgeable enough to speak "without embarrassment." She didn't know how to handle a press conference. And she missed her mother.

At a formal dinner with pageant officials on her first day, she was uncomfortable with the hard-partying crowd around her. She knew they weren't happy about her win and didn't approve of conducting as her choice of talent (or was it that she had done it in tails without pants?). She was a music major but had never actually wanted to be a conductor—in fact she'd never conducted before; her state pageant director had put it on her entry form for her. Rumor had it that the musicians followed house conductor Glenn Osser's lead anyway, discounting her routine as a gimmick. "Finally," writes Jayroe, "the dinner conversation turned to my lackluster attitude." She was told how much money she would make and how appreciative she should be, and that "if I did not want to be Miss America, Miss California was more than ready to take my place."

Like Van Derbur, Jayroe found the year to be terribly lonely, but also, finally, consummately enriching. She, too, came to like doing public events and got better at them; the experience led her to a career as a news anchor. But first, there were dark times. She had bought the Cinderella myth and was focused entirely on finding her prince. She met him on her return to Oklahoma City University and married him in 1968. "I was truly a completely submissive wife to a husband I had known less than a year . . . I assumed that because marriage had been my ultimate goal, everything else would just happen. My parents had taken care of me, the Miss America managers had taken care of me, and now it was my husband's turn."

A year later, when she finished her degree at Oklahoma City University (avoiding the cafeteria, where other students whispered about her as she ate), she was bored and depressed in a failing marriage with a workaholic who didn't want her to work. "I was so disappointed in myself. I had been something. Now I was nothing," she writes. It would take years, a women's studies course en route to her master's degree, and a Christian rebirth for her to get out of her marriage and find the community support and confidence she needed to become something.

Jayroe stood at a crossroads of women's history. The postwar boom had opened opportunities for women, but they had few professional role models, and though they'd been marrying later and having fewer children since the late 1950s, many were unsure of how to balance work with family or navigate male-dominated workplaces. As the writer Patricia Lynden, one of forty-six plaintiffs in a historic sex discrimination lawsuit filed against *Newsweek* in 1970, put it, "Our generation was raised to be attractive and smart—but not too smart. We were to be deferential to men, to get married, raise children, and be ornamental wives dedicated to our husbands' careers."

"Yet here we were," writes Lynden's co-plaintiff, the journalist Lynn Povich, "entering the workplace in the 1960s questioning— and often rejecting—many of the values we had been taught. We were the polite, perfectionist 'good girls,' who never showed our drive or our desires around men. Now we were becoming mad women, discovering and confronting our own ambitions, a quality praised in men but stigmatized—still—in women."

The pageant, too, was in flux. Following Jayroe's crowning, Slaughter retired after thirty-two years with Miss America, taking Brad Frapart, her husband and business manager, with her. But even at its smoothest running, the Miss America organization didn't generally think beyond sending its winners ricocheting around the country to sell cars and make speeches about how dreams really do come true and anything is possible. After the crowning, said Mercer, "It never occurs to anyone, least of all the girl, what must come next, so she heads off to do something for which she is perfectly inadequate, since she has no training." Most of all, as a gender-segregated contest, it didn't prepare women to compete in a world with men.

A FUNNY THING HAPPENED DURING Miss Idaho's magic act at the 1968 pageant. She had trained twenty-four white doves to follow her commands, but when the stage lights came on with a boom, the spooked birds darted away, flew around the rafters, and "left their calling cards everywhere," according to the new executive director, Albert Marks.

The fugitive doves were an apt symbol for a country in turmoil and transition. The January Tet Offensive had curdled many Americans' support of the Vietnam war, now claiming 1,000 soldiers a month and registering 49 percent disapproval in a Gallup poll. Anti-war protests were escalating; Students for a Democratic Society (SDS) were organizing campus sit-ins, strikes, and rallies. Riots wracked the country after the assassination of Martin Luther King Jr. in April; Bobby Kennedy was killed in June. The Black Power movement was in full swing (with women now constituting 60 percent of the Black Panther Party). Richard Nixon won the Republican nomination for president. The Democratic National Convention opened with Aretha Franklin singing "The Star-Spangled Banner" and ended in violence and police brutality. And *Hair*, a countercultural rock musical with an interracial cast and full-frontal nudity, premiered on Broadway. It was the dawning of the Age of Aquarius.

None of this was of any concern at the pageant, except insofar as the winners now embarked on USO tours to entertain troops. Jayroe had been the first to go, spending seventeen days in the war zone during the Summer of Love, doing a musical revue called, unironically, "What's Going on Back Home." She and the five state winners who joined her elicited boos from soldiers by first appearing in military fatigues ("the last thing they wanted to see"), then slipped backstage to don "cute little dresses" instead.

Whatever their thoughts on the war, the winners were expected to keep their political views, like their romantic dalliances, under their Miss Dior hats. But in September 1968, politics hit the pageant like a spitball when the feminist activist group New York Radical Women (NYRW) arrived with pluck and picket signs to condemn Miss America's retrograde vision of women. Though feminists had staged other demonstrations (a year earlier, NOW had picketed *The New York Times* for its gender-segregated help-wanted ads), the pageant protest commanded national attention and, many felt, kick-started second-wave feminism.

"The 1960s," protester Robin Morgan wrote in her memoir, "had already seen two streams of the Women's Movement emerge: a reform-oriented 'equality feminism,' represented by such dues-paying, formalized membership groups as NOW, and a radical feminism represented by us, younger women activists seasoned in the student, civil rights, and anti-war movements."

The name New York Radical Women said it all. They wanted to turn their energies to the sexism they saw swirling around them—

including among their own political brethren, some of whose idea of engaging women in their cause was sending them for coffee and mimeographs. When twenty-seven-year-old Morgan showed up at a meeting of New Left activists that included Jerry Rubin, Tom Hayden, and Abbie Hoffman and announced what the NYRW women were planning, most of the men couldn't understand "why I might prefer attacking silly old sexism when I could continue to be a token woman in their impending apocalypse."

In August, NYRW sent out a press release inviting women "of every political persuasion" to picket the pageant not only for its sexism, but also for its racism and consumerism. "[We] do not plan heavy disruptive tactics and so do not expect a bad police scene. It should be a groovy day on the boardwalk in the sun with our sisters," it read. A ten-point manifesto followed, listing among its targets "The degrading Mindless-Boob-Girlie Symbol" the queens personified, "Miss America as Military Death Mascot" (for touring Vietnam), and "The Unbeatable Madonna-Whore Combination" the winners embodied. Point two condemned the pageant's "racism with roses": "There has never been a Puerto Rican, Alaskan, Hawaiian, or Mexican American winner. Nor has there ever been a *true* Miss America—an American Indian."

Morgan requested a permit from the mayor, identifying the protest sponsors as "Women's Liberation," a term yet to enter popular speech, and Florynce Kennedy's Media Workshop, a group that fought racism in advertising and media, from discriminatory practices in hiring to stereotyping and tokenism. Kennedy was a pathbreaking, charismatic black civil rights lawyer who forged links between the Black Power and early feminist movements, bringing the tactics of the former to the latter. She later founded the Feminist Party, which nominated Shirley Chisholm, the first black congresswoman, for president. Fearless and flamboyant, Kennedy called the boardwalk action "the best fun I can imagine anyone wanting to have on any single day of her life."

Coming to Atlantic City from as far as Iowa, they arrived by bus—over a hundred women, many of whom later became well-known feminists, including Alix Kates Shulman and Kate Millett. They wore summery shifts and shirt dresses, A-line skirts or shorts, sandals and tennis shoes. Some brought their mothers; one brought her grandmother; another pushed a stroller. Marching in a circle outside Convention Hall, they carried signs that read WELCOME TO THE MISS AMERICA CATTLE AUCTION, MISS AMERICA SELLS IT, MISS AMERICA IS ALIVE AND ANGRY IN HARLEM, and GIRLS CROWNED—BOYS KILLED. They chanted ("Atlantic City is a town with class. They raise your morals and they judge your ass!") and sang ("Ain't she sweet, makin' profit off her meat").

For a bit of guerrilla theater, they brought a sheep from a New Jersey farm and festooned it with a Miss America sash to parody the human cattle auction going on in Convention Hall. (Alas, it turned out be male.) Standing guard, a police officer petted it absentmindedly. Kennedy and others were chained to an eight-foot-tall Miss America marionette in a star-spangled swimsuit as slaves to beauty and puppets of capitalism, while a mock auctioneer, comically dressed in an oversized men's suit and hat, cattle-rattled, "You can use her to push your products, push your politics, or push your war!"

As historian Georgia Page Welch observes, the auction skit dramatized black women's double oppression through its slavery conceit, showing how "white beauty perpetuated racial, as well as sexual, subjugation." It may also explain why Kennedy wore all white—slacks, turtleneck, and jacket. Kennedy herself was thoughtful and irreverent about the politics of fashion. She was in her fifties, older than most of her fellow picketers, and, as Welch explains, "rejected the civil rights ethos of using respectability to earn citizenship" yet "refused to comply with the politically correct dress codes imposed by the anti-establishment left." Unlike other middle-aged feminist leaders like Betty Friedan, who dressed conservatively, Kennedy typically wore a cowboy hat atop her short Afro, jeans and graphic tees or pantsuits with political buttons pinned to the lapels, outsized jewelry, and gleaming red fingernails.

But it was the image of the "Freedom Trash Can" that lodged in the national consciousness and spawned a stubborn myth about "women's libbers." The women gathered playfully around a garbage can, laughing as they tossed in the symbols of their oppression: women's magazines (including *Cosmo*), men's magazines (including *Playboy*), steno pads, dishwashing detergent, "falsies," floor wax, hair curlers, false eyelashes, stockings, girdles, and, significantly, bras. Had they not been denied a permit, they would have dropped a match into the can and burned it all, just as anti-war protesters burned their draft cards. But they might as well have: their plan was leaked to the press, which seized on it, making the term "bra-burners" an all-purpose slur for feminists, still circulating in conservative circles today, though no bras were ever burned.

Over the course of the afternoon, 600 spectators pressed against police barricades to take in the spectacle. Some—mostly women—were sympathetic, carrying buttons and leaflets away with them; most—mainly men—were not. "Dykes, Commies, Lezzies!" they yelled. "You don't deserve to be Americans!" "If they were married, they wouldn't have time for all this!" (Many were indeed married.) A small counter-protest blossomed nearby; Terry Meeuwsen, a Wisconsin beauty queen wearing a NIXON FOR PRESIDENT button, had come as a fan (and returned, in 1972, to be crowned Miss America). Her sign read 36-24-36 IS HARD TO BEAT, BRA OR NO BRA.

The contestants, who entered the convention hall on the street side, missed the protest but heard about it inside. "I think at one point we kind of snuck out and peeked outside to see what was going on," says Judi Ford (now Ford Nash), Miss Illinois, who was crowned that night. "But we really didn't get to see or hear a lot about it."

Ford, who was eighteen, knew virtually nothing about the history of the pageant or its racist legacy, having been drafted to compete in her first pageant at a county fair only six weeks earlier. As for being a "Mindless-Boob-Girlie," she wasn't. She was a straight-A student, the first woman to compete on the men's gymnastics team at her college, and the first in the school's history to earn a varsity letter. (At a modeling school session preparing her for Atlantic City, she was told she walked like an athlete. "Thank you!" she said and was crisply informed this was not a compliment.) Instead of scrambling to organize a singing or dancing act, she planned a trampoline routine despite her state sponsors' warning that an athletic performance might be seen as unfeminine and knock her out of the running. Miss America wasn't supposed to sweat, but this one, who did twenty-foot flips wearing a wiglet-enhanced beehive hairdo, was counting on it.

When the finals started at 8:30, word had reached Parks that a protestor inside intended to disrupt the evening. "I'll grab her by the throat," he said, "and keep right on singing." That year's theme was "Once Upon a Someday," a fairy tale about a little girl dreaming of becoming Miss America, who travels her "Someday Road" over a rainbow bridge to find her "Someday"—or *something*. ("I guess you had to be there!" Ford Nash laughs.) A group of picketers who'd bought tickets and changed into evening clothes were now in their seats, prepared for a bigger action. But first, one of them pulled her own rogue stunt and sprayed the mayor's box with foul-smelling

Toni home-permanent spray. She was arrested for disorderly conduct and "emanating a noxious odor."

Ford won the swimsuit. Ford won the talent. And at midnight, just before Ford took the crown, Debra Snodgrass was delivering her farewell speech when the protestors dropped a bedsheet from a balcony demanding WOMEN'S LIBERATION. In unison, they yelled, "Freedom for women!" and "No more Miss America!"

"Being on stage with spotlights in your face," says Ford Nash, "we couldn't see anything that was happening and Debbie was kind of startled but continued with her speech." The camera crew ignored it, so home viewers heard distant voices and merely saw the audience reacting as police removed the hecklers. But national newspapers and radio stations covered it all, running stories with photos of the banner, releasing the term "women's liberation" into the American lexicon.

Because one of the NYRW's labor critiques centered on discrimination against women reporters, generally consigned to fashion and home pages (*if* they managed to climb out of the secretarial pool), their members pledged to address only female journalists at the boardwalk protest. The decision echoed Eleanor Roosevelt's women-only press conferences of the 1930s, organized for basically the same reason. They stopped talking when men approached, giving women the best stories; some even got front-page bylines. *Life* magazine's first female staff writer and columnist Shana Alexander used her perch, a column called "The Feminine Eye," to blast the broadcast: "So many things seem wrong and boring and silly about the Miss America pageant as it comes across on t.v. . . . it is dull and pretentious and racist and exploitative and icky and sad. It is fake in everything from wigs to talents to sentiments. It does not worship beauty but beauty products . . . Beauty contests are not so much anti-female as anti-human."

By contrast, a fulminating response by syndicated humorist Art Buchwald registered the depths of casual misogyny at play in mainstream media. A few years earlier Buchwald had also called the pageant broadcast dull, imagining, tongue in cheek, how it could be enlivened if it were covered more like a political convention. But news of the 1968 Freedom Trash Can short-circuited his sense of humor and left him sizzling with derision. "If the average American female gave up all her beauty products she would look like Tiny Tim, and there would be no reason for the American male to have anything to do with her at all," he fumed, adding this flourish: "[T]here is no better excuse for hitting a woman than the fact that she looks just like a man."

More surprising, perhaps, as a nasty slice of just the kind of internalized misogyny the picketers hoped to abolish was columnist Harriet Van Horne's reaction in the (then liberal) *New York Post*: "As my father used to say . . . if they can't be pretty, dammit, they can at least be quiet!" Most women, she elaborated, "would rather be some dear man's boob-girl than nobody's cum laude scholar."

Pageant officials were unruffled—publicly—by the protest, dismissing it as the work of publicity hounds piggybacking on the contest's media coverage for their own self-promotion. But as Miss America Kate Shindle (1998) has written, "the visual was insurmountable. A new type of woman was outside, raging against the machine; a traditional type of woman was inside, blithely competing in swimsuit, talent and evening gown." It had opened "a visible split between the old and the new, one that would inexorably alter the pageant's image and reputation."

It also empowered women to question their own representation in popular culture. In *Where the Girls Are: Growing Up Female with the Mass Media*, media critic Susan J. Douglas, a college freshman in 1968, says she was transformed by the protest, which she called "the opening salvo in a revolutionary social movement that would change our lives forever." It was a roadmap for a kind of rebellion, she writes, that "few outside of the New Left knew of," linking the personal with the political. The protesters "put us on notice that the politically innocent word 'girl' was about to give way to the politically conscious word 'woman.'"

Still, some of the organizers regretted parts of their strategy. Robin Morgan later wrote that "our leaflets, press statements, and guerrilla-theater actions didn't make clear that we were not demonstrating against the pageant contestants . . . but that our adversaries were the pageant organizers and the pageant concept and process itself."

Carol Hanisch, who'd hatched the idea, wrote a postmortem expressing remorse that some of the posters (which had not been group-approved) were "anti-woman" and "really harmed the cause of sisterhood." They didn't clarify, she explained, that "we women are FORCED to play the Miss America roll [sic]—not by beautiful women, but by men we have to act that way for and by a system that has so well institutionalized male supremacy for its own ends." Hanisch said the best slogan emerged a month after the demonstration, when feminist Rosalyn Baxandall said on TV, "Every day in a woman's life is a walking Miss America contest."

For their part, Snodgrass and Ford Nash didn't appreciate being called tools of exploitation. "First of all, I entered this voluntarily," says Ford Nash, now a retired physical education teacher who served for eight years on the President's Council on Physical Fitness and Sports after her reign. "No one put a gun to my head and said you will do this. I [had] an opportunity to get an education—my college education was totally paid for . . . [and] because it was a non-profit organization, I was paid for every appearance that I made and they didn't take a cut out of it. And I said, if that's exploiting, go ahead, exploit me."

Both women felt the two groups had parallel aims, as Ford Nash puts it, "to empower women and to give them opportunities to further their education and to realize goals and ambitions that they otherwise might not have been able to." Both had working mothers; both achieved exactly the careers they set out to pursue as Miss Americas—without defaulting, as many others did, into jobs as motivational speakers or spokesqueens, though, says Snodgrass, "it would've been very tempting had I not had a passion for teaching."

When Ford Nash was later divorced and learned that her credit card company would permit her husband to use both of their joint cards, but wouldn't let her keep one, she understood better, firsthand, what the feminists were fighting. And she was happy to see the swimsuit axed in 2018, as was Snodgrass, who says, "I think that we have really made a good move, because we are concentrating on what makes a girl special, not her body. You're born with your body . . . And I don't want to concentrate on that. I want to concentrate on the character, and morals, and ambition, and education."

Calling the winner a "Military Death Mascot" was also dubious (and surely didn't warm the heart of Miss Iowa, whose father was leaving for a second tour of duty in Vietnam that month). Snodgrass, who ended up visiting Korea because Vietnam was deemed too dangerous in the summer of 1968, believed in supporting the troops as a matter of patriotism. But she didn't comment publicly about the wisdom of U.S. involvement there, both because she'd been advised not to and because as a college student she didn't feel qualified to opine about it, though she was routinely asked to. "Like all of us at that time who weren't actually doing the fighting," she says, "I had no idea the extremely high price our soldiers and their families were paying."

Likewise, Ford Nash didn't consider the USO trip to be an endorsement of the war. On the tour, she had asked a general over dinner, "So, seriously, should we be here?" Her focus was on the troops, who "didn't go there because—most of them anyway—they really wanted to." Some of the men she met were her own high school classmates. She calls it "probably the most rewarding experience I've ever had. We visited patients in hospitals and on hospital ships and we did our shows at major bases like Bob Hope stages and on flatbed trailer trucks." Some still write to her. "Maybe they were cleaning out a drawer and saw a picture and . . . took the time to find me just to say thank you and how much it meant to them that we were there."

Two points were overlooked in this initial face-off between pageant boosters and their feminist foes. First, for all the pageant talk about opportunity, no one acknowledged that the contest discriminated against worthy women *without* the looks to compete for scholarships. Trading on beauty in realms irrelevant to beauty is a devil's bargain women have been making forever, but it smacked of pure hypocrisy in an institution claiming to be a meritocracy.

Conversely, the protesters failed to see that for many women, a different trade-off was at play. Beauty pageants were, for some, a necessary evil in a world of scarce professional opportunity for women. The journalists Diane Sawyer and Judy Woodruff, for example, competed in pageants in the South in the 1960s, and Oprah Winfrey was Miss Black Tennessee in 1971. They were especially tempting to low-income women. Gloria Steinem competed as a teen in Toledo, Ohio, because it seemed "like a way out of a not too great life in a pretty poor neighborhood," though it required standing on a beer keg in a swimsuit.

Even for the many women who entered contests because they found them fun, status played a role in their appeal—winning afforded not just an opportunity but a kind of culturally approved prestige for women, an unempowered underclass. Pageants formalized that power in a society that gridlocked women through institutionalized sexism. ("Real power to control our lives is restricted to men, while women get patronizing pseudo-power," the NYRW manifesto read.) The protesters hoped to overhaul the institutions; the contestants just wanted to seize an opportunity.

For some women, merely witnessing the ascent of beauty queens planted a seed of ambition. Professor and self-described "card-carrying feminist" Mari Boor Tonn has written about growing up in rural Kansas about forty miles from Debra (Barnes) Snodgrass, who became her "personal hero" as Miss America 1968. Tonn was a first-generation high school student who, at age thirteen when Snodgrass was crowned, had never seen any woman except Jacqueline Kennedy "generate such heightened regional media interest or community conversation." (A first lady was a little like Miss America. She ascended, through good breeding and popularity, to a figurehead position of privilege in which she had no formal power and was expected to remain politically neutral. But she ascended.) Boor Tonn writes:

In my socially conservative world in which female inferiority was literally an article of religious faith, female aspirations were hardly encouraged. And I had watched my bright and gifted oldest sister who, when forbidden to apply to college or even to take purportedly "impractical" high school courses no woman would ever need, decide to marry at 17, take up years of factory work, and embark on a long struggle to keep a corrosive mix of disappointments and sense of inadequacy at bay. Thus, odd as it may now seem, through Barnes I entertained the subversive possibility of female mobility—higher education, travel, perhaps professional opportunity, and exposure to diverse intriguing people—that had appeared beyond my reach.

The role-modeling Snodgrass offered Tonn, of course, was of little value to women of color, who didn't see their potential reflected on a national stage. Which is why the boardwalk rebellion was just half the story of the 1968 protests.

———

ON THE AFTERNOON OF THE Miss America finals, as the contestants prepared inside and the feminists marched outside, eighteen young black women in formal wear were out riding in open convertibles through the business district, down the boardwalk, and around Convention Hall, cheered on by spellbound bystanders. "They waved white-gloved hands, smiled perfect smiles and showed off themselves as well as their elegant evening gowns in the afternoon sun," *The New York Times* reported.

These were the first contestants in the Miss Black America contest. The brainchild of a Philadelphia businessman, J. Morris Anderson, whose African American daughters had told him they wanted to be Miss America when they grew up, it was organized with the support of tri-state area NAACP director Phillip Savage and sponsored by the National Association of Colored Women's Clubs. The idea was a pivot from pressuring Miss America to integrate, something the Atlantic City NAACP had attempted with pitiful results: a $1,000 pledge to the NAACP to attract black state participants and the addition of a black board member, a local reverend. (The pageant had also, unbelievably, invited black superstars Diahann Carroll, Leslie Uggams, and Lena Horne to judge, all of whom—no surprise—declined.)

"We want to be in Atlantic City at the same time the hypocritical Miss America contest is being held," Savage said when the pageant was announced in August. Theirs, he said, "will be lily white and ours will be all black."

The motorcade was a kind of Freedom Ride, considering that when the Miss America pageant came to town, writes Georgia Page Welch, "African Americans experienced it as a segregated event that used their hometown as a site for reproducing national white supremacy." Until just two years earlier, blacks were banned from appearing in floats in the Miss America boardwalk parade. As a jubilant public assertion of self-esteem, the motorcade's symbolism reached beyond the pageant, since civil rights leaders had been pushing for systemic reforms in a city whose African American population had doubled since the 1920s: the first black school principal, rent control, an end to redlining and surging police brutality. When the cortège reached the Northside black neighborhood, bongos, cowbells, and flutes heralded its arrival; the women hopped down and headed to a beachfront cabana party to celebrate the birth of a pageant that continues today.

That night, after Parks finished his serenade, the press hustled over to the Ritz-Carlton ballroom, four blocks away, to see Miss Black America crowned before a few hundred spectators. She was Saundra Williams, a nineteen-year-old Philadelphia college student who sported short, natural hair, wore a white beaded dress she'd made by hand, and performed an African dance wearing a yellow jumpsuit and bells on her ankles. She could play violin, piano, and drums, and had delivered, during the semifinals Friday night, an original poem set to music, "Awareness," which described feeling bad about her appearance until she overheard people talking about their pride in being black. She told the press, "Miss America does not represent us . . . With my title, I can show black women they, too, are beautiful even though they have large noses and thick lips. There is a need to keep saying it over and over because for so long none of us believed it."

Williams and Judi Ford were wedded in the press coverage—two faces of beauty, two sides of a divided America. Just as the feminists had timed their event to capitalize on coverage of the Miss America pageant, so had the Miss Black America pageant. But they weren't exactly aligned. Williams had little to say to reporters about the boardwalk revolt, and Robin Morgan told them her group condemned *all* beauty pageants, including black ones, hedging, "but we understand the black issue involved."

The next day, when journalists asked her about the other pageant, Ford was stopped twice by her press coordinator. "No questions about the Miss Black America pageant," he said, "because Miss America is in our own Miss America Pageant and she has nothing to do with that," which was precisely the problem.

So while Miss America was claiming its white monopoly on beauty and the boardwalk protesters were decreeing pageants oppressive to all women, Miss Black America was asserting something else entirely: the *right* to be beautiful.

As culture critic Tricia Rose told PBS, "Miss Black America is of course an effort to say well, look, trying to be like a white person is not what's at stake. But appreciating what is black is quite important ... saying, we exist as both a market and as a kind of esthetic ..." From the early 1960s, when top designer Pauline Trigère started using black models, to the watershed moment in 1974 when Beverly Johnson became the first black cover model for American *Vogue*, the Black is Beautiful movement expressed exactly that.

Although it was conceived as a challenge to Miss America, Miss Black America swiftly claimed a meaning and momentum all its own. Miss America's win was a triumph of individualism;

Miss Black America's was a collective victory. Miss America was concertedly apolitical; Miss Black America was inherently political, though hardly radical in its mimicry of the time-honored Convention Hall format. Some black activists didn't consider it a sign of progress at all; New York City radio host Clayton Riley called it "[all] that same Atlantic City bullshit revisited in the company of Afro princesses . . ."

But it was an instant success, repeated in 1969 at Madison Square Garden, with appearances by Stevie Wonder and the Jackson 5 in their first televised performance. Michael Jackson sang "It's Your Thing," the Isley Brothers' first number one hit, to an audience of over 4,000 people from a stage lined with flower pots. The judges included Shirley Chisholm and Betty Shabazz, and Curtis Mayfield wrote the pageant anthem ("You're such wonderful people / and so beautifully equal / Miss Black America"). Who even needed Miss America, staged in a declining beach town with its girlish themes, orchestral music, and aging judges? Miss Black America was not just beautiful, she was cool. She was *now*.

With 72 million TV viewers confirming Miss America's popularity, it was easy for the pageant to dismiss the boardwalk protesters as wild-eyed opportunists and to deflect Miss Black America's challenge by saying there was nothing preventing women of color from entering. But its image took a hit, driven home in 1969 when Pepsi pulled its national sponsorship, stating, "Miss America as run today does not represent the changing values of our society." Though it continued to offer some state funding, a Pepsi spokesperson said the pageant "no longer has big-city appeal. It is a waste of time, for instance, to try to do anything with Miss America in New York City."

As executive director, Albert Marks, an Atlantic City stockbroker, understood that it had to adapt (for starters, it drew $2 million a year to Atlantic City). But you wouldn't know it by some of the clueless comments he gave the press. "We are for normalcy," he said in 1969, the year of Woodstock and the Stonewall riots—and continued student protests. "We have no interest in minorities or causes. SDS has its thing. We have no thing. If that is a crime in today's society, so be it. Our youngsters are interested in plain American idealism." (That year, when a sociologist named Zelma George became the first black pageant judge, Marks announced, hilariously, "We are now integrated in every aspect of the pageant except that we've never had a [black] contestant here.")

Board member Leonard Horn, one of the more enlightened pageant leaders (who became CEO in 1987), later said the feminist protest had a delayed but palpable effect. "We didn't understand them and they didn't understand us back in 1968. But the women's movement helped effectuate tremendous change in the lives of women and it was inevitable that we change our focus to accommodate those changes."

In an effort to swing with the kids, the 1969 pageant theme was "The Sound of Young," driven by a rock medley composed by Osser and his songwriter wife, who dreamed up the lyrics in the bathtub. (The title was both opportunistic and tone-deaf; Motown's slogan "The Sound of Young America" intentionally elided the racial divisions that Miss America still enforced.) It featured songs like "Where is the Real" and "Just You Do Your Thing" and involved bell bottoms, granny glasses, and psychedelic lights. The women were liberated from knee-length skirts. Two played drums for talent; one sang a folk song. There was even a rumbling of subversion when seventeen-year-old runner-up Susan Anton of California, thunderstruck at being asked to name the proper time to marry, paused and answered, "When you're pregnant!"

But what the pageant organizers didn't grasp was that youth

culture wasn't something that could be scripted by a middle-aged orchestra conductor and kitted out with festival fashion, or that a typical American girl wasn't typical in 1969 if she was forbidden from wearing her hair down, sporting frayed jeans, smoking, dating, discussing the war or weed or the Manson murders or the sexual revolution or civil rights and belting out "Respect" or "White Rabbit" with a tie-dyed scarf wrapped around her head. Too much had changed. And it had changed in response to everything Miss America signified.

SIX

Trailblazers

A FORMER CHEERLEADER, PRESIDENT OF HER Methodist Youth Fellowship, and a pianist with fourteen years of classical training, Phyllis George was crowned the Miss America in 1970 after playing "Raindrops Keep Falling on My Head" with a jazzy twist. She had *a* talent, but did she have talent? Certainly not like that other Texan, Janis Joplin, who'd become a global superstar making $50,000 a night without being beautiful. As Frank Deford wrote the following year, "Great dancers or singers do not show up at *Miss America* any more than great bodies do. If she is that good at something . . . she does not have to depend on a beauty contest for approbation and reward."

Still, George's crowning was a step forward during the heady early days of second-wave feminism. Unabashedly ambitious, she became one of the big-name Miss Americas. After acting lessons and commercial TV work, she was hired in 1975 to appear on

CBS's *The NFL Today*, becoming one of the first female network sportscasters. She stayed for eight years. This was a time when a pioneering generation of women reporters were being humiliated and harassed by players and coaches who didn't want them in the press box, much less in the locker room getting quotes. But George wasn't a journalist, and learning on the job resulted in high-profile gaffes that pained some of the women who'd fought hard to break in and prove their worth in this profession. She was thumped in the media for it. But, says Lesley Visser, the first female NFL beat writer and one of a handful of women in the Female Sports Broadcasting Hall of Fame, "most people have no idea how difficult live television is at that level. Phyllis had many qualities that made her a star—a magnetic personality, a quick mind and a disciplined work ethic." Her very presence as a woman sportscaster on national television helped move the needle of progress.

Like so many of her forerunners, George was overwhelmed by her win. That night she called her mother and gasped, "What have I done?" But a month in, she began to see her future unfolding. "Before then I was living a happy existence in Denton, Texas, thinking I knew everything about myself and what I wanted," she writes in her memoir, *Never Say Never—Yes You Can!* "But venturing out of my small world, I realized I was just a little pea in the grand scheme of things and maybe I didn't know so much after all. This change gave me the opportunity to open my eyes and see that the pie was a lot bigger than I thought—and so was the piece I wanted."

George was crowned weeks after the Women's Strike for Equality, the biggest women's rights demonstration since the suffragists demanded the vote fifty years earlier, with sister marches coordinated across the country. The day she won, pageant protesters were back on the boardwalk. George had mixed feelings about them. "Even though I'd won the swimsuit competition, I despised that

Wearing her Lady Liberty crown, Margaret Gorman, Miss America 1921, receives the key to Atlantic City from King Neptune in preparation for the 1922 pageant. Neptune's mermaids attend. *Photograph courtesy of the author*

A "beach cop" measuring for modesty in 1922 at the Washington, D.C., Tidal Basin Bathing Beach, where suits revealing more than six inches of skin above the knee were forbidden. *Photograph courtesy of the National Photo Company*

A 1922 postcard shows Steel Pier, where the early pageants were held.

Photograph courtesy of the author

Miss America 1924 Ruth Malcomson of Philadelphia poses in a Hinds Cream advertising shot. *Photograph courtesy of the George Eastman Museum*

The crowning of Norma Smallwood, Miss America 1926, with (left to right) Miss Atlantic City, King Neptune, outgoing queen Fay Lanphier, and "guest of honor" Jessie Jim, Princess America II. Smallwood's winning mermaid trophy is at her feet. *Photograph courtesy of the author*

In celebration of her twenty-five years of service to the pageant, Lenora Slaughter wears a chiffon anniversary gown, courtesy of pageant sponsor Bancroft & Sons, appliquéd with roses representing each contestant of 1959.
Photograph courtesy of the Lenora Slaughter Papers, Archives Center, National Museum of American History, Smithsonian Institution

Atlantic City's Steel Pier on the day of Bette Cooper's fraught 1937 crowning.
Photograph courtesy of the Lake Hopatcong Historical Museum

Miss Americas Bette Cooper, Marilyn Meseke, and Patricia Donnelly.
Photograph courtesy of the Lake Hopatcong Historical Museum

Bess Myerson in the 1945
Miss America Parade in
Atlantic City.
*Photograph courtesy of UPI/Alamy
Stock Photo*

Yolande Betbeze, Miss America
1951. She refused to wear a swimsuit
in public during her reign year,
causing key sponsor Catalina to
withdraw from Miss America and
launch Miss USA. Lenora Slaughter
called her "the sexiest, most
glamorous thing I ever laid my eyes
on." *Photograph courtesy of Dolly Fox*

When Marilyn Monroe served as grand marshal at the 1952 Miss America Parade, her publicist claimed "she murdered those poor little Miss Americas," but Monroe said she was intimidated by them. *Photograph courtesy of Bettman via Getty Images*

Pageant host Bert Parks, "Mr. Miss America," with Miss America 1966 Deborah Bryant. *Photograph courtesy of ZUMA Press, Inc./Alamy Stock Photo*

THE *Miss America* PAGEANT PRESENTS "ONCE UPON A SOMEDAY"

ATLANTIC CITY, N.J.

SEPT. 2-8, 1968

Copyright 1968 Miss America Pageant

ONE DOLLAR

Delaware Valley Printers, Inc., Philadelphia, Pa.

Debra Barnes, Miss America 1968. *Photograph courtesy of the author*

Women's liberation protesters gather around the Freedom Trash Can outside the 1968 pageant. Contrary to popular myth, no bras were burned.

Photograph courtesy of Bev Grant Photography/Getty Images

Cheryl Browne, Miss Iowa 1970, the first African American Miss America contestant, on the Atlantic City boardwalk with Miss Maryland, Sharon Ann Cannon.

Photograph courtesy of AP Photo

Susan Supernaw, Miss Oklahoma 1971, wearing buckskin regalia in a portrait used as an alternate Miss Oklahoma photo for her Native American events.

Photograph courtesy of the Robert M. McCormack photographic studio archive, 1935–2000. University of Tulsa, McFarlin Library, Department of Special Collections and University Archives (utulsa .as.atlas-sys.com/repositories/2 /resources/35)

Kathy Huppe, Miss Montana 1970, who resigned her title six weeks before the Miss America pageant after being told to suppress her anti-war comments. This photo appeared in *Life* magazine shortly afterward.

Photograph courtesy of Vernon Meritt III/The LIFE Picture Collection via Getty Images

Vanessa Williams, Miss America 1984. She made history as the first African American to win the title. *Photograph courtesy of Shutterstock*

Kate Shindle, Miss America 1998. *Photograph courtesy of the author*

Filipina American Angela Perez Baraquio, Miss America 2001, was the first Asian American winner.

Photograph courtesy of AP Photo/Chris Polk

Deidre Downs Gunn, Miss America 2005, was both the first winner to become a doctor and the first to marry a woman.

Photograph courtesy of 2b|Photography

Miss America 2014 Nina Davuluri, the first South Asian American Miss America, performing a Bollywood dance during the talent competition.
Photograph courtesy of UPI/Alamy Stock Photo

Gabriela Taveras, the first Afro Latina Miss Massachusetts, was fourth runner-up in the 2018 Miss America competition.
Photograph courtesy of WENN Rights Ltd/ Alamy Stock Photo

Miss America 2018 Cara Mund, the last winner to compete in a swimsuit, crowning Nia Franklin, the last to be crowned in Atlantic City's Boardwalk Hall.

Photograph courtesy of UPI/Alamy Stock Photo

part of it; most of the other contestants did as well," she writes. But though the swimsuit remained, the reign rules had changed. George was able to wear pants and say what she wanted, "which is good," she told a reporter, sans crown, "because I think my generation wants to speak out today." And she did. Asked if the pageant was marked for death because of women's lib, she gave him a bracing earful about the scholarships and travel it afforded. Still, she added with an edge of irritation, "I don't feel like I need to defend it at all."

With her relaxed wardrobe and assertive personality, she was a refreshingly contemporary Miss America, if a traditionalist (a husband and children, she said, would be her greatest accomplishment—the media had been asking winners this question since the 1920s). But she still fit a narrow, exclusive demographic of winners.

As the women's movement gained traction, criticism of pageantry spread. Even contestants themselves had their beefs. In 1970, Miss Montana Kathy Huppe resigned her title six weeks before the Miss America pageant after being told to put a lid on her anti-war statements and activism. At a pageant week news conference in September, Miss New York Katherine Jean Karlsrud pronounced the swimsuit exploitative. (Albert Marks agreed; as the new executive director, he predicted that "certain changes will be made in the next three years." It would take forty-five.) A finalist in the Miss Rochester (Michigan) pageant, peeved at being coached to change her walk, wear a swimsuit "like a prostitute selling her product," and glob on makeup that made her look ten years older, quit in disgust. "I have found the emphasis on the body personally degrading," she fumed.

Some women entered with the express purpose of sabotage. Dory (then Louise Piccard) Dickson was a freshman at Ohio University when a fraternity put out a call for participants in the 1970 campus pageant. Having grown up in the Philadelphia area, she knew about the '68 feminist protest and the Miss Black America pageant. Dickson, who opposed pageants, saw an opportunity. When she arrived for her interview, she was seated next to a woman who was, she says, "poised and self-possessed, with coiffed hair, excellent posture, and wearing a tailored business suit." She was Laurel Lea Schaefer, who was crowned Miss America the following year.

Before the semifinals, Dickson persuaded another student to walk out with her—if they both made the finals—after she read a pageant protest statement. But her overzealous anti-war saxophone-and-spoken-word routine, created in response to the assigned talent theme (current events), ensured that the finals would not be in her future. Schaefer, who made runner-up, later found her way to Miss America through the state contest.

The mother of all pageant protests, which echoed the Atlantic City rebellion and inspired the 2020 Keira Knightley movie *Misbehaviour*, stopped the 1970 Miss World pageant in London cold, just after the swimsuit-clad contestants had taken the stage. Aware of demonstrators outside who had brought a cow mannequin, the host, comedian Bob Hope, then in his late sixties, taunted them with painful jokes. "I am very, very happy to be here at this cattle market tonight. *Mooooo* . . . I've been back there checking calves." Fifty activists who'd infiltrated the auditorium watched, awaiting the shake of a soccer noisemaker by a woman tapped to start the disruption, which came early because Hope's cracks were so infuriating she couldn't help herself. (To wit: "I don't want you to think I'm a dirty old man because I never give women a second thought. My first thought covers everything.")

Confused by the whirring rattle of noisemakers around him, Hope paused and scanned the audience, then flinched when he saw flour, smoke, and ink bombs flying toward him. "We're not beautiful, we're not ugly, we're angry!" the protesters shouted, rushing the stage and sending Hope scurrying backstage. A shower of leaflets rained down from the balconies as arrests were made and the dissenters were booed and removed. Reluctantly coaxed back out to finish the job, Hope groused to the bewildered audience, "Anybody that would try to break up an affair as wonderful as this . . . [has] got to be on some kind of dope." Then he turned from the mic and asked, "Who are these bastards, anyway?"

The Miss America pageant had deftly suppressed its own backyard uprisings by slapping a restraining order on a second wave of rebels in 1969. But they kept coming. In 1974, the National Organization for Women held its Eastern Regional Convention in Atlantic City during pageant week and invited the contestants to attend their meetings and workshops, which they did not. (Too busy, said Marks. Very demanding schedules.) Inside the convention, the feminists addressed equal pay, rape, access to abortion, women in prison, women in government, lesbians in the movement, and the ratification of the Equal Rights Amendment. Policy was their focus, but there was time for fun; instead of slamming the pageant, they threw their own Wonder Woman–themed boardwalk parade, accompanied by a coed bugle corps. Two thousand people turned out for it.

In the early 1970s, the women's movement had something Miss America didn't: momentum. With George's victory in 1970, the pageant ratings peaked, then began a chronic if fitful decline. By contrast, feminism was ascendant. "I Am Woman," Helen Reddy roared in her explicitly feminist anthem, claiming the numbers were "too big to ignore," hitting number one on the Billboard Hot 100 and clinching a 1971 Grammy Award. That year, Don McLean's international hit "American Pie" mourned the death of American innocence in the wake of the tumultuous 1960s. (A rumor later circulated that its refrain, "Bye, bye, Miss American Pie," referenced a beauty queen McLean had dated.) In eliding "Miss America" and "American as apple pie," McLean's point was clear: Miss America—and all she represented—was a thing of the past.

Women were making monumental progress, from Title IX in 1972, which banned sex discrimination in federally funded schools (and was co-written by the first woman of color in Congress, Patsy Takemoto Mink), to *Roe v. Wade* in 1973, to the 1974 Equal Credit Opportunity Act, which ended discriminatory practices like withholding credit cards from unmarried women. In 1972, Shirley Chisholm became the first female major party candidate for president. "Ms." was approved as the honorific for government documents, carrying, like "Mr.", no marital designation. Billie Jean King and eight other major tennis players created the Virginia Slims Tennis circuit in 1970 in response to the pay gap in their field. (Three years later, 50 million Americans watched King cream Bobby Riggs in "the battle of the sexes.") From 1970 to 1977, *The Mary Tyler Moore Show*, fueled by the experiences of a historic number of female writers, starred a single working woman in her thirties whose life didn't revolve around family. Women's studies programs mushroomed and women's clinics, banks, shelters, rape centers, and publications—notably *Ms.* magazine—emerged.

"The sleepwalkers are coming awake," the poet Adrienne Rich famously wrote, "and for the first time this awakening has a collective reality; it is no longer such a lonely thing to open one's eyes." Even Barbie was jolted into consciousness: in 1971, Mattel redesigned her face, lifting her deferential downward gaze to a direct, level stare.

Just as World War II gave beauty culture a renewed mission— to inoculate women against masculinization in the workplace—so did the growing women's movement, which inspired fears that women, in gaining parity with men, would become them. (The blurring of gender divisions wasn't just a male worry. In 1976, discussing the plight of female sportswriters, Phyllis George said, "I'd like to see more women get involved, as long as they retain their femininity.") Women's mounting social and economic might was tempered by beauty in television shows like *The Bionic Woman* and *Wonder Woman*, which starred heroines with superhuman powers *and* bodacious bodies. Lynda Carter's Wonder Woman bustier barely contained the luscious curves that had made her Miss World USA in 1972. Beauty pageants showcased conventional womanhood in the midst of turbulent change—and offered comfort in the spectacle of women competing with each other instead of men.

Meanwhile, pop culture—and its gender biases—was becoming the stuff of scholarly inquiry and journalistic commentary. In his tremendously popular 1972 book and TV series *Ways of Seeing*, British art critic John Berger analyzed images of women in art history and advertising as they reflected male cultural power, asserting that "men act and women appear. Men look at women. Women watch themselves being looked at." (Three years later, feminist theorist Laura Mulvey tracked this dynamic in cinema when she theorized the male gaze.) *Ways of Seeing* showed images of women on public streets, in modeling shoots, in girdle ads, as nudes in paintings, in pornography, and in a beauty contest. "[H]ow she appears to others, and ultimately how she appears to men," wrote Berger, "is of crucial importance for what is normally thought of as the success of her life."

Even though it was framed as the embodiment of national identity, Miss America's flawless femininity was a triumph of individual achievement. Hers was a private body submitted for one-off public consumption, not a social body, like the women's movement, whose power was collective (if factionalized) and cumulative. And in the early 1970s, as the self-designated mascot of a country divided over war, feminism, and civil rights, she stood, symbolically at least, with the "silent majority," a term Nixon debuted in a 1969 speech advocating continued U.S. involvement in Vietnam after a massive anti-war march in Washington. As historian Rick Perlstein told NPR, Nixon saw "two kinds of Americans—the ordinary middle-class folks with the white picket fence who play by the rules and pay their taxes and don't protest" (the silent majority) and a "noisy minority" of anti-war activists, feminists, racial minorities, and urban elites. "It was students who were smoking drugs. It was rock 'n' roll bands. It was everything that threatened that kind of 1950s *Leave It to Beaver* vision of what America was like before everything literally and figuratively went to pot."

As a well-groomed, patriotic, corporate-friendly, USO-ready national icon, Miss America belonged to Nixon. (In 1972, Nixon supporters Laurel Lea Schaefer and Terry Meeuwsen enjoyed a deluxe tour of the White House with him.) But as the counterculture was swiftly being mainstreamed, the pageant was losing its footing, beginning what Kate Shindle calls a "long, strange trip into the realm of cultural irrelevance." With shocking levels of corruption exposed in Nixon's administration, America's withdrawal in defeat from it's least popular war, and a slumping economy marking the end of postwar prosperity, cynicism colored the mood of the era. Hollywood had entered a period of disillusionment and moral ambiguity, expressed in films such as *Midnight Cowboy*, *Easy Rider*, *The Last Picture Show*, and *The Godfather*. In the 1970s, punk music channeled white-knuckled anger and nihilistic despair, and *Saturday Night Live* lampooned celebrities and politicians.

But the pageant clung tight to a showbiz formula buoyed by nostalgia, sidestepping political allusions onstage even as the winners were being liberated to air their own opinions offstage. Nobody really knew what Miss America thought in the days when Slaughter kept the misses muzzled. Now their generally conservative views tumbled forth. As Miss America 1972, Schaefer promptly declared herself a bootstrapper who believed a woman could be whatever she wanted, "with dedication and perseverance," and if she failed to transcend the status of private secretary, well, "she shouldn't blame others, but see what's lacking in herself."

There were, as always, exceptions. Rebecca Ann King (1974) knocked pageant mavens sideways by openly supporting *Roe v. Wade*, even as a Republican who admired Barry Goldwater and claimed Nixon was wrongly persecuted for Watergate. Worse yet, she said she'd entered mainly for the money. ("I didn't think it was strange at all," she reflected years later on PBS. "It's a scholarship program, right? Isn't that what we're here for?") King was set on becoming a lawyer (she was the pageant's first) and was indifferent in response to questions about marriage and children. Like a true queen, she took the crown calmly, without crying. Forgoing the usual performative humility in her Cinderella moment, she treated her win as her due, claiming it with confidence. "I think my mother received maybe a hundred letters because I didn't cry," she said. "What kind of Miss America do we have here on our hands walking down the runway not crying?"

Bicentennial Miss America Tawny Godin, the first New Yorker to win after Bess Myerson, was also an iconoclast. She revealed she'd smoked pot and supported choice in abortion, premarital sex, and sexual preference. Both she and King lost bookings because of their views. But by then, as pageant diehards skewed right and into the arms of the emerging evangelical movement, the public was losing interest in Miss America's convictions, whatever their leanings. As more direct avenues of opportunity opened for women, the whole exercise started to seem like a sort of desperate bid for fame, though most people—focused on the women's looks and talents—weren't aware that the money they earned could be life-changing. Yet the academic level of contestants was rising. In 1974, half were on their high school or college dean's lists or belonged to the National Honor Society.

"I think that a large number of people began not watching the Miss American pageant probably about the mid-seventies," said Leonard Horn, who succeeded Marks as CEO in 1987. "The ideals upon which the Miss America pageant appeared to rest no longer seemed very exciting or relevant. And I think we lost a generation of people."

As moral indignation about pageantry cooled in the 1970s, it gave way to amusement, mockery, or knowing appropriation. Miss Gay America, launched in 1972, followed the pageant's format, presenting female impersonators whose schtick wasn't so different from Miss America's, though it was much more permissive; competitors could be fat, middle-aged, racially diverse, and, despite the name, gay or straight. It became the largest drag pageant system in the U.S., though it's been eclipsed in the new millennium by TV pageantry like *RuPaul's Drag Race*. Miss Gay America has demonstrated, for nearly half a century, that the performance of gender is a game anyone can play—a truism that also explains many gay men's long-standing interest and involvement in the Miss America pageant.

Hollywood also began spoofing beauty queens, a trend that's accelerated in the twenty-first century. In Woody Allen's 1973 sci-fi parody *Sleeper*, a cryogenically preserved man (Allen) wakes up in a global police state in 2173, forced to conform. His assimilation is deemed complete when he wins the Miss America pageant, wires springing from a metal cap clamped on his head, after delivering a properly generic answer to the question of what "Miss Montana" would do for mankind if she won. "I would use my title to bring peace to all nations of the world, be it black, be they white, be it colored, be it whatever," he says, goggle-eyed, and cries dopily when he's anointed.

If Allen took an easy whack at the ritual itself, Bob Rafelson's *The King of Marvin Gardens* (1972) exposed, with dark nuance, the impoverished afterlife of women whose sole currency is beauty, introducing the trope of the unhinged former beauty queen. The film uses Miss America as a framing device for the squashed options of its female leads, Sally and Jessica (Ellen Burstyn and Julia Anne Robinson), two prostitutes staying with two brothers, Jason and David (Bruce Dern and Jack Nicholson) in off-season Atlantic City as it spirals into economic defeat before the first casinos opened in 1978. Set in and around the shabby Marlborough Blenheim Hotel, it featured views of the nearby Traymore, which was demolished months later in a single heart-stopping blast, reducing the Castle by the Sea to dust and rubble and taking with it the rooms of presidents and Miss Americas who'd stayed there over the previous half century.

The women answer to—and sleep with—Jason, a hustler whose attentions are shifting entirely to Jessica, whom Sally, her stepmother, as it happens, grooms as her professional successor. The foursome stage a crackbrained mock pageant in Convention Hall: Jessica clacks through an awkward tap routine, Sally ("last year's queen") crowns her, David sings "There She Is," and the others join him for a spin in a golf cart, crooning together as they career around the yawning empty space. The pageant theme continues back at the hotel, where Sally announces, "No more competition," dropping all her cosmetics into a trashcan that she extends to the sweetly vacant Jessica. "Here, you pick out something for your old age," she says with bitter congeniality. "This will be your hope chest."

Reprising the Freedom Trash Can "bra-burning" at the 1968

protest, Sally carries the can out to the beach and throws the products, one by one, into a bonfire. "Tame, you go first," she says to her creme rinse—a wink at the Toni Company, still a major pageant sponsor when the film was made. Lipstick, nail polish, and Jean Naté Bath Splash follow, then she stops, blinking back tears, digs a hole, buries her eye makeup in the sand, delivers a kooky eulogy for her youth, then whips out a pair of scissors and madly cuts off her hair.

The film hits nearly every point in the feminist protest playbook: interchangeably pretty women competing for men; consumer exploitation of their anxieties about their looks; the commodification of female bodies; the pitting of tender youth against shameful age—always the loser in the beauty sweepstakes. And it distills, painfully, the utter disposability of middle-aged women.

With the release of *Smile* in 1975, just two years after *The King of Marvin Gardens*, Miss America was enshrined in pop culture mythology—a calcified national tradition to be goofed on, like square dancing or sock hops. Parodying the America's Junior Miss pageant (formerly called Junior Miss America), a Jaycee-sponsored scholarship pageant for teens, *Smile* is an affectionate send-up, though stinging enough that the people of Santa Rosa, California, where it was shot (many of whom were cast in minor roles), weren't smiling after its release.

It opens with a girl demonstrating how to pack a suitcase (something once actually "performed" at Miss America) during the talent section. One of the girls strips in the spirit of Mary Ann Mobley; another, in one of the all-time great pageant parody moments, warbles Helen Reddy's "Delta Dawn," skewering adolescent queens and Reddy herself in a single direct hit. *Smile* pokes fun at the adults in charge (an over-earnest head judge—Dern again—and an unhappy former queen wrangling the girls) much more than the self-aware contestants, who treat it like a talent show, only half-heartedly mouthing the platitudes expected of them: "We're not really competing with each other, we're more friends."

Warmly reviewed, *Smile* inspired some critics to reflect on their own relationships to beauty pageants. Roger Ebert remembered a county fair he saw as a teen, where he was struck by the similarities between the livestock contest and the beauty pageant, which had overlapping judges. "Here were girls I'd grown up with," he wrote, "and this dreary and demeaning ritual was forcing them to walk around in bathing suits on a stock-car track." He thought *Smile* effectively showed "the hypocrisy and sexism" of it all.

Writing in *The New Yorker*, Pauline Kael saw it more as an everywoman tale. She wondered if beauty pageants were too easy to target and decided they were not. "Who doesn't get stuck in false positions? Who hasn't been through stupid rituals? If many of us can't resist turning on the TV to watch at least one or two beauty contests each year, perhaps it's because these competitions seem like pockets of the past—pure fifties—and link in with our own memories."

Smile, which became a Broadway musical in 1986, set the formula for pageant parodies to come, with half-baked talent acts, leering sidemen, cynical production directors, and tightly wound former queens terrifying everyone in their orbit. Shallow, overbearing pageant moms became a staple of these films, from *Drop Dead Gorgeous* in 1999 to *Dumplin'* in 2018. Mothers had always been key players. (In the 1950s, Miss America contestants' guidelines routinely prescribed the mothers' pageant week activities along with their daughters'.)

But not all pageant moms were, as these films imply, redeeming their own dashed dreams through their kids. Some were focused on the scholarship, or propelling their daughters out of dead-end towns, or even helping them skirt dependence on unreliable men. Only one series, *Queen America*, which launched in 2018, explores poverty as a motivator for pageantry, as it affects both a (motherless) teen aspirant and the bitchy former queen (an AWOL mother played by Catherine Zeta-Jones) who trains her. The show marks a turning point from merely dumping on the musty rituals of pageantry to probing why it still exists. Some of the teen queens it tracks seek not just an escape from poverty, but also a lifeline to a community or family.

———

EVEN AS ITS STAR WAS dimming in the 1970s, the pageant was progressing, quietly, in a few ways. During her 1972 reign, Laurel Lea Schaefer became a spokesperson for families of missing veterans and POWs, anticipating the social issues platform that became an entry requirement in 1990. In 1974, the pageant added a modest scholarship for women pursuing careers in medicine. The interview questions got tougher on current events, though they were asked behind closed doors. Women were introduced by their college affiliations. The robe was retired, the roses scrapped. ("We're eliminating the robe to tell America we are not crowning Queen Elizabeth in the middle of the eighteenth century," Marks told the 1974 contestants, scrambling his history and forgetting . . . the crown?)

The ceremony still struck chords of obliviousness, notably a 1974 production number called "A Good Year" (never mind that Nixon had just resigned in disgrace after months of impeachment proceedings). But it was also finally on a path to diversity. In 1968, of 70,000 women entering state pageants, forty to fifty were black; now the numbers were inching up and more women of color were placing in them. With Lenora Slaughter as her witness, an African American beauty made it to Atlantic City in 1970. She was Cheryl Browne, Miss Iowa, a state where 1 percent of the population was black.

Browne was actually from Queens, New York, attending Luther College in Decorah, Iowa, where she won the campus title that led her to the state crown. And she was as New York as Junior's cheesecake. Her mother was a hospital clinic manager in Queens, her father a narcotics officer at Kennedy Airport. She had attended Manhattan's High School of Performing Arts and had been a freelance fashion model. She was extroverted, with a natural smile and a careful but game approach to the media. "I know all the reporters want me to say something controversial," she said. "But I'm going to fool them. I'm not going to." That said, she was up front about being a Democrat who supported the women's movement (but didn't grasp its opposition to Miss America). She had marched on campus in support of starting a black studies program. ("I'm not a militant," she said. "I fall somewhere in between the Urban League and the Black Panthers.") She hoped her win would "show the radicals in the black power movement that things aren't so bad." She opposed the Vietnam war, though unlike Miss Montana Kathy Huppe, she wasn't censored for saying so.

Browne was confident about nearly everything, it appeared, except her unequivocally good looks. She was at pains, in an Iowa Public Television interview, to say she didn't believe she was beautiful. Her comments could be dismissed as mere boilerplate about how Miss America isn't really a beauty contest, but for a historical coincidence that invites a double take: the publication, that year, of Toni Morrison's harrowing first novel, *The Bluest Eye*, about a black child who wishes for blue eyes so she can be as pretty as a white girl. Coming from a black woman making history by breaking the race barrier in a beauty pageant, Browne's comment seemed tinged with more than modesty. As Morrison said of her character Pecola Breedlove, she was not *seen* by herself. And how could she be, when popular culture offered so few reflections of her? The Miss America pageant (just like Barbie, who remained resolutely white until 1980) had never once recognized black beauty.

Browne didn't win. She didn't even make the top ten, perhaps because she was black, perhaps because she was only five feet four, perhaps because of talent or interview or swimsuit, perhaps because she wasn't really from Iowa, perhaps because Iowa has never once delivered a winner, perhaps because she was too real, too natural, too mellow—she didn't have that switched-on pageant personality. But she'd kicked open the door, and others soon breezed through. "I'm sure that in the future a black girl will win the crown, but I don't feel the country is quite ready for that now," she said. She was chosen to go on the USO tour as part of Phyllis George's troupe, which was meaningful to her because "those black guys over there never get to see a black woman and they really seemed glad to see me."

Miss America's white bias was typically called out as a slight against black women, which it was, but very few Latinas or Asians had alighted in Atlantic City either, and no Native American had competed since Miss Oklahoma Mifaunwy Shunatona in 1941. But in 1971, another Native American, also from Oklahoma, seized the state crown and was on her way. Susan Supernaw was a Muscogee (Creek) Native American from Tulsa, who had survived poverty, the terrifying violence of an alcoholic father and stepfather, and a fall from a horse that broke her back and left her temporarily paralyzed. She became a cheerleader, gymnast, and class valedictorian who won a National Merit Scholarship. As a presidential scholar, she spent a summer in Washington interning for the House Majority Leader, Democrat Carl Albert.

"Super Sue" was terrifically outspoken, which was one reason Albert picked her as his intern. At a welcome luncheon for the scholars, she was seated next to Nixon himself. She took the conversational lead, telling him that Native American religious practices were in jeopardy and needed constitutional protection. Though she hadn't been raised in a traditional Muscogee home (her mother was white; her father had been largely absent before her parents separated), she had learned Muscogee customs from her grandmother and belonged to the Native American Church, a syncretic religion combining native beliefs and Christianity.

When one of the other scholars loudly asked when the Vietnam war would end, Nixon asked for the students' thoughts. Supernaw told him she opposed America's involvement and described its devastating impact on her community, starting with a boy widely considered the best local hunter, who became a sharpshooter in Vietnam and came home in a coffin. "The boys who have returned," she said, "are like Eddie Begay, who had a severe reaction to Agent Orange, or Bruce King, who came back addicted to heroin . . . or Edward Skeet, who's deaf in one ear . . ." She stopped, fearing she'd gone too far. But the president was listening intently. Supernaw had traveled a long way since the first grade, where a teacher had told her, when she failed to answer a question, "Well, that's OK. You're nothing but a dumb Indian anyway."

As a sophomore at Phillips University in Enid, Oklahoma, she was nominated to compete in the campus pageant by the members of the Indian Club she and the four other students had started. She agreed, though she'd never seen a beauty pageant and didn't know Miss America from Miss Universe. Because she usually wore jeans and bare feet and couldn't afford to buy a pageant wardrobe, friends lent her clothes to compete in. She did a tumbling routine and delivered a smart interview answer about her major, anthropology, and its importance for understanding cultural differences. Against the roar of applause that erupted when she was named the winner, she heard a rival snarl, "It's so dehumanizing to be beaten by an Indian!"

At the Miss Oklahoma contest, her major was again a point of interest, but this time she was asked, astoundingly, "Since anthropologists study the American Indian, why are you studying anthropology?" She wanted to crack, "To study the white man," but knew better and repurposed her original response, cutting a reference to world peace so as not to appear to be anti-government.

Supernaw was learning to be more politic in her responses and—sometimes—to curb her wonderfully wicked sense of humor. At a Tulsa event where she would address Kiwanis Club members—key sponsors of Miss Oklahoma—the club president introduced her, whispering in an aside that she should give them a typical Indian greeting. She took the mic, turned to the audience, and repeated what he'd asked, saying, "I didn't know whether he meant [one] like the one the Wampanoag Indians gave the Pilgrims at Plymouth Rock—or [one] like the Lakota and Cheyenne Indians gave Custer at Little Big Horn." Her humor, even when it was politically inflected, didn't seem to rankle her fans at all.

As Miss Oklahoma, Supernaw had the attention of the same state executive director, Toni Spencer, who'd groomed Jayroe for success, and decades before that had competed herself, becoming first runner-up to Bess Myerson. Spencer would schedule Supernaw's bookings that year and organize her dance and runway training.

Crowned and gowned and ready to dazzle on a rainy June night before her first appearance, Supernaw made a dash for her limo across a flooded street, but her sash fell and she tripped, crashing to the ground and ripping both sash and dress. She sprang back up and darted toward the limo door, forgetting to lower her head for the crown, which cracked against the opening and sent her reeling backward into the street, water pooling around her ankles. It was her first lesson in being a beauty queen: mishaps, weather, wardrobe malfunctions, and mortification were part of the job. She made her debut "looking like a drowned rat," she writes in her memoir, but entered the room regally, the broken crown turned with the crack hidden in the back.

Spencer enlightened Supernaw about the secrets of pageant judging, like stacking points—where judges who liked a contestant's personality voted for them in the preliminary gown and swimsuit portion whether they looked good or not, just to push them into the finals. This explained why the curveless but charismatic Supernaw had won the swimsuit competition both times she'd competed. Spencer said doing the same talent as the previous year's winner reduced a hopeful's chances of winning, since comparisons would be inevitable and probably unfavorable against a winner. She taught her table manners and how to sit properly, breaking her of the habit of kicking her shoes off when she was seated. And she helped Supernaw gain ten pounds for Miss America. Unlike most contestants, who dieted and exercised ad nauseam, Supernaw ate and exercised, working with an instructor to translate her gymnastic talent into a jazz routine she could perform with a forty-piece orchestra.

As a girl, when she lay semiconscious in the grass, crushed by her injured horse after the riding accident that left her paralyzed for months, Supernaw had had a vision: A Native woman dressed in white buckskin beaded with blue turquoise approached her carrying a bear cub with a broken leg. "You must fight yourself," she told Supernaw. "It is a battle within your body."

"Why?"

"To earn your name."

"I don't have any name to earn."

The woman shushed her and released the cub, healed now, which ran, turned toward Supernaw, reared up, roared, waved, and danced. When it finished and bowed, Supernaw saw herself in its face.

"This bear cub is your totem. Your name is 'Ellia Ponna.'" The name meant Dancing Feet of the Bear People. Supernaw would later envision the bear whenever she performed.

For a hundred years, her state's eastern and western tribes had been in conflict because of the Medicine Lodge Treaty that pushed many Plains Indians into western Oklahoma to clear the way for white expansion. But Supernaw's Miss Oklahoma win brought them together to support her. They organized a ceremonial pow-wow with singing, dancing, food, and prayer and fronted $1,000 to sponsor an ad for her in the annual pageant program, recognizing that she had, as Supernaw writes, "endured the prejudice of the majority population, poverty, alcoholism, and domestic violence, and yet remained true to my culture's spiritual teachings." They wanted America to know that "I was not just the state's queen but the Indian tribes' ambassador, their queen."

Supernaw represented a state with one of the highest Indigenous populations in the country. And the timing of her win was significant. That year, in a now-notorious *Playboy* interview, John Wayne had come out as a white supremacist who said of Native Americans, "Our so-called stealing of this country from them was just a matter of survival. There were great numbers of people who needed new land, and the Indians were selfishly trying to keep it for themselves." (When a Hollywood talent agent later came sniffing around about casting Supernaw as an Indian, she said her dream was to shoot Wayne as he rode off into the sunset.)

She packed her gowns and matching shoes, jeans and hot pants (which she was later forbidden to wear), and beaded gifts for pageant officials (later stolen backstage) and flew off. Her arrival in Atlantic City was heralded with an appalling Associated Press photo titled "War Cry" and a caption stating Supernaw wanted "the Miss America scalp as a contribution to the Image of the Native American Indian."

Supernaw competed with just two other women of color: the second ever black contestant, Patricia Patterson of Indiana, and Aurora Joan Kaawa, a Native Hawaiian. Many of her white rivals, she discovered, either disapproved of her being there or thought she was cute, "more like an oddity than an equal," she wrote. Miss Connecticut, a white woman, had been named "Princess Soft Sunshine" by the Easter Seals Society for the disabled, and brought along a headdress they'd inexplicably given her to wear at the pageant, which she did. Supernaw tried, in vain, to explain that it was for a man.

She was paired, traveling between the hotel and Convention Hall every day, with the unlikeliest of companions: Laurel Lea Schaefer, the Ohio University student who'd been crowned Miss Ohio on her third try, now days away from becoming Miss America. Supernaw waited each morning while Schaefer spent three hours getting ready—two on her hair alone, which, Supernaw marveled, was "so ratted and rigid from hairspray that I figured it must take her that long to comb it out again." Schaefer was such a pageant pro, in fact, that there were media mutterings that she'd manipulated the judges when they asked about her father, who had died twelve years earlier, by crying so vigorously she'd had to leave the room.

At a time when at least 65 percent of women were having sex before marriage, Schaefer told the press she didn't believe in premarital sex or doing drugs and felt she represented the majority of youth. But it was her claim that she'd never owned a pair of jeans that flummoxed Supernaw, who until then "would not have believed it possible for someone to go through life without wearing jeans."

One of Supernaw's charms was that she could get along with anyone, including Schaefer. And though she never felt comfortable with most of her competitors—they were formal, unfriendly, superficial backstabbers—she still had fun, and met a few who, she reflects today, were "the nicest girls in the world" and didn't behave like their lives depended on winning. During one rehearsal, a group of contestants sang:

> We're the Miss America girls, sweet and jolly
> We don't cuss, we just say "golly!"
> We don't smoke, drink or screw,
> And we don't go with guys that do.
> Now you may think we don't have fun,
> Hell, we don't!

A prim pageant matron rushed over to ask Supernaw if they'd just used the word "screw." Quick on her feet, she told her, no—they'd sung, "We don't smoke, drink, or *chew*." As in tobacco. She was discovering that stretching the truth was essential to pageantry. But "something inside gnawed at my spirit, and I knew I couldn't compete with those social debutantes on their level because I was unwilling to change certain parts of myself." Then there was the cold truth that she could never rate as the girl next door at a pageant where no one had lived next door to a Native American.

A pulled muscle nixed her chances of placing anyway. She won a $1,000 Judges Special Award, which her African American friend Pat Patterson also received. Neither knew what it was for, but Supernaw hoped to God Miss Hawaii hadn't received it too, which would make them all winners of an ethnic minority consolation prize. Hawaii's award, it turned out, was for talent.

Supernaw finished school, got a master's degree in education, and became a teacher and computer programmer who consulted on education projects for rural Native Americans. For her, the benefit of winning the state crown wasn't state fame or career boosting or giving back to the pageant. It was a matter of leveraging her public profile, she says, to rebuild Indigenous communities.

———

WHEN WOULD A WOMAN OF color become a finalist? Miss USA was already way ahead of Miss America in embracing diversity; its first Asian American winner, Macel Wilson of Hawaii, took that crown in 1962. Jayne Kennedy, the first black Miss Ohio USA, was a semifinalist at Miss USA in 1970. Miss America was mulishly slow to evolve.

Throughout the 1970s, black women made sporadic progress as four more won their states. In 1973, Lydia Lewis of Kentucky became the first black Southerner to compete. Miss Wyoming, Cheryl Johnson, followed in 1974 and found a nasty note in her Atlantic City dressing room labeled TICKET BACK TO AFRICA. Johnson was a football player—football!—on a female team at Laramie Community College, probably the only one in Miss America's history. ("I'm no women's liberationist," she said in a caveat that would be echoed by generations of reluctant feminists, in and out of the pageant world, through the decades, "but I guess you could call me a sympathizer as far as jobs are concerned.")

Finally, in 1976, Delaware's Deborah Lipford became the first black woman to break into the top ten. In 1980, Lencola Sullivan, Miss Arkansas, hit the top five. After almost sixty years, the crowning of a black Miss America finally seemed possible. And with Doris Janell Hayes (Miss Washington) arriving the same year as Sullivan, the job of the trailblazing black contestant became a little less lonely.

Sullivan's grandparents, who had eleven children and no college education themselves, had worked picking cotton and beans to put their kids through college. But they only earned enough for one child's education. The oldest of five, Sullivan decided to pay her own way by competing in pageants, where she not only determined she could make good money even as a runner-up, but also had fun and enjoyed "discovering things about myself," she told me. She won three locals, making history as the first black winner in each, then went on to the state competition. After twice making the top ten at Miss Arkansas without winning, Sullivan planned another try, but her mother, convinced that a black Miss Arkansas simply wouldn't be crowned, questioned the decision. Why not enter a pageant like Miss Black America, she asked, where her chances were better? Sullivan wasn't interested; not only were the winnings much smaller, but she wanted to be prepared for the real world, "and the real world has more than only my culture represented," she said.

Racism, subtle and overt, awaited Sullivan and Hayes in Atlantic City. Hayes was harassed at the opening parade. "Oh go take a bath, Miss Washington," a bystander taunted her. "You're too dirty to be in the parade." They fielded endless questions from journalists about race ("How does it feel to be a black contestant?") and were often pitted against each other. Asked, "What do you think your chances are against Miss Washington?" Sullivan wanted to say, "Well, there are fifty other women in this pageant!" Her chaperone finally snapped and told reporters their line of questioning was rude. But Sullivan said it was okay, because her parents had taught her not to let racism get in her way. "They said, 'Life isn't fair. You just have to be twice as good.'"

She won her least favorite part of the pageant: swimsuit. Her discomfort about it still crackles forty years later in a phone interview from her home in the Netherlands, where she works as a diversity and inclusion trainer for Shell International. "We had to walk and stand in front of the judges and let them look at us to see and compare us to all the others. And that was horrible. When I think about it now, I think, *Oh my God.* And some girls—I could see their knees knocking, they were so nervous to stand there. [The judges] looked you up [and down], head to toe, to make sure you had what they call the three diamonds" (spaces between the upper thighs, knees, and ankles). "And then you could not leave until the head judge nodded his head to say you could go."

Earlier that year, sixty-five-year-old Bert Parks had been rudely sacked without warning, after twenty-five years as host, causing the pageant switchboard to light up with furious callers and prompting Johnny Carson to launch a "We Want Bert" campaign. Marks had made the decision in hopes of drawing younger viewers and boosting droopy ratings after the sponsors told him Parks was too old. He approached several dashing younger potential successors, including John Davidson, an actor and game show host who responded, "I wouldn't sing that lousy song for a million dollars." Former Tarzan Ron Ely took the job, serving respectably for the next three years, though no one since Parks has ever so perfectly matched the occasion.

When Ely called Hayes out as a semifinalist, Sullivan assumed she herself wouldn't advance further "because I never thought they would have two [black women] in the Top 10." Then her name was announced. She strode across the stage in her sleek black beaded gown. Minutes later she was named fourth runner-up, making history as the first black woman to place that high. But the crown went to Miss Oklahoma, Susan Powell.

Sullivan's disappointment was crushing, but the pageant sent her on an unexpectedly varied career path. She had already been working as a TV anchor when she competed, and she continued off and on. But she also sang, having picked this as her talent in Atlantic City even though she had no training. "All those other people competing with me had years of dance, years of classical piano, years of voice lessons," she says. "And I had nothing. I just had guts." She later went on to sing with Lionel Hampton, Kool & the Gang, and Stevie Wonder, whom she dated in 1988. (When she took him home to meet her parents that year, he sang at her church, causing a two-day traffic jam after word spread that he was in town.) Her background in TV and public speaking led to her job at Shell, where her diversity work has brought her full circle after her Miss America breakthrough. Since then, she says, many black Miss Americas have thanked her for opening the door.

Even, she says, Vanessa.

SEVEN

Iconoclasts

I N A DELICIOUS BIT OF kismet, the birth announcement of the most famous Miss America of all time shows a crowned baby under bunting emblazoned with the words HERE SHE IS—MISS AMERICA! Born to schoolteachers in small-town Millwood, New York, Vanessa Williams was the queen who fell hardest, then flew farthest, becoming a Grammy-nominated singer and actress beloved both because of and in spite of her scandalous 1984 reign.

"I never had any desire to be a beauty queen, let alone Miss America," she writes in her 2012 memoir, *You Have No Idea*. But . . . scholarships. She thought she could win a little money to help fund her junior year semester abroad. As a sophomore studying musical theater at Syracuse University, she'd been drafted into a feeder pageant that delivered her to Atlantic City, where she met "girls who had starved themselves, girls who had practiced the same routine since they were children, girls who'd been coached by their moms since birth, girls who'd been in hundreds of pageants." She bonded with the few rookies she met, never thinking she could win with so little pageant experience. "We were naïve and ready to have fun." Like Sullivan and Hayes in 1980, she and the three other black contestants were posed together in photos that emphasized their difference while purporting to highlight the pageant's inclusiveness.

The moment she won, she thought, "There goes my junior year abroad in London." And as she walked the runway, she wondered what would happen next. No one had told her about the relentless plane-hopping and glad-handing. At first, she writes, "I had no emotion—I wasn't happy. I wasn't excited. I wasn't there." But as it sank in that she had just made history as the first black Miss America, she was thrilled.

It's hard to overstate the impact of her win on the thousands of black girls and women who watched it. "I was not the kind of girl who cared about pageants or being a beauty queen," Roxane Gay writes in *Bad Feminist: Essays*, "but watching Williams and her perfect cheekbones and glittering teeth as she accepted the crown gave girls like me ideas. That moment made us believe we too could be beautiful."

As a child witnessing Williams's crowning, Miss America 1994 Kimberly Aiken, the fifth black winner, thought, "Wow, she looks like me. This is something that I could do. I had never to that point thought that Miss America was something that was for me or something that I could do."

Though he was a pageant skeptic, Gerald Early, an African American studies professor at Washington University, had watched the crowning with his wife and daughters in St. Louis and even had their photo taken with Williams when she came to town.

"We went, my wife and I, to celebrate the grand moment when white American popular culture decided to embrace black women as something other than sexual subversives or as fat, kindly maids cleaning up and caring for white families," he later wrote. "We had our own, well, royalty, and royal origins mean a great deal to people who have been denied their myths and their right to human blood."

Benjamin L. Hooks, executive director of the NAACP, compared her win to Jackie Robinson breaking the color barrier in baseball and hoped it would hasten progress in other areas, like law, medicine, and physics. Shirley Chisholm thanked God she had lived long enough "that this nation has been able to select the beautiful young woman of color to be Miss America."

The Nation was wary about the positive reaction, marveling, in an unbylined editorial, that "a society which is still profoundly racist along its entire institutional base … can thrill to the symbolic success of an individual from an excluded minority," given that "[m]inority heroes tend to lose their appeal when they travel in large groups." Still, the writer granted the resonance of Williams's win in a year that had seen a revival "of black demands for power and privilege after a decade of battered quiescence." That year, Martin Luther King Jr.'s birthday became a national holiday, Chicago elected its first black mayor, Jesse Jackson planned his presidential run, and Alice Walker coined the term "womanist" to describe feminists of color.

There was indeed an illogic to touting Williams's crowning as a civil rights triumph when the whole pageant was predicated on individual achievement. Both Williams and the pageant authorities trumpeted it as such, the scholar Sarah Banet-Weiser explains, "in a historical moment when affirmative action policies and hires were under attack for tokenism and reverse racism." The judges repeatedly said she had won "on her own merits," something that would have gone unsaid about a white winner.

The confused state of popular feminism, deflated now in the "post-feminist" 1980s, was also evident. In one of the rare instances of the F-word ever being uttered in the broadcast, Miss Kentucky said, "I'm not an activist but I do believe in feminism." The statement, however—a clip from her prerecorded interview segment—was inset on the TV screen as she teetered across the stage in heels and a pink swimsuit. And after making nods to "women's lib" in the 1970s (a 1974 production number named "Call Me Ms." seemed to forget this was *Miss* America), the pageant now expressed little commitment to women's empowerment—or, for that matter, patriotism. Because of a copyright controversy over the use of "There She Is, Miss America," Williams walked the runway as host Gary Collins sang "Look at Her," a goopy tribute to the "radiant beauty" "carrying our hearts," with no mention of Miss America or America, period.

People loved that Williams was black, people hated that she was black, people said she won because she was black, people said she won in spite of being black, people said she wasn't black enough, with her light skin and her green eyes and her white boyfriend. Her win may have marked a milestone in black history, but it also tapped a vein of virulent racism, including among pageant people. The night she was crowned, Mary Ann Mobley pulled Williams's chaperone aside and asked, "Are you ready to go to Harlem now?" That week, Johnny Carson joked, "Did you hear we have a black Miss America? I bet you didn't know that Mr. T was one of the judges." Until then, Williams says, she hadn't experienced bald-faced bigotry. Her parents told her, "Well, we can't shelter you anymore, Ness."

An initial flood of congratulatory letters to Williams was soon polluted with a slurry of death threats, semen, spit, and pubic hair. Armed guards were posted outside her hotel room in Alabama; sharpshooters stood watch on rooftops during her celebratory hometown parade through Millwood and nearby Chappaqua. "We had no idea that her Miss America reign would quickly become a reign of terror for us," writes her mother, Helen Williams, who coauthored Vanessa's memoir.

And that was just the start of her travails. Ten months in, as the most in-demand Miss America ever, her crown fell. *Penthouse* announced it would publish nude pictures of her, some in explicit poses with another woman, taken when she was nineteen. Williams said she hadn't given permission for publication (the photographer claimed she signed a release), and days after they were shot, she'd returned to retrieve the negatives—receiving, she later discovered, an incomplete set. Once the magazine hit newsstands, the pageant gave her seventy-two hours to resign, and she did, though her ever-supportive parents encouraged her not to. Leonard Horn, the pageant's attorney at the time, said sponsors were threatening to pull out if she didn't step down. And Marks explained, "Vanessa is a lovely young woman. Nobody is going to crucify her for a mistake. But this put us in a position of having to act to protect sixty-three years of the Miss America pageant."

Celebrities from Gloria Steinem to Jesse Jackson called Williams to commiserate, and former queens Laurel Lea Schaefer and Lee Meriwether sent their support. ("Remember, you will always be a Miss America and I will always be proud of you," Meriwether wrote.) The photos made her another inadvertent first: hers was the biggest-selling issue in *Penthouse* history, earning $24 million, none of which was hers. The pageant allowed her to keep her scholarship and earnings thus far, but she lost about $2 million, she says, in canceled contracts with Gillette, Diet Coke, and Kellogg's. Her first runner-up, Suzette Charles, who entered her first pageant when she was seven, assumed the throne, saying she would represent "the wholesome American image."

Thus began a second frenzy of punditry about Williams. She

was merely a foolish girl who made a mistake. She was a slut who should never have been crowned in the first place. She was a threat to children who might be tempted to follow her path to perdition and—the implication was clear—lesbianism. She was a disgrace to her race (a charge only slightly mitigated by the fact that her successor was also black). She had single-handedly reinvigorated the Jezebel stereotype. She was an ambitious woman who'd only done what many women in entertainment did to get ahead—used her body in pursuit of an opportunity, something akin to wearing a swimsuit and heels in a beauty pageant. She was a victim—of the photographer who betrayed her, the magazine that exploited her, and the pageant that dumped her back on her parents' doorstep before dropping all contact with her. "They just wiped their hands of her because they felt she was no longer of any value to them," her mother writes.

Williams made her confession: she was naïve and misguided, and she had let the pageant down. But, she says in her memoir, she had done nothing wrong. In entering the pageant, she'd signed a contract that guaranteed she hadn't committed acts of "moral turpitude," phrasing of a Slaughter-era vintage, but no acts were specified. Horn even conceded that there was "no specific language in the contract saying that she cannot pose in the nude" but said her resignation was a matter of moral responsibility.

In a 1984 *Vogue* profile of Williams, cultural critic Margo Jefferson noted the correlation between *Penthouse*'s hard-core porn and Miss America's soft-core sexuality. (An inexplicable number of women in dance routines performed without pants or skirts that year, their legs exposed up to the panty line.) "One gives us the Whore, one the Virgin. But though they sustain each other in myth, they are not allowed to eat at the same table or to inhabit the same persona in life."

The sexual revolution of the 1970s had set a foundation for women's erotic self-expression, and they were freer to do so in the 1980s—or so they thought. "The most interesting thing about Vanessa Williams," Jefferson wrote, "is the fact that she seems equally removed from both *Penthouse* and the pageant stereotypes— too sensible and reserved for the one, too brisk and unsentimental for the other. She struck me as intelligent and self-assured in a way I've come to associate with the young women often called post-feminists: they view their ambition and their resourcefulness as a right, not as a battle or a frontier. I find this very appealing, but I also find that they can be less aware of their fallibility and more sure of their worldliness than might be wise."

Williams was the pageant's own Hester Prynne, the first and only winner to be dethroned, whose transgression only intensified her aura. (A year later, Madonna, too, would have a Vanessa moment when both *Playboy* and *Penthouse* published nude pictures of her taken years earlier under similar circumstances. Like a sullied Miss America, she was told her hometown had reneged on plans to grant her the ceremonial keys to the city.)

———

DISHONORABLY DISCHARGED, WILLIAMS STRUGGLED TO get her life back on track, facing obstacles at almost every turn: a co-op board refusing her application because of the incident; a successful audition for *My One and Only* torpedoed when the executive director heard Williams was the director's choice ("I don't want that whore in my play," she snarled). Her plight anticipated the wave of twenty-first-century revenge porn scandals in which private photos have ruined women's lives.

But once Williams became the pageant's most successful

alumna, people questioned whether she'd ever needed it in the first place. Her 1988 debut album *The Right Stuff* went platinum, igniting a career during which she has won ten Grammy nominations for her buttery pop songs and R&B albums. She has also acted, receiving Tony and Emmy nominations for *Into the Woods* and *Ugly Betty*, respectively. To her delight, journalists finally stopped referring to her as a former beauty queen. And for some fans, seeing her transcend the pageant was a gauge of her success. Comedian Margaret Cho told PBS she found a hero in Williams, "the only winner anyone remembers," because she had "the most kiss-my-ass story that you can triumph over anything."

Given the chance to be twenty-one and compete again, Williams says she would not. She told *Huffpost* that being a beauty queen "really hurt my brand . . . a lot of people assume if you have a Miss anything in front of your name, it negates any sort of talent or intellect you have." When Williams was invited back to the pageant in 2015 to receive a public apology from Executive Director Sam Haskell, Suzette Charles wondered why she needed it, having so successfully transcended pageantry. The gesture added a crowning irony to Williams's saga: Haskell was forced to resign two years later because of his own scandal—a monumentally nasty affair that did far more damage to Miss America's reputation than Williams's dethroning ever had. But that's a story for chapter 8.

———

WILLIAMS HAD DONE MISS AMERICA a colossal favor in jolting the moribund pageant back to life and returning it to public awareness. In 1980 the first Miss America, Margaret Gorman herself, at seventy-five, had said she might not stay up for that year's crowning: "It can be so boring." Now people who'd tuned out were curious to see what new intrigue it might offer; others were impressed that a highly talented, thoroughly modern winner had been crowned. (In her first press conference, Williams had said she was pro-ERA without hedging, though she was coached to answer the obligatory swimsuit question with the perennial dodge, "A fit body reflects a fit mind.") The pageant gained renewed value as a dowsing rod for attitudes about race, sexuality, and gender. Ticket sales jumped 20 percent in 1984. Viewership briefly leapt back to 74 million. But in 1984, anyone looking for more scandal was disappointed: the new Miss America was a Mormon.

Sharlene Wells was the first Miss America born abroad, in Paraguay. She spent much of her childhood in South America, where her American father worked first as a Citibank executive, then as a missionary. Wells didn't smoke or drink, supported school prayer, and opposed the ERA, which she said "would make us a neuter society." She was against abortion and premarital sex—*even*, she told a reporter who pressed the issue, for an unmarried woman of thirty-five. (Here she likely lost a good share of ladies who'd spent their formative years grinding to Donna Summer's multiply orgasmic "Love to Love You Baby" or thrilling to Joan Jett's "Bad Reputation.") "I believe very strongly in God and country," Wells said. "I follow the flag with my whole body."

"What a relief," sighed a pageant official. "She is almost too good to be true."

A five-foot-eight blonde with an elegant nose and china-blue eyes, Wells appeared for a New York press conference wearing a pink suit with matching stockings and shoes, paired with a pearl necklace and earrings. (Oh, for the days of Jacque Mercer in her sexy cowgirl regalia!) Her crowning had not only rectified the Williams debacle, but averted a whole new one. The week of the pageant, *Penthouse* publisher Bob Guccione announced that he had 350 nude pictures of one of the contestants, ready for publication if she won. (Guccione had been making mischief for Miss America even before Williams; in 1979, he ran a satiric story about a baton-twirling Miss Wyoming whose oral prowess could make men levitate, which she demonstrated on her baton during the talent section. The woman was clearly identifiable as an actual contestant—who responded by filing a $26.5 million lawsuit.)

The swimsuit competition posed a problem for Wells's father in light of Mormon church president Spencer Kimball's decree, decades earlier, that Mormons should not enter "bathing beauty contests." But, he figured, Kimball was probably referring to "the girly-type competitions of years ago." (Little did he know that his daughter's measurements would run in the pageant program.) Furthermore, a modest swimsuit, the type college swim teams actually swim in, would make it acceptable, he said. Such a suit, oddly, couldn't be found, so a seamstress was hired to create a double-lined one-piece in white. After she won Swimsuit, Wells took Talent (worth 50 percent) as well, playing a medley of folk songs on the Paraguayan harp and singing in Spanish, which inspired Paraguay's president to send her a congratulatory telegram and invite her to visit.

And so it was that Wells, a foreign-born Miss America who had spent most of her life outside the U.S., returned the pageant to godliness and patriotism. "I think what has happened is we have redefined what Miss America stands for," she said. "Miss America has always stood for certain ethics, I would have to say, the traditional values." Perhaps, but was Wells better qualified to exemplify them than a Latina born and raised in the United States? Not one had ever won—or has since. By contrast, Miss USA has crowned four, the first in 1985.

By the time Wells triumphed, Latinas had their own pageant. Miss Latin America began in Florida in 1981 and went national in 1983, with individual state representatives feeding into it, ultimately aligning with the Miss Universe pageant. Some Latinas felt more welcome at other pageants. And one found Miss America openly racist. Ane Romero, Miss New Mexico, was one of two Latinas competing in 2005. The pair were booked in a room together, and directed, when the hopefuls met the press, to Spanish-language publications, though neither was fluent in Spanish. That week, says Romero, she was interviewed by Sue Lowden, a former Miss New Jersey, who asked question after disparaging question about Mexican mothers and their "illegal babies" on the assumption that Romero was an immigrant, though her family had been on the land that became New Mexico since 1598. She'd expected to discuss her suicide prevention platform and was "nearly paralyzed in shock and anger" as she realized that because of Lowden, she didn't stand a chance of winning.

Even in 2018, Miss Massachusetts Gabriela Taveras, a finalist, was advised to tone down her accent to improve her chances and avoid making people "feel uncomfortable." She did not.

On the other hand, Wells's foreign experience made her a much more worldly Miss America than most, better informed about international politics, thus able to field questions about student protests against apartheid in South Africa or Reagan's controversial trip to a cemetery in Germany where members of the Waffen-SS were buried. She had been in the minority of Americans at her international school abroad, and told one interviewer, "I grew up with friends from all over the world, so issues that affected them affected me ... It surprised me when I came back to the United States how my friends my own age really didn't know anything that was going on past our own little community."

Wells may have seemed like the perfect pageanteer for that tumultuous year, but her experience was anything but perfect, as a

graduate student at the University of Nebraska Omaha learned over
a decade later. Debra Deitering Maddox wrote her 2001 sociology/
anthropology master's thesis on that year's contest, gauging its
impact on eleven 1984 contestants she interviewed between 1998
and 2001. It's a rare public postmortem, one Deitering Maddox was
uniquely positioned to write, since she'd competed with them herself: she was Miss Iowa. Speaking with a fellow alum, her subjects
were much more honest about pageant life—searingly so—than
most are in media interviews.

Deitering Maddox used a sample group of contestants from all
over the country, with top to bottom levels of success. She chron-
icled their run and its effect on their self-image and career paths,
concluding that ultimately "there are no winners at Miss America.
Those who do not win struggle with residual self-esteem and failure issues." Even Wells herself, wrote Deitering Maddox, "struggles
with these same issues. [She] entered the pageant self-assured with
a strong sense of family and self. She completed her reign emotion-
ally bankrupt."

Wells, who became a reporter for ESPN before going into business, has enjoyed a successful career and rich family life, having
raised four children. But the pageant, she told Deitering Maddox,
was just "a little side trip off her lifepath," one that seemed largely
unenjoyable, from the mean-girls antics of some of the other contestants to her reign year, which was so stressful she considered
quitting and at one point feared she would be fired. Unlike some
winners who bonded with their chaperones, she found it lonely to
travel with a stranger. Because she hated wearing the crown, she
sometimes pretended to forget it. Later, she couldn't stand to look at
the scrapbooks her mother made about her year. She had applied to
Harvard but changed her mind after getting an interview and went

to Brigham Young University to be close to home. "It just wasn't
the right time to go out and be alone again after that year," she said.

Then there was the Vanessa factor. Wells could never know for
sure whether she'd won on her own merit or because she was Mormon. She became the butt of jokes; Bob Hope riffed on it on his
TV show. "She's so religious she has a stained glass in her compact,
and she has nude pictures of Bob Guccione. She says the next time
he opens his mouth she'll publish them in the *Ladies' Home Journal*." Likewise, the losers wondered if their failure resulted from
the controversy. Maryline Blackburn, Miss Alaska, one of the few
black entrants (who bested Sarah Palin for the state crown), knew
there was no way a black queen would be chosen after the scandal.
Another regretted choosing a torch song instead of something more
wholesome. One wished she'd picked a more discreet gown. "Every
former contestant interviewed believed the dethroning of Vanessa
Williams had enormous impact upon the competition," writes Deitering Maddox.

But though their particular year was exceptional, their experience as losers wasn't. The public defeat—something the finalists
had to endure while smiling—was humiliating, leaving them not
just with disappointment, but also "depression, indescribable pain,
self-blame, shame and abandonment." One feared she'd let down
everyone who'd supported her. One briefly wondered if her parents
would still love her. One was embarrassed that she cried when she
didn't make the top ten. One went home and slept clenched in a
fetal ball between her mother and sister and suffered stomachaches
for the next six weeks. One become bulimic during her pageant
years and struggled thereafter. Donna Cherry, Miss California,
who had been discovered in a nightclub by Miss America 1983
Debra Maffett, lost thirty pounds to compete, then gained it all

back, plus twenty more, in rebellion. "The whole thing about being yourself. It's the stupidest thing I've ever heard," she said. "In the pageant, it's all about marketing yourself. Go in and market the heck out of yourself, but don't be yourself."

There were benefits. Blackburn found she could both sing and play piano and embarked on a music career. Wells discovered she didn't like being in the limelight, Deitering Maddox reported, and later adjusted her career choices accordingly. They learned various skills—makeup and fashion, public speaking, self-presentation—that helped them professionally, or in some cases attracted million-aire husbands. One said competing had made her more confident. (Another, who had gone into it with no expectation whatsoever of winning, had found it to be great fun.) Blackburn's responses may best summarize the contradictions of competing and losing: it was a "wonderful opportunity" and "good experience" that damaged her self-confidence and "stripped me of my innocence."

The pageant hadn't offered most of them any direct opportunities, except for one local news reporter, Kathy Manning, who said she was hired because of her title. But her colleagues who'd worked their way up the professional ladder resented that she'd landed a high-profile slot with no experience. Wells also got a job in local TV when ESPN later recruited her without knowing she'd been Miss America (which she'd left off her résumé), but she felt the sting of derision as people found out, and "had to prove her professional credibility not once, but every time she entered a new industry, market or arena," wrote Deitering Maddox. "They assume you're here only because of the title," Wells told her.

Most surprising of all, none of Deitering Maddox's interviewees cited the scholarship as a benefit. And Wells (who got her master's degree years after Deitering Maddox interviewed her) told her "she would have done a lot more academically had she not won the Miss America title."

Deitering Maddox's research must be balanced with the testimony of state winners like Sullivan and Supernaw, who said nothing in our interviews about damaged self-confidence or lingering resentment about the pageant. It also correlates differently with lower-stakes local pageants, where, according to one 1985 winner, Donelle Ruwe, a feminist English professor, the benefits were virtually accidental and "unexpectedly positive." In an essay about her experience called "I Was Miss Meridian 1985," Ruwe explains that though she considers pageants to be oppressive and degrading (she was coached to behave in a less self-assured, more decorous and submissive way, for example), they can also have "idiosyncratic and unpredictable" payoffs—even subversive potential. The impact, she argues, is different on different people.

Ruwe entered local pageants in Idaho not for scholarships (her six wins yielded just $1,300), but because she wanted to wear glamorous clothes and feel beautiful. As a child, she'd worn glasses, a back brace for curvature of the spine, and an orthodontic head brace. She writes that pageantry training gave her the confidence in her looks and self-presentation to *stop* thinking about appearance, to "interact with others in non-physical ways" that led her to both "challenge and to be challenged intellectually." The gendered behaviors she was required to adopt ("not a version of gender that I respect") were something she believes contestants do with self-awareness; competing taught her not just to master it but also to critique it. Having grown up in a small, largely Mormon town, she writes, "I did not have access to feminist-oriented, alternative discourses of beauty and womanhood. It is ironic but nonetheless true that my success at a beauty pageant helped me to understand

beauty as a performance that I could choose or not choose to give."
(Deitering Maddox found no such self-awareness in her interviewees, none of whom, she noticed, used the word "objectification" or
ever acknowledged the pageant's patriarchal view of womanhood.)

Trelynda Kerr, a state winner who lost to Vanessa Williams,
was also the beneficiary of one of Ruwe's "unpredictable" effects,"
though unlike Ruwe, she's an unequivocal pageant champion. A
lesbian who wasn't out when she competed, she hadn't even fully
grasped her sexual orientation. "I was from Oklahoma and I was
very naïve," she told me. "I wasn't around anybody [who was gay]."
After the Miss America pageant, she moved to Dallas to perform
at Six Flags. "That was the first time I was around a bunch of gay
people," she says, and there she found her community. For Kerr,
the benefits of pageantry—cultivating confidence, commanding respect in her state, polishing her professional demeanor—also put
her in touch with her sexuality.

But the body issues Deitering Maddox unpacked in her thesis
applied to one Miss America herself. Elizabeth Ward (now Gracen), Miss America 1982, says competing—and winning—had
profoundly negative effects on her self-image. "I consider my pageant career and its outdated, misogynistic template of objectification and Barbie-doll emphasis on physical appearance as the origin
of what would constitute many years of self-destructive, misplaced
energy and wasted time," she wrote in a 2018 blog post.

The daughter of a nurse and a poultry worker, she'd entered
small pageants starting in her senior year in high school. Wearing a
borrowed, too-long green chiffon dress she had to kick forward onstage to avoid tripping as she walked, she won first runner-up in one
pageant, was soon being crowned Miss Arkansas by Lencola Sullivan, then walked the Miss America runway in a peach lace gown
she'd hand-sewn with rhinestones. She saw the pageant system, she

told me, as "a viable way of paying for school, stretching into the world outside the small town I grew up in, and, if I'm totally honest, to receive positive feedback from the people around me. It fueled my ambition to 'be somebody.'"

And it worked. She made about $150,000, which, with her scholarship money, funded acting lessons that started her on her way as an actress, notably in the *Highlander* TV series. (She had intended to become a corporate lawyer, but being in the limelight every day for a year gave her "the showbiz bug" and she never returned to college.) Miss America, she says, "trains you to be 'on' and to perform. It helps you develop that particular set of muscles." She's grateful for that and considers the pageant worthwhile because of it. But it all came at a price. It took her years of therapy, she wrote, "to shake off the Miss America cloak of what I consider harmful body shaming, objectification and misogynistic 'ideals.'"

The "misplaced energy and wasted time" Gracen referenced are among the hidden costs of high-maintenance femininity. It can not only work against these women's professional ambitions, as so many Miss America memoirs reveal with their myriad accounts of dieting, exercising, coaching sessions, and shopping, but may also derail them entirely from whatever their primary aspiration was to begin with.

Gracen was both competitive and ambitious. The 1982 pageant yearbook noted that she preferred to think of her title as "a goal she strove for and achieved" rather than "a dream come true." But a palliative cocktail of conformity and neutrality was essential to blunting the appearance of careerism. "I guess I was brainwashed to a certain extent to give the right kind of answers," she said in 1992. "You say the right things, you don't offend anyone and you're likable . . ." She was briefly a born-again Christian who lost her religion once Pat Robertson's *700 Club*, the Christian Broadcasting Network's flagship program, recruited her, post-pageant, to groom her as a cohost. During a telethon, she found herself unprepared to deal with desperate, sometimes suicidal callers. She'd been coached to read them Bible verses indexed to particular problems, concluding with a sales pitch. Toward the end, as the Robertson family spurred the telethon staff on to shorten the prayers and crank up the sales, a chill went down her spine; she realized this was crass business, not meaningful religion, and her trust in people, along with her faith, took a serious hit.

If Donna Cherry rebelled after her loss by gaining weight, Gracen did so after her win by posing naked for *Playboy* a decade later. It was both a way of distancing herself from the pageant world and a strategy for boosting her career, something she noticed Sharon Stone and Kim Basinger (a former Junior Miss) had done. (In a prescient coincidence, her year's pageant program—loaded, as was customary, with photographs of Gracen, the outgoing queen—also included an ad for the Playboy Hotel and Casino in Atlantic City. "Don't Miss the Playboy Fantasy Revue in the Cabaret," it read.) But Gracen's *Playboy* spread was as much a symptom of her experience as a rebellion against it—one more concession to the demands of being the ultimate woman.

"It's pretty obvious that I think the old model of Miss A is harmful to women," she says. "Yes, it gives them scholarships, but what it requires of them to get those scholarships is very harmful to women in general." The emphasis on looks was just part of the problem. It took years for her to stop trying to be charming, making everyone in the room feel comfortable, catering dutifully to other people, and striving toward an impossible perfection at the cost of her own identity. Though she returned to the pageant in 2018 for the first time in almost thirty years, reconnecting with other formers and hopeful that the scuttling of the swimsuit that year foretold broader reforms, she still believes this people-pleaser aspect of the pageant should end.

GRACEN ADMITTED TO USING A *teeny* bit of padding to enhance her curves in the pageant, but that was the slightest deception, and the oldest. In the 1980s, taping and padding, then nipping and tucking, gave way to liposuction, rib removal, and breast implants—adjustments that did essentially what the corset had done a century earlier by pinching the waist and amplifying the breasts. By the late 1980s, surgery was de rigueur; five 1989 contestants bounced into Atlantic City refashioned by the same surgeon. One judge called it "the American way." It was a very different America from the days of Margaret Gorman, when visible makeup could get a beauty booted.

Naomi Wolf's influential 1991 book *The Beauty Myth* drew attention to the way beauty culture functioned as a form of social control by usurping women's time and exploiting their insecurities for profit. Wolf attributed it mainly to a backlash against feminism, which Susan Faludi so comprehensively documented in her classic of the same year, *Backlash: The Undeclared War Against American Women*. In the Reagan 1980s, Faludi explained, women were told feminism was over, that it had only left them unhappy—lonely, frustrated, barren, bitter, unloved, and, worst of all, unmarried. Its triumphs were a threat to men and family, its failures the fault of feminists themselves. Two hallmarks of the backlash were the reassertion of control of women's bodies (notably through renewed assaults on abortion) and a growing emphasis on fitness as a measure of women's worth.

In an iconic image made for the 1989 pro-choice Women's March on Washington, artist Barbara Kruger proclaimed, "Your body is a battleground." The battle went far beyond abortion. Women were the subject of ceaseless debates about breast implants and face-lifts, surrogate motherhood, pornography, eating disorders, and ticking biological clocks. Sheath-like suits with shoulder pads armored women warriors in the corporate workplace. But the bodies beneath them had become—in their ideal form, anyway—exaggeratedly feminine: long, lithe, and stacked. In the 1960s, the average Miss America was five feet six and 120 pounds; in the 1980s, she was the same weight, but two inches taller.

In 1987, *The Washington Post* devoted most of an article to 1986 Miss America Susan Akin's rear end. Firm Grip, the adhesive she'd used to keep her swimsuit in place (also good for securing toupees), was on hand for almost everyone; there were thirty cans backstage, in fact, to be sprayed and pressed where the women's suits met the leg. Akins said it was helpful "if your behind is flabby, if you didn't lose as much weight as you should have"—something hard to imagine for a five-foot-nine, 114-pound twenty-one-year-old, but she wanted "protection." (And that was just one piece of her architecture. "I'll admit to a boob job," she shared.)

As the standard of perfection rose in the 1980s, so did the amount of labor required to achieve it, diverting women's energies away from work that could make them more than magnificent bodies. (A classic of second-wave feminism, Susie Orbach's 1978 book, *Fat Is a Feminist Issue*, said it all.)

In 1988, Gretchen Carlson took a leave from her studies at Stanford to prepare for the pageant, to which her flabbergasted dean responded, "That's absolutely the most ridiculous thing I've ever heard." Over the next nine months she spent two hours a day working out, two more getting coached in pageantry, and three to four practicing her violin, with additional time studying current events to prepare for the interview. (There was simply no logic to a "scholarship program" that forced women to leave college to earn a scholarship.) Carlson was exercising so hard, she said, she "could have eaten a farm," but she was also dieting, trying to lose twenty pounds, and always hungry. When she thought she was in good shape, her coach sized up her thighs and butt ("Absolutely not!"), announced that she needed to be "rehabbed" to get the right "cut," and prescribed a routine that consigned this Ivy League–caliber scholar and classical violinist to spending so much time jumping around in the family basement that her father asked, "Is she going to die down there from working out too hard?"

Achieving the perfect form, however, was just one ingredient of successful pageantry. The fit body required proper piloting. Standing, walking, sitting, turning, smiling, and gesturing were all matters of somber study. A 1989 pageant preparation guide called *The Crowning Touch*, written by pageant director and former contestant Anna Stanley, laid out the mind-boggling choreographies a hopeful had to master, starting with the "Suck-and-Tuck Glide":

> The *Miss America* walk is the Suck-and-Tuck Glide. You suck in your stomach and tuck in your derriere, walking briskly. At the same time, you swing your arms in time with the alternate legs. This helps to mask big thighs. In the swimsuit, stand so that no light shines between your legs. The only two spaces permitted are below the knees and ankles. Stand in the basic pageant stance so that your legs are together. When properly executed, this elongates and slims your body and legs . . . Prior to stepping forward, take several deep breaths so you can build every move to the next point on stage. Look natural, don't hurry to your next position, maintain eye contact with the judges, and [italics mine] *enjoy your moment.*

Pivoting like a model, tilting the head for the most flattering angle, standing to camouflage knock-knees—Stanley imparted her trade secrets *and* the racial and religious assumptions baked into them. A healthy glow was good; dark tanning was not. A coach could help "dampen" a "Mexican" accent. A good answer to a question about religion might touch on "Christian music that's vibrant and uplifting."

Gesticulating was to be avoided. Undisciplined hands betrayed the kind of class markers beauty queens hope to erase. When screenwriter William Goldman judged at the 1988 pageant that Carlson won, he noticed all the women did the same thing during the interview, placing the left hand on the right thigh and the right palm on the left hand. One smart, strong contestant battling the impulse to gesture as she spoke kept stopping herself by grabbing one hand with the other and pulling it down like Peter Sellers in the war room scene in *Dr. Strangelove*. In the end, Goldman reflected in his book *Hype and Glory*, she "so outclassed the winner in all the categories" but for her wandering hands. "I wanted to leave my chair and go hug her and tell her it was okay, what was a stupid beauty contest anyway," he wrote; "she'd get a Ph.D. and an M.D. and maybe win a Nobel Prize down the line." As it happens, she's now a doctor—her hands happily liberated to do their work.

In *The Crowning Touch*, Stanley called beauty queens the symbol of American sweetness, femininity, and innocence, clarifying that "[a] true winner is made, she is not born . . ." She was in perfect harmony with the feminist philosopher Judith Butler, whose groundbreaking 1990 book *Gender Trouble: Feminism and the Subversion of Identity* built on Simone de Beauvoir's claim that "[o]ne is not born, but rather becomes, a woman." Butler argued that gender is performed. Male/female binaries, she wrote, are socially constructed and artificial, perpetuating power differences that oppress women, along with gay and transgender people. The book became a key text of queer theory, a discipline that emerged in the 1990s, opening the way to contemporary acceptance of more fluid gender expression in dress, speech, and behavior. To this day, the Miss America competition enforces that binary, even after Miss Universe announced, in 2012, that it would welcome trans contestants; even after the arrival of the Miss America pageant's first openly gay contestant in 2016.

By the time Leonard Horn replaced Albert Marks as CEO in 1987, the pageant's sagging mystique was badly in need of Firm Grip. The queens publicly discussed not only the state of their saddlebags but also smearing Preparation H under their sleep-deprived eyes. A University of Mississippi professor studying pageant culture determined that 85 percent of the state's contestants believed their crowning had been ordained, unglamorously enough, by God. Sportsmanship had wilted once the cameras clicked off after the 1986 pageant: Ohio claimed she was "robbed," Montana alleged a bias toward deep-pocketed Southerners, and Louisiana declared, "If you don't get out there and shake your booty, you don't win."

Horn commissioned a study of public perceptions of the broadcast and learned that Miss America was a "turn-off." "That panicked me," he said. But it shouldn't have come as a surprise. Women were moving on. Former teen queen Diane Sawyer told *People*, "A friend and I were trying to remember what it was that made us watch the Miss America pageant in the '50s, and why Miss America seemed the dreamiest thing to be, why it seemed to matter in a way it doesn't anymore. I suppose it was because options were so limited then, and it was the quickest way to vault out of ordinariness. Now there are so many ways, including merit. Isn't that a shock?"

Feminists revived their complaints, especially in California,

where protesters hounded the state pageant throughout the 1980s—
first just four, then over a thousand, parading through the streets of
Santa Cruz in parody costumes. One year, former *Sports Illustrated*
swimsuit model Ann Simonton joined them wearing a thirty-pound
gown made of sliced bologna and pimento loaf, with a wiener-link
crown and matching necklace, beaming as she swanned along the
town's main drag. A Chicana protester dressed as a blonde bride in a
bird cage carried a sign asking, AM I WHITE ENOUGH FOR YOU?
In 1988, a California undergrad named Michelle Anderson infiltrated
the pageant as a contestant after much bleaching, dieting, training,
tanning, and feigning fundamentalist beliefs to get into the running.
Just before the winner was announced, she pulled a silk banner from
her décolletage that read, PAGEANTS HURT ALL WOMEN. (Anderson became a lawyer specializing in rape and sexual assault.)

For the first time, the pageant struggled to sell TV advertising. Horn set out to improve its image, entice new sponsors, and
replenish its coffers. He and his board renamed it the Miss America Organization (MAO), consigning pageantry to its bathing
beauty past; established a women's advisory committee; and funded
achievement awards for humanitarian work by women who might
otherwise have had no truck with Miss America. He announced a
greater focus on talent and a keen interest in attracting Ivy League
contestants.

When Gretchen Carlson's mother read about the changes in
the newspaper in 1988, she pushed her daughter to compete, even
though Carlson was spending a semester at Oxford and had been
accepted into a summer program that would allow her to continue
there.

"Hear me out," her mother said, reading from the paper. "'Miss
America is a relevant, socially responsible achiever whose message

to women all over the world is that in American society a woman can do or be anything she wants.'" Carlson was sold.

When William Goldman arrived to judge that year, flush with the success of his novel–turned–feature film *The Princess Bride*, he discovered the pageant had another problem: no one (else) of consequence wanted to judge. "These weren't celebrities," he realized, looking at his fellow judges, "they were a bunch of NBC employees, or would-be employees."

Not surprisingly, celebrities didn't want to spend a week in Atlantic City for the preliminaries; after decades of economic deterioration, "The World's Playground" was not just decrepit, it was downright dangerous. *Money* magazine had just named it the single worst place to live in America. Its decline could be traced to the rise of air travel in the 1960s (whisking East Coast tourists to other attractions like Las Vegas and Disney World), along with white flight, which cut the city's population by 25 percent between 1940 and 1970. The influx of casinos in 1978 attracted huge numbers of hit-and-run visitors, but also triggered an 80 percent surge in crime. Goldman marveled at the slums and sleaze, the muggers and panhandlers right outside the casinos. When he stopped in front of the recently built Trump Plaza to ask a bellhop where he might find a bookstore, there was a long pause. "You mean porn, right? Dirty stuff?" No, he didn't. "Sorry, can't help you."

Like Frank Deford, who judged four pageants in the 1970s after the publication of his book *There She Is: The Life and Times of Miss America*, Goldman wanted to have it both ways, granting that this was more than a skin show while leering at the ladies like a creepy old guy in a strip club. If the pageant hadn't reconciled the cheesecake with the scholarships, it had at least finessed the euphemisms to downplay it. Not so Deford and Goldman, who toggled between paternalistic pity and grudging respect for the "bright" contestants, between mocking their talent and cheering them on after seeing them sweat through eighteen-hour days. Unsure of how to narrow down a swimsuit winner from a dozen or so nearly identical women, Deford was at a loss. "You don't want to be a pig and just go for the biggest boobs. What do you do?"

Goldman was rooting for Miss Colorado—smart, impressive, and different. He was dead set against Gretchen Carlson, a "God-clutcher" who "would have made the most dedicated Sunday school teacher in the history of the Western World." He was also convinced that had the judges not been split in two groups, preliminary (weekday) and celebrity (weekend), to allow them shorter stays in Atlantic City, she would have lost because his cohort didn't like her. Favoring a more sophisticated winner was fine; calling Carlson "Miss Piggy," as Goldman did, was, well, piggish. He wondered why smart Miss Utah had ever gotten involved in a pageant; the same could have been asked of him, considering his conclusion, after judging it, that it was sexist.

Carlson abandoned plans to become a lawyer, went into broadcasting, served as a cohost on *Fox & Friends*, won a $20 million sexual harassment settlement that toppled Fox News CEO Roger Ailes in 2016, and now campaigns against sexual harassment. She's one of the brightest stars in Miss America's firmament. (She also became, incidentally, a Sunday school teacher.) Goldman couldn't predict the scope of her ambition or the reach of her influence. But she wasn't the only winner he misread. The queen who crowned Carlson, Kaye Lani Rae Rafko, inspired the pageant's biggest change since the addition of the scholarship, right in front of him.

Rafko, Miss America 1988, was an oncology nurse from Monroe, Michigan, who'd entered fourteen regional pageants over four years to earn $45,000 to pay for college. Her mother was a former

Miss Dairy Queen; her father owned an auto parts shop. Crowned in a donated, revamped wedding dress in 1987, she was a proud blue-collar winner who broke pageant protocol by combining her Miss America duties with her nursing work. She had no interest in show business before or after her reign. "I can't imagine doing anything else," she said. "I love my coworkers, and I find it especially fulfilling to work with patients who are dying and to help them accept their death."

As she waited to crown her successor, a drama unfolded: there was a tie in the judging of the runners-up, causing an epic eleven-minute delay, during which Gary Collins and his cohost wife, Mary Ann Mobley, Miss America 1959 herself, bantered nervously on live television. "You're dying well, my dear," Mobley joked as Collins nattered away, shooting worried glances at the judges, who were busy whispering and penciling in recalculations while Horn drummed his fingers on the stage beside them. Collins wandered over to chat up the petrified contestants, one of whom cheekily asked if he remembered her name. Then the two cohosts began thanking people—the states, the "young ladies," the parents, the volunteers, the television viewers—everyone but the ushers. And the clock ticked.

Goldman, off duty now as a first-shift judge, regarded the spectacle from the front row. "I was just so happy being there, watching this great fuck-up." In a desperate bid for help, Collins turned to Rafko and said, "Tell us about hospice." She announced that she intended to get her master's degree in oncology, "so that one day I *will* open a hospice center, for all terminally ill patients, both cancer as well as AIDS."

The audience roared. Goldman recoiled. "What were they clapping for?" he wondered. "Cancer? Death?" No: Dignity. Truth. The first International AIDS conference had been held just three years earlier, and Reagan had only finally deigned to utter the acronym publicly a year hence. Rafko had stood by her first love, nursing, something the vanity of the title hadn't knocked out of her on the beauty trail. In fact, she had preferred charity appearances to sponsorship events, and still made $150,000 during her reign.

When she finished her degree, she opened that hospice.

After seeing the scope of the respect she garnered and the substance of the appearances she made, including addressing a congressional sub-committee about nursing issues, Horn seized an opportunity. Starting in 1990, contestants—from the local level to the national competition—would be required to adopt a cause, a "platform issue" like cancer, literacy, or poverty, and advocate for it as Rafko had. Like the addition of the scholarship in the 1940s, the platform gave the pageant an invigorating new mission and a moral justification for the business of crowning beauty. The reign year became the "year of service," and the winner's ribbon-cuttings and autograph signings were supplemented with nonprofit fundraisers and advocacy outreach.

Debbye Turner (1990), a doctoral candidate in veterinary medicine, was the first to win with a platform, "Motivating Youth to Excellence," which was mainly about role-modeling. She was also the third black winner—one of six women of color competing that year. (Remarkably little was made of the fact that her runner-up was Korean American Virginia Cha, a Princeton grad and Fulbright scholar who was the first Asian American to place so high.) Turner was predictably asked about her race, to which she responded, "I'm Debbye Turner. I'm from Arkansas. I attended school in Missouri. I'm a born-again Christian. That's who I am. Being black is not my identity." She claimed only journalists were concerned with her race; her fans didn't care. But she did tell children she met "not [to] be limited by being black or being female or being from the South or any other limiting minority status that someone could attach to me."

In his 1990 essay "Life With Daughters: Watching the Miss America Pageant," Gerald Early noted that his young black daughters watched the pageant every year because "it's funny" and because "they cannot understand . . . why the women are trying so hard to please, to be pleasing"—exactly what Gracen worked so hard to unlearn. The girls were indifferent to the fact that Turner was black; one had predicted her win because she was simply "the best."

But Early and his wife, seeing it with the hindsight of history, considered her win important. "We laughed during the contest, but we did not laugh when she was chosen. We wanted her to win very much." Even though he thought Turner was "intended to be the supersession of Vanessa Williams—a religious vet student whose ambitions are properly, well, postmodernist Victorianism," and even if the pageant was "a reaffirmation of bourgeois cultural conditioning," it mattered. "It is impossible for blacks not to want to see their black daughters elevated to the platforms where the white women are," he wrote.

But his daughters had very different assumptions about race and, significantly, about beauty. Early wrote about comforting one of them after a bad day at school by telling her, in what he called "a father's patronizing way," that she was the most beautiful girl in the world. It was a gift she didn't need or value. She looked at him "strangely" and replied, "I don't think I'm beautiful at all. I think I'm just ordinary. There is nothing wrong with that, is there, Daddy?"

EIGHT

Believers

THE PLATFORM. IT SOUNDED GOOD: political, substantial, uplifting, forward-thinking. It put wind in Miss America's sails by recasting the pageant as more than a talent show, but also compounded a problem that had dogged it for so long: How did beauty relate to achievement—first scholarships, now public service? And though platforms modernized the focus, they also turned back the clock to a time, a century earlier, when women were the nation's moral guardians, advocating (on the sidelines of public policymaking) for family, health, and children.

Yet not all the platforms were the kind of safe, First Lady–like charitable causes people might have expected. Marjorie Vincent (1991) chose domestic violence. "When I was competing," she told me, "the only time the media really covered this issue was to report a tragedy which resulted from family violence. During my year, I had countless numbers of people thank me for shedding light on the issue and its magnitude in this country. And I vividly recall speaking with one man after a speaking engagement who thanked me for mentioning that men also are victims of domestic violence."

Kate Shindle (1998) advocated for HIV/AIDS prevention and education after taking a sociology class at Northwestern University called "Rhetoric of Social Movements." She endorsed condoms in schools and needle exchanges for addicts and was invited to address the 1998 International AIDS Conference. Shindle told a reporter that Miss America's squeaky-clean image opened doors "to places where AIDS activists had been trying to get in for years, and nobody would let them ... even in some of the conservative, rural or suburban areas." (It helped that she was a pro-life Republican—*and* a virgin.)

But the literal crown had functioned differently for Leanza Cornett (1993), the first to choose HIV/AIDS education as her cause. At public events, she held it instead of wearing it because she felt it undermined her credibility ("How do you talk about practicing safe sex when you've got this thing on top of your head?"). Heather Whitestone (1995), who made history as the first Miss America with a disability (she was deaf), did the same when she visited schools to address deaf children. "I'd learned that carrying instead of wearing it made a better impression."

Some of the new socially conscious winners adopted platforms rooted in their own or their relatives' lives: sexual abuse, homelessness, depression, diabetes. Others went through a virtual speed-shopping exercise in picking a random cause. One winner, Erika Harold (2003), did a bait and switch. She won on a platform called "Preventing Youth Violence and Bullying," but once in office she also promoted sexual abstinence, which had been her state cause until she was advised to choose something less partisan in pursuit of Miss America. Harold, a religious conservative who went to Harvard Law School, had lost a state pageant after (reportedly) saying a foster child would be better placed in a home with abusive straight parents than with a gay couple. She muzzled her homophobia in Atlantic City, but the comment came back to bite her in her losing run for Illinois Attorney General in 2018.

At its best, the platform hearkened back to Myerson's "You Can't Be Beautiful and Hate" campaign in the 1940s and Laurel Lea Schaefer's work with families of veterans in the 1970s. (Some of the older Miss Americas I interviewed said they wished the platform had been in place when they won.) It betokened the new millennium, when a number of winners would run for office in their states, including one, Heather French Henry (2000), who won the 2019 Democratic nomination for secretary of state in Kentucky. With the addition of the platform, Miss America became a philanthropic crusader. Still, 30 percent of her score, between the swimsuit and evening gown, hinged on her appearance. And whether she wanted to be a nurse, an activist, or a businesswoman, she still had to perform a talent. Skills that couldn't be demonstrated dramatically, like writing or drawing—or *thinking*—didn't rate.

The platform was just one in a suite of modifications Horn oversaw during his time as CEO from 1987 to 1998. There was the pageant's rebranding as a "scholarship program," the change from "reign" to "year of service," the renaming of "evening gown" as "evening wear," a push toward more natural hair and makeup, and the trimming of the talent section, whose quality had decreased, according to Shindle, because "more women were choosing to go to college to pursue non-artistic careers and just had fewer hours to practice the piano."

Horn also brought in, after thirty-one years, a new TV producer, Jeff Margolis, who'd overseen the Academy Awards. Margolis, who vowed to update the live show, didn't want "45-year-old

Stepford Wives marching like robots across the stage," he said. "Women of the '90s have a much more natural, realistic look." But though Kimberly Aiken (1994) won with an understated style well suited to her stop-in-your-tracks beauty, many still clung to the lacquered look of the 1980s.

Dated fashion wasn't all that kept the pageant out of step with the sensibility of the decade. Body modification, sex-positive feminism, and growing recognition of multiculturalism were trampling the chaste, vanilla womanhood of pageant culture. In 1992, grunge landed on the covers of most major fashion magazines but never mussed Miss America's tresses. Riot Grrls—a Gen-X subculture of feminists who wore baby doll dresses and combat boots—emerged from the punk music scene of the early 1990s to claim "girl power." The grunge breakout band Hole posed a mock beauty queen on the cover of its 1994 album *Live Through This*, hugging her bouquet and crying rivulets of mascara. Singer Courtney Love said the image captured "the look on a woman's face as she's being crowned . . . 'I won! I have hemorrhoid cream under my eyes and adhesive tape on my butt, and I had to scratch and claw and fuck my way up, but I won Miss Congeniality!' That's the essence of the sickness in this culture that I'd like to capture."

Likewise, the Grammy-winning video for TLC's 1999 chart-topping hit "Unpretty" showed women paging through women's magazines, stuffing their bras, stress-eating, contemplating breast implants, and feeling "unpretty." The song, a critique of the crushing pressure on women to look conventionally attractive, was timely. That year cosmetic surgery procedures leapt 66 percent, and women were getting 89 percent of them.

Horn publicly called the swimsuit "our Achilles heel," but couldn't do much about it—for many fans, it *was* the pageant. At a July 1995 press conference at the Plaza Hotel, he announced a call-in vote during the broadcast to determine whether it should stay. "[W]e hope to engage the American people, including many ardent supporters and feminist opponents, in a national debate on this topic." There was neither debate nor surprise: the swimsuit stayed. (Seventy-nine percent of voters wanted it, as did forty-one of the contestants.)

That year, forty-one ex-Miss Americas turned out for the seventy-fifth anniversary—a testament to the formers' fealty. Even swimsuit apostate Yolande Betbeze Fox had started returning in 1985, blinged out with diamonds, mobbed by grabby fans, and trailed by undercover cops. She was forgiving now, in light of the pageant's greater inclusiveness (though unwilling to submit to the annual autograph signing). "I was embarrassed for so many years about it because people didn't take me seriously," she said. "But now it's all changed and come around. And I'm here. And I'm rather proud to have been Miss America, all things considered." (Williams ignored the invite, and Bess Myerson, asked if she would go, snorted, "Are you kidding? It's totally irrelevant.")

Lenora Slaughter, then eighty-four and living in Arizona, was too frail to attend. After Betbeze Fox sent her flowers, she wrote back:

What a happy surprise . . . They arrived as I was feeling very lonely, for my thoughts were far away—remembering my years in Atlantic City and knowing many of my Miss Americas were there. I was invited, but of course I could not accept for the old crippled body could not make the trip . . . I was so thrilled to know you were there and you looked beautiful as I would expect you to. I'll always love you in a special way for I was so proud of my Miss Americas that year and our friendship continued long after. Thank you honey for the flowers, the remembering, and your friendship.

Slaughter told Betbeze Fox the pageant had grown "beyond my wildest dreams." But as she was fading with age, so was her creation. Unlike golden age Miss Americas, the winners who set their sights on entertainment careers in the late 1980s and '90s failed to become big names, something underscored when Vanessa Williams outshone and outranked her successors by singing the national anthem at the 1996 Super Bowl.

A steady march of pageant spoofs didn't help its image, from the irritatingly chipper, culturally illiterate Corky Sherwood, a former Miss America, on *Murphy Brown*, to a 1992 episode of *The Simpsons* ("Lisa the Beauty Queen"), in which Lisa enters a beauty contest and strips, recalling Mary Ann Mobley, to the 1999 teen pageant mockumentary *Drop Dead Gorgeous*, written by a former Junior Miss, Lona Williams. With a star-studded cast (including Kirsten Dunst, Ellen Barkin, Allison Janney, Kirstie Alley, and a then unknown Amy Adams), *Drop Dead Gorgeous* features preposterous patriotic themes (Barbie as Lady Liberty) and ludicrous talent (one hopeful dances with a life-sized Christ puppet nailed to a cross). The film toggles between absurdist hilarity and moments of transcendently bad taste that helped make it a box-office flop. But it found a passionate cult following by sending up pageantry's absurdist clichés, prompting Hulu to rerelease it in 2019.

Meanwhile, the Miss America pageant's ratings were tanking. In 1996, NBC dropped the broadcast; ABC picked it up (only to drop it in 2004). Part of the decline, to be fair, was a matter of changing media. The explosion of cable TV diced viewer demographics into smaller and smaller shares, as did the arrival of the internet, a mounting distraction from network TV, where pretty ladies in any state of dress or undress were available at the click of a mouse, which punctured the thrill of the annual swimsuit reveal.

While pageant devotees grew older and fewer, a younger demographic watched on the lookout for butt-glue mishaps, comical cry-faces, or campy talent, which reached a jaw-dropping apotheosis in 1995 when Miss Colorado (platform: disability awareness) sang "Can You Feel the Love Tonight?" to a puppet in a wheelchair. Though the new social advocacy winners worked tirelessly during their terms, this kind of kitsch lingered in memory once they dropped out of sight the day after the broadcast.

Just when Miss America was losing its hold on the American imagination, Philip Roth enshrined it as a Nixon-era relic of national identity. His 1997 novel *American Pastoral*, about a rural New Jersey couple whose daughter becomes a radical terrorist in the late 1960s, features the only substantial literary depiction of a Miss America contestant, Dawn Levov (the girl's mother). She's convincing for good reason: Roth used Betbeze Fox as the primary source for his character, a 1949 hopeful. The two spent an afternoon talking in his apartment, where, said Roth, "she just opened up whole ideas for me that I couldn't have had on my own." (He also made a pass at her, according to Dolly Fox.)

A former Miss New Jersey, Dawn had lost in Atlantic City, then married Seymour Levov, a ruggedly handsome former high school athlete and hometown hero who, despite being Jewish, looked so convincingly Nordic that he'd been nicknamed "the Swede." Dawn is the Swede's prize, a Venus to match "the household Apollo of the Weequahic [New Jersey] Jews," and a "shiksa" to complete his assimilationist American dream. They settle among WASPs in rural New Jersey. But their dream explodes in 1968 when their sixteen-year-old daughter Merry—Dawn's diabolical inverse—joins the anti-war movement, blows up the local general store, and goes underground, severing ties with her parents.

With the fabric of her life shredded, Dawn exposes the truth about Miss America's empty promise. Hospitalized and sedated after a breakdown, she rages, "Do you know what Miss New Jersey did for my life? It ruined it!" She'd wanted to be a music teacher, but people pushed her to compete in the local pageant, so she did and kept winning, even though she hated it—hated being told how to glide when she walked, hated learning "tricks of the trade" that made her paralyzingly self-conscious, hated her rivals. Here her words come straight from a 1960 *Cosmopolitan* interview with Betbeze Fox: "I hated them and they hated me."

Above all, Dawn resents the Swede for worshipping her as a beauty queen. "You had to make me into a *princess*," she vents. "Well, look where I ended up! In a madhouse!"

She speaks for many contestants, including, of course, Betbeze Fox, though disappointingly, Dawn displays none of her spring-loaded wit. Both competed to advance their music careers and bristled at being dismissed as mere beauty queens. She also channels Jacque Mercer, who told Frank Deford that women always thought she wanted to steal their husbands (Dawn stopped going to her beach club for this reason); AWOL winner Bette Cooper ("How can I back out of this?" Dawn says as she advances unexpectedly toward Miss America); and Vanessa Williams ("Why is it that if a girl takes her clothes off in Atlantic City it's for a scholarship and makes her an American goddess," a dinner guest asks Dawn, "but if she takes her clothes off in a sex flick it's for filthy money and makes her a whore?").

Paradoxically, the most humiliating piece of the pageant—the swimsuit competition—also strengthens Dawn. Before she meets the Swede's brash, disapproving father, she says she's not afraid:

I walked out on that runway in a bathing suit, didn't I? It wasn't easy, in case you didn't know. Twenty-five thousand people. It's not a very dignified feeling, in a bright white bathing suit and bright white heels, being looked at by twenty-five thousand people. I appeared in a *parade* in a bathing suit. In Camden. Fourth of July. I had to. I hated that day. My father almost died. But I did it. I taped the back of that damn bathing suit to my skin, Seymour, so it wouldn't ride up on me—masking tape on my own behind. I felt like a *freak*.

If she could overcome *that* fear, her logic goes, she can do anything. The very year *American Pastoral* was published, Kate Shindle said as much. "I worked so hard to be ready to compete in swimsuit that I didn't dread it. You know, I actually found it kind of empowering because I figured that once I could get over enough issues to walk around on the stage in a bathing suit in front of twenty million people, I could pretty much do anything I wanted to."

Though he would have cringed at the comparison, Roth's poisoned pastoral echoes Don McLean's 1971 "American Pie" as a requiem for the Eisenhower-era American dream. But instead of mourning Miss America's passing, he deploys Dawn to refute its very premise. Miss America had appeared in pop songs throughout the twentieth century, starting with the Beach Boys' starry-eyed "Little Girl (You're My Miss America)" in 1962. But by the end of the century, her symbolism was collapsing. David Byrne used her as an inverted Lady Liberty figure in his 1997 "Miss America," a song about immigration in which a beauty queen represents the false promise of the American dream, as did rapper Hasan Salaam's 2011 "Miss America": "Her ethics are deceptive, silicone synthetic." And McLean's own "American Pie" was subverted in Flatbush Zombies'

"Amerikkkan Pie" (2013), a screed about deep-seated American racism, citing the whiteness of the pageant as just one example.

If pop music was any measure, Miss America's mythos lived exclusively in the eyes—and minds—of men for over half a century. When women finally addressed it, they renounced it, defiantly, in the first person. Singer Leikeli47's 2012 "Miss America" affirms her right to "dress like a boy and talk like a girl." Ingrid Michaelson's 2016 song of the same name claims she needs no crown to be a queen, and quotes her mother telling her there are many ways to be beautiful. Kacey Musgraves's "Pageant Material" (announcing that she isn't it) takes a swipe at Miss America by saying she could never be Miss Congeniality and claiming she'd rather lose for what she is than win "for what I ain't." These women share Dawn Levov's desire to be more than pageant pretty, but unlike Dawn, who caves and gets a face-lift, putting on "a new crown" in order to remarry and start a new life, they reject the beauty myth outright.

———

IN THE EARLY 2000S, FOR the first time, women outnumbered men as college graduates, which meant the pageant's scholarships were more important than ever. More degrees conferred meant more women carrying loans after college, which meant more need for assistance. Their debt load mushroomed steadily until the American Association of University Women called it a crisis in 2019, with women carrying almost two-thirds of the national burden, and the gender pay gap making it more difficult for them to pay off loans than men. It was a whole new marketing opportunity, and a missed one for Miss America.

Despite Horn's adjustments of the 1990s, the pageant—er,

scholarship program—couldn't get its message on point, its finances in order, or its leadership in line. Thus began a parade of changing CEOs, networks, and emcees. (One CEO was fired after proposing, for fear of discrimination lawsuits, to relax the rule against contestants who'd been divorced or pregnant, which had prompted an uprising by tradition-bound state pageant directors.) The year 2000 marked a new ratings low—8.8 million viewers, down from 22 million in 1970.

This was a time when Miss America couldn't afford to slip. Reality TV, a newly minted American obsession, was set to beat it at its own game. When *American Idol* premiered in 2002, it offered weekly what the pageant delivered annually: the chance to see people picked off in an elimination talent competition—but also the opportunity to watch winners become international stars afterward. Elimination shows like *America's Top Model*, dating competitions like *The Bachelor*, and makeover shows like *The Swan* and *Extreme Makeover* tapped interest in women's aspirational beauty and cashed in on the Cinderella fantasy that had carried the pageant through the twentieth century. But when the Miss America Organization tried to ride the trend with a reality show format on the Learning Channel, the hopefuls were force-marched through fashion critiques and pressed to engage in catfights until they rebelled and refused.

The crowning of the first Asian American winner, Filipina American Angela Perez Baraquio (2001), was a milestone, if a belated one. Miss USA had crowned its first Asian American nearly forty years earlier. But the pageant's racial advances clearly still mattered to fans; on Baraquio's first media tour, people yelled, "We're so proud of you!" "I'm Thai!" "I'm Korean!" "We're Vietnamese!"

Still, the pageant's take on inclusion was weirdly constricted, with no regard for diversity in hair (notably braids, twists, and locs), fashion, talent, body shape, or religion. Christian winners dominated the aughts. Muslims and Jews, Hindus and Buddhists, atheists and agnostics, by the looks of it, didn't represent America.

In 2001, when the swimsuit competition was renamed "Lifestyle and Fitness," everyone knew "fitness" meant rail-thin bodies with rock-hard abs. The latter had become a centerpiece of the ritual since bikinis were first permitted in 1997. (As a crowning humiliation, the non-finalists repaired to the "Losers' Lounge" to be offered—no joke—donuts on a silver platter.) The American Medical Association published a study showing that the winners' body mass index had decreased by 12 percent from 1922 to 1999 and concluded that since 1980, Miss America had been clinically undernourished.

In *Miss Congeniality*, a Miss America spoof about a frumpy career-minded FBI agent (Sandra Bullock) who goes undercover as a beauty queen to avert a bomb threat at a pageant, scholarships are a punchline. "It is *not* a beauty pageant, it is a scholarship program!" Bullock snaps, as does the villainous pageant director (Candice Bergen), a former queen, who fights "the feminists, the intellectuals, and the ugly women" who oppose her pageant. (Still, the film ends with a reactionary message: Bullock's makeover attracts men and earns her a happy ending—i.e., a marriage proposal.)

Baraquio, who is five feet four, competed in pageants for six years before entering Miss America, losing thirty pounds in the year between her Miss Hawaii and Miss America runs. In her memoir, *Amazing Win, Amazing Loss: Miss America Living Happily, EVEN After*, she calls her story "a tale of American girlhood, of dieting and mirror gazing, of false eyelashes, high heels, and inside-out beauty," as well as one of race, faith, and ambition. (The loss in the title refers to a death in her family, but carries a telling subtext.) As a grade-school teacher and a strict Catholic, she fretted about appearing in public in a swimsuit. When her mother objected, she went to her priest, who assured her it posed no moral obstacle—but even if it did, he said, "Don't worry—I'll get your back. I've got an in with the guy upstairs." Like Cheryl Prewitt before her, Baraquio used the language of religion to justify what her church explicitly opposed. "I love a well-sculpted body because it's God's artwork," she writes, "and being at my physical peak, I felt I showcased it in a pure way." That is, in a high-cut canary-yellow bikini and heels.

The pageant retailed Miss America's body offstage as well. Though the MAO once forbade hopefuls from even entering a casino, it now not only booked them into free rooms in casino hotels, but also approved, in 2002, a Miss America slot machine at Harrah's. A lucky coin drop lined up parts of Miss America's perfect figure and delivered an orgasmic dividend—up to $650—as Bert Parks crooned "There She Is" and rolled over in his grave. A number of formers objected, including Jean Bartel, mindful of the scholarship legacy she and Slaughter had established, as did 2002 Miss America Katie Harman, who was dismissed out of hand by CEO Robert Renneisen, a former casino executive. "By the time it comes out she won't be Miss America anymore and her vote won't count anyway," he said.

The board struggled to reconcile its decisions with a network of thousands of national grassroots organizers who could—and did—rise up as one when they wanted to. When state pageant directors challenged Renneisen's leadership, he called it "the rebellion of the beauty queens" and said the MAO was staffed "by people who are predominantly volunteers, many of whom are deeply passionate about the pageant, and some of whom, frankly, have no other life than this." No CEO had ever been so brazenly contemptuous of the pageant community.

Harman, one of the most beleaguered modern Miss Americas (crowned days after the 9/11 terrorist attacks and protested as a commencement speaker at her college in 2002), complained publicly not only that she was under-scheduled, but that she'd received a bill for her crowning night party. (When he retired in 1998, Horn had left the pageant a $10 million "reserve." In 2002, it was operating $1 million in the red.)

While Miss America lurched around in the broadcast boondocks, Miss USA, which Donald Trump had bought in 1996 as part of the Miss Universe franchise, was airing first on CBS, then on NBC, which outbid other networks for the rights. Though Trump had been a Miss America judge in 1990 and had made news by attending the 1991 pageant and boorishly demanding to see "the bodies that won the swimsuit contest," it was the greater visibility of Miss USA that sowed confusion between the two pageants and forever linked him, incorrectly, to Miss America. Miss USA's scandals, including reports of Trump harassing contestants and fat-shaming a former Miss Universe, often redounded, mistakenly, to Miss America, which was generally free of any such vulgarity— until its own epic scandal broke in 2017.

As the winners hustled for money by upping their sponsorship appearances at the cost of their platform work, the pageant began to look a bit like it had in the era before Rafko revolutionized it. But here's the thing about Miss America: just when it seems to have capsized under mismanagement or drifted off into obscurity, somebody interesting wins. As the first winner to become a doctor, Deidre Downs (2005) fulfilled Slaughter's long-ago dream. The doe-eyed daughter of a single mom, Downs worked through college and competed for five years in Alabama before her crowning there, earning, with her Miss America winnings, close to $110,000—not what queens took home in the late twentieth century, but enough to help a medical student graduate debt-free. A self-described "left-to-center feminist" and progressive Baptist (her church welcomes members of any gender identity), she went on to become an obstetrician-gynecologist.

Downs wore her dark-brown shoulder-length hair natural during the finals, and reacted to her win with none of the usual jumping, crying, squatting, or mouth-covering; she merely smiled with joy, hugged her runner-up, then bent over to be crowned, saying, "Thank you." She'd been accepted to medical school and was a Rhodes scholar finalist but had deferred to compete in Miss America. Her platform was pediatric cancer research, so she appeared at children's hospitals and medical nonprofits along with doing 4-H Club dates and other civic events.

Unlike some of her predecessors, who charged they were manipulated by the MAO, Downs felt supported. Even in 2018, when she married a woman and became the first lesbian former, she said the pageant community embraced her, though there was reportedly some tut-tutting behind the scenes. And not everyone warmed to a lesbian queen. Chatting with a garrulous elderly pageant fan in line at an autograph signing at the 2018 competition, I referenced Downs's marriage, which stopped her cold for a few uncomprehending beats. "I didn't know they . . . *did* that," she finally said.

"I was terrified, frankly, of the publicity," Downs (now Downs Gunn) told me, "because I live in a conservative state and I did not know how it would be received. And [I] actually tried to just get married and not have [the media] find out about it." But a week before the wedding, word got out, and "people responded in such a positive way." Her sexual orientation wasn't an issue during the pageant, because, like Trelynda Kerr in 1983, "I didn't even realize I was gay." The first openly gay contestant, Miss Missouri Erin O'Flaherty, competed in 2017 and was rightly celebrated as a pathbreaker, but like so many of Miss America's advances, it raised the question: *Now?* When Ellen DeGeneres had been out for two decades? Six years after Lady Gaga's historic LGBT Pride anthem "Born This Way" worked its way into the hearts of little monsters around the globe? Was the pageant so timid that it took the 2015 legalization of same-sex marriage for a lesbian to claim a state title?

Unlike the Miss Americas who went into broadcast news without experience and faced skepticism or hostility at work, Downs Gunn had solid training after medical school. But she still worried that she would be "treated differently on rounds when I went to each little subspecialty," she says, "because a lot of people have pretty negative perceptions about the pageant, and who you're going to be." She feared her colleagues would assume she was a diva, which she wasn't and which they didn't.

Nina Davuluri (2014) also competed to win money for medical school, but her crowning as the first Indian American Miss America was so extraordinary—such a lightning rod for unfiltered, culturally illiterate American bigotry—that it set her on an entirely different course, one that made her anti-bullying platform, "Celebrating Diversity Through Cultural Competency," supremely relevant. Davuluri was judged for what she wasn't: a Muslim Arab. Born in Syracuse, New York, and raised in Oklahoma and Michigan, she's the daughter of Hindu Indian immigrants. But her brown skin told a different story to equal opportunity racists who called her a foreigner and a terrorist and dubbed her "Miss 7-11" and "Miss Al Qaeda." A meme circulated claiming that Miss Kansas Theresa Vail, who made the top ten that year, should have won because she was blonde, tattooed (another first), loved hunting, and was in the

National Guard. Fox News's Todd Starnes complained, "The liberal Miss America judges won't say this—but Miss Kansas lost because she actually represented American values."

Women of color had for years been excluded as exemplars of "real" American beauty. Now Davuluri's very citizenship was challenged—just like the brown-skinned president then in office, just like singer Marc Anthony, who'd been attacked for singing the national anthem days after 9/11 at a major league baseball game. Davuluri told *The Times of India* she grew up "feeling like I could never be in this role because I didn't look like the 'stereotypical' Miss America." But she hoped her win would affect "a new demographic of young women that is representative of America today" and show them they didn't have to fit a stereotype.

One of my Lehman College students, Asha Jagmohan, was one such young woman. Her Bronx family was excited about Davuluri's win even though they didn't generally watch pageants. Davuluri's treatment was so ugly that Asha didn't want to tell her younger cousins about it. In the end, she says of the crowning, "We couldn't see it as a win because society didn't see it as a win. It hurts to see that some people are seen as less American than others."

Writing in *The Nation*, Samhita Mukhopadhyay, now executive editor of *Teen Vogue*, didn't consider Davuluri's crowning to be such a breakthrough. "As tempting as it might be," she wrote, "to suggest that Davuluri's win signifies progress for South Asians in America is to defend the Miss America pageant itself. And there isn't really much about Miss America that could be considered progress for anyone ... Miss America's role in the public imagination has always been the product of objectification."

Davuluri didn't go to medical school after her win (she said her parents had pressured her); she decided instead to get a master's degree in business administration. But she didn't do that either.

She became a motivational speaker, then hosted a reality show for South Asian American women that trained them for international pageantry, confirming Mukhopadhyay's skepticism about her symbolism. Like Miss America, her show *Made in America* wasn't called a beauty pageant, but it sure looked like one. Each episode opened with women (referred to as "young girls" in the trailer) getting made up, learning to walk, and discussing workouts, swimsuits, and rivalries. The winner was promised an acting course and a modeling contract. When the show ended in 2018, Davuluri shifted her energies to her skin-care line for South Asian women, Aavrani.

One of the chronic pitfalls of the pageant formula is that winners who excel in non-entertainment professions (like Downs, or Kimberly Aiken Cockerham, now a health care executive, or Marjorie Vincent Tripp, an assistant attorney general in Florida) melt away from public view after their scholarships set them on their career paths. And though Shindle launched a successful acting career and is now president of the Actors Equity Association, none of the performing winners who've followed her have enjoyed celebrity, despite all the singing and dancing the pageant rewards. By the time Davuluri won, the days of queens who became household names were long gone, making scholarships the key attraction for hopefuls.

But even academic achievement wasn't vaunted the way it had once been. The winner profiles on the 2014 pageant site didn't even say where most went to college or what they'd studied, and the "Become a Contestant" page beckoned to low-achievers with this quote from 1987 queen Kellye Cash: "I did lots of things. I was a pianist, but not quite good enough to get a music scholarship; an athlete, but I didn't play a varsity sport; smart, but not smart enough to get an academic scholarship. So competing in the Miss America program was an opportunity to get a scholarship for school."

The next year, in the Parade of States, college affiliations were replaced with silly state-themed introductions (New Hampshire: "from the state that brings you Velcro") and, in one case, a malodorous pun by Miss Wisconsin: "Representing the Dairy State—come smell our dairy air." (Any true fan of "women's empowerment" might have preferred hearing that Wisconsin was the first state to pass an equal rights bill.)

And many queens made news for the wrong reasons. One of Davuluri's rivals claimed she'd caught her on tape calling her predecessor "fat as fuck." Kira Kazantsev (2015) triumphed after getting booted from her college sorority for hazing. Miss Puerto Rico (2015) was suspended for making an anti-Muslim comment.

On the upside, winners were becoming more honest about their challenges, dispelling the illusion of Miss America's perfection. Kirsten Haglund (2008) revealed she'd been anorexic; Davuluri said she'd struggled with bulimia. After a year of relentless touring and vicious internet jibes—a liability for social media era winners—Teresa Scanlan (2011) was pushed to the brink of suicide, then faced disapproval on her return to her conservative Christian college, all of which she addressed publicly. In her 2019 memoir *Miss Unlikely: From Farm Girl to Miss America*, Betty (née Cantrell) Maxwell (2016) reports getting cyberbullied about her appearance during her year, especially when she cut her hair short (something she had to get MAO approval to do). "The pressure of having to wake up every morning and look the part of Miss America, whose image is one of beauty and perfection, was more pressure than I can describe," she writes.

Being Miss America no longer seemed like the cakewalk it had been for the golden age winners. For the queens of the 1920s, the win itself was overwhelming—Gorman burst into tears when crowds swarmed her on her return home post-pageant in 1921, and Malcomson's mother took her to rest in the Poconos after her 1924 victory. (Her daughter had not actually had a nervous breakdown, she said, but "was tired of mind and body from the excitement and turmoil of the pageant, and of the thousands of curious eyes that have searched her person from head to foot ever since she won the title of Miss America.")

The title was now promoted as a "job," but it offered no job security afterward and little preparation for the post-tour letdown, which could be shattering. Whitestone, whose 1995 reign was especially difficult because she was deaf, wrote, "There were times when I wept and begged God to take my life away." On her return to Hawaii after her year, Baraquio saw that her friends and family "wanted me to be the same local girl I was before I left, but I was no longer that girl. I was different in so many ways I didn't even know how to deal with the loss of who I once was to the people I cared so deeply about." She found herself staring at the pool outside her ninth-floor condo in Honolulu, hearing a voice in her head say, "Just do it. Jump and see what happens."

In her 2014 memoir-cum-exposé, *Being Miss America: Behind the Rhinestone Curtain*, Shindle diagnosed the ailing pageant she still loved. She described the eating disorder her training produced, calling herself a hypocrite for insisting that "Miss America was all about the big picture while privately striving for an impossible aesthetic." She detailed the MAO's financial and administrative woes, with executive salaries disproportionate to pageant revenue, and exposed the semantic sleight of hand that extracted money from contestants without technically requiring an entrance fee as Miss USA did. Starting in 2007, after the MAO partnered with the Children's Miracle Network Hospitals, a nonprofit supporting children's hospitals and research, contestants were required to "raise" money to compete. Shindle calls it "pay to play" and feels that "balancing the books on the backs of kids with terminal illnesses [is] not only ethically reprehensible, it's borderline fraudulent."

"Raising money," in pageant parlance, means soliciting donations from friends, family, or businesses. As of 2019, that meant raising $100 to compete at the local level, $250 at the state level, and $1,000 at Miss America itself. Greg Petroff, a lawyer for the Miss America Foundation, the pageant's scholarship arm (and chair of its board of trustees), says that 40 percent of that money goes to Children's Miracle Network Hospitals. Once the remaining 60 percent is dispersed to scholarships at all levels, he confirms, contestants themselves have funded 85 percent of Miss America's scholarships, totaling, in 2019, $1.3–$1.4 million. It looks a lot like a lottery.

Though he declined to comment directly on Miss America, Mark Kantrowitz, a nationally recognized expert on college financial aid, told me he considers any scholarship that requires an application fee "problematic," especially ones where the major source of funds comes from applicants themselves, as opposed to third parties.

The rest of the funding is secured through "in-kind" tuition waivers. For years, the pageant claimed it granted $45 million to winners at all levels. That number backfired in 2014, when a John Oliver "How Is This Still a Thing?" segment debunked it. The MAO got this number by multiplying every in-kind scholarship available to winners by the number of contestants each year. The amount could only be feasible were each contestant to accept multiple awards and attend multiple colleges simultaneously. The money actually given, Oliver estimated, was less than $4 million. Petroff put it at $3 million in 2019, saying they believe it's still the biggest, by comparison to other nonprofits offering scholarships.

Oliver's fifteen-minute report criticized not just the scholarship claim but also the ritual itself. "[T]hrough it all, the swimsuits, the dance numbers, the inexplicable ventriloquism . . . it was very difficult not to think 'How the fuck is this still happening?'" The problem, he said, wasn't that contestants could be vapid—it was that they were forced into swimsuits *and* talent acts *and* expected to answer insanely difficult questions in twenty seconds while standing in evening gowns. It was that it required them to be, as he put it, "unmarried with a mint condition uterus." And it was the implicit bias of limiting a scholarship to beauty queens. (If granting scholarships with a built-in age and appearance bias seems discriminatory, it's not—legally anyway, thanks to a beauty pageant exemption added to the Higher Education Act in 1976.)

The segment went viral, sparking discussion and making it a thing to ask why Miss America was still a thing. But Oliver didn't fully unpack the pageant's discrimination against mothers. Because more young mothers, statistically, come from lower-income backgrounds, they need scholarships far more than women who postpone childbearing, who tend to be more privileged, thus better able to pay for college before having children. Barring pageant-age mothers from competing denies help to the very women who need it most. Oliver also failed to mention that Miss America's scholarship award had been stalled at $50,000 for nearly two decades—and it still is.

As the conceptual chasm between the scholarships and the swimsuits widened, the bikinis shrank. The very garment that had freed active women from bulky beachwear a century earlier didn't look so liberatory now, worn with mile-high Lucite heels. Betbeze Fox, then in her eighties, felt the pageant had taken it too far. "She was horrified that the women were in bikinis and hooker pumps," says Dolly Fox. "She said, you might as well be Miss USA."

Furthermore, the bodies wearing the swimsuits didn't reflect evolving visions of American women. In 2016, after doing the kind of soul-searching Miss America should have undertaken, Mattel released new "curvy," "tall," and "petite" Barbies to model a broader cross-section of the populace for girls. *Sports Illustrated* put its first plus-sized model, Ashley Graham, on its 2016 Swimsuit Issue cover. By contrast, the Victoria's Secret Fashion Show, unconcerned with any pretense of body inclusivity, carried on like Miss America, likewise shedding viewers as the spectacle of hungry bodies on parade lost its charm for a woke generation. The big difference, however, was that Miss America was selling itself as a college and career pipeline. Once the Harvey Weinstein accusations brought the #MeToo movement to a crescendo in 2017, asking women to show their swimsuit-ready physiques in a bid for a professional opportunity seemed positively benighted.

———

JOHN OLIVER HAD BEEN A thorn in its side, but the pageant would soon have a much, much bigger problem: its own CEO, Sam Haskell. The former worldwide head of television at the William Morris Agency, Haskell had married a onetime Miss Mississippi and judged Miss America twice in the 1980s, along with many state pageants. In 2005, after ABC dropped the broadcast, Phyllis George called to ask him to help secure a new deal and sit on the board. He served as it jumped to basic cable and back to network TV and moved from Atlantic City to Las Vegas and back. He oversaw the Children's Miracle Network partnership and the ill-fated reality show and in 2014 arranged for Dick Clark Productions to fund and produce the telecast. He extended a public apology to Vanessa Williams when she returned as a judge at the 2015 pageant.

Haskell was generally considered an effective, if over-reaching, leader; as board chair, he'd also taken on the role of CEO, unconcerned about the clear conflict in being a chair overseeing himself as a paid employee. "I was determined to take my responsibilities seriously and 'polish' what had become a very tarnished crown," he wrote in his 2009 memoir, *Promises I Made My Mother.*

Instead, he basically drop-kicked it, as a 2017 *Huffpost* exposé explained in toe-curling detail. The piece distilled three years of leaked emails in which Haskell and other key administrators fat-shamed, slut-shamed, and ridiculed former Miss Americas, in one case calling some "a pile of malcontents and has-beens who blame the program for not getting them where they think they can go," and adding, "80 percent of the winners do not have the class, smarts and model for success." He directed special venom at Kate Shindle because of her memoir, which criticized his management style and questioned his bloated paycheck when the MAO was in the red, and Gretchen Carlson, who wanted to modernize the pageant and refused to publicly denounce Shindle's book. The two had helped organize a group of formers who addressed the board about how to save the ailing contest.

When he received an internal email suggesting that instead of calling formers "forevers" in the telecast, they should be called "cunts," Haskell responded, "Perfect . . . bahahaha." He had also tried to persuade a pageant employee, Brent Adams, to date his daughter instead of 2013 Miss America Mallory Hagan, saying, "You don't need a piece of trash like Mallory. You need someone with class and money like my daughter."

The day after the *Huffpost* piece ran, forty-nine formers sent a letter calling for Haskell's resignation, and he stepped down. He deleted his Twitter and Instagram accounts and scrubbed Miss America from his LinkedIn profile. ("Trying to live a principled life can be difficult," he'd written with earnest prescience in his memoir.) Dick Clark Productions cut ties to Miss America. Novelist Jennifer Weiner, a self-described "highly conflicted" pageant fan, wrote in *The New York Times*, "I've been bracing myself, waiting for this particular high-heeled shoe to drop. It's not surprising that a contest with objectification baked into its DNA has spawned this kind of talk, and behavior, from the men in charge."

In 2018, a new, mostly female board was named, with Gretchen Carlson as the unpaid chair. With women at the helm and arguably the most famous former leading them in reclaiming the organization, it seemed like a new day for Miss America, though not everyone was convinced Carlson was the woman for the job. Journalist and *Jezebel* cofounder Anna Holmes found it difficult to see how Carlson could update an antiquated institution given the regressive culture of Fox News that she had sprung from. "[I]t's really hard for me to look at her as some sort of savior or women's rights advocate . . . after the years and years and years she spent spewing either falsehoods or hatred on one of the most destructive media companies that we've had in some time," she said on Slate's podcast *The Waves*.

Others, however, thought Carlson's conservative leanings (though she was a political independent) would provide balance in an overhaul that required radical changes. They felt her activist credentials could only empower the new pageant, which was re-branded Miss America 2.0. And the changes were indeed radical. In June, her board did the unthinkable: they scrapped the swimsuit. "We will no longer judge our candidates on their outward physical appearance," Carlson told *Good Morning America*. "We've heard from a lot of young women who say, 'We'd love to be a part of your program, but we don't want to be out there in high heels and a swimsuit' . . . So guess what? You don't have to do that anymore." She hoped the change would attract contestants of "all shapes and sizes." The evening gown portion was also revamped to allow what-

ever women wanted to wear. Miss America had finally been un-
hitched from its bathing beauty beginnings.

Some found it revolutionary. Others found it ridiculous, like
Playboy's 2015 announcement that it would no longer publish photos of naked women. "Instead of trying to change its spots, Miss
America and other organizations like it . . . should die a proper
death like the dinosaurs they are," columnist Tricia Bishop wrote
in the *Baltimore Sun*.

Pageant fans were divided—some were happy to see it go,
while others were shocked to see tradition trashed. Holdouts
claimed the swimsuit was necessary to show physical fitness, but
why in the name of athleisurewear a bikini was necessary for that,
no one could say. The best I could get out of the fans, formers,
and contestants I asked was that it just wasn't the same. Since
the 1980s, the pageant had absorbed the language of feminism—
ambition, achievement, independence—while studiously avoiding
the F-word itself. Now, suddenly, former titleholders were writing editorials claiming women could be feminists and compete in
swimsuits. Some genuinely enjoyed getting their bodies ripped and
vogueing on TV, which they found "empowering." (Ericka Dun-
lap, Miss America 2004, dispensed with the scholarship program
lingo altogether and declared, "It's a beauty pageant . . . period.")

Mallory Hagan endorsed its removal in a *Vox* editorial explaining that in the six months of training leading to her win,
her self-image was bruised every time she was reminded that her
body wasn't good enough yet; she would rather have spent her energies on her platform, preventing child sexual abuse. Ultimately,
she said, none of this had anything to do with her duties as Miss
America anyway. Kirsten Haglund (2008) wrote a *Daily News* editorial saying the swimsuit portion not only promoted unhealthy
behaviors and objectified women, but also diminished Miss Amer-

ica's ability to be taken seriously as a public figure and alienated potential sponsors.

When a full-fledged civil war erupted weeks after Carlson's announcement, it wasn't just the bikini ban that caused it; it was Carlson herself. The new leadership was crumbling as quickly as it had taken shape. Two board members claimed they'd been forced to step down (Carlson said their contracts were temporary); two more, including Shindle, quit over what they called Carlson's lack of transparency and top-down leadership style. Twenty-two state pageant directors launched a petition calling for the board and the new CEO, Regina Hopper, to resign, drumming up 18,000 signatures within a week. Thirty former Miss Americas expressed their support for Carlson and Hopper. State directors threatened to keep their winners home. Marjorie Vincent Tripp, a Carlson ally appointed to head up the scholarships, quit without explanation.

And to complicate it all, that year's Miss America, Cara Mund, a Brown University graduate, claimed Carlson, the anti-harassment heroine, had bullied her. Mund aired her complaints in a five-page public letter, saying, "Our chair and CEO have systematically silenced me, reduced me, marginalized me, and essentially erased me in my role as Miss America in subtle and not-so-subtle ways on a daily basis." It was indeed odd that the titleholder herself had hardly been seen during this historic transition. She said she'd been told she was bad at using social media and that posts—with misspellings—were made in her name. She said Regina Hopper had told her what to wear. (Betty Maxwell's memoir confirms the latter two practices were standard before Carlson and Hopper came on the scene.) She said she'd been coached to say Carlson had started the #MeToo movement.

Mund, who mouthed the usual moldy maxims right after her win ("If you can dream it, you can become it," she said, forgetting all the Latinas who'd been dreaming it since 1937), now sang a different tune. The pageant had created the kind of winner it had historically stifled: one who broke ranks and publicly defied authority.

It looked like the historic 2018 pageant—renamed "competition," refreshed with "candidates" instead of contestants now vying for a "job" instead of a crown, and rebranded as Miss America 2.0—was either going to be a giant step forward or an absolute disaster. It turned out to be both.

NINE

Survivors

THE DAY BEFORE THE 2018 pageant finals, it was raining on Miss America's parade. The "Show Us Your Shoes" parade had evolved from a procession of giant state-themed floats rolling down the boardwalk in the 1920s, complemented by spiffy convertibles carrying the state queens after midcentury, to a footwear-focused affair in the 1970s after spectators in balconies above the boardwalk noticed bare feet or flats hidden beneath the women's dresses. They catcalled them, demanding to see their feet, sparking a tradition of decorated shoes and, in time, themed costumes. A raised foot also afforded a look at their legs—or more. Some who wore the shortest skirts in the 2018 parade hoisted their platform heels highest, offering a generous upskirt view. (By contrast, two women expressing state pride wore football uniforms and sneakers.) Cara Mund had been told to wear a gown—traditional for the incumbent—instead of the Wonder Woman costume she'd prepared for the parade, but she wore it anyway, outfitted with glittery boots, sword, shield, and pageant crown.

Seventy years after her crowning, BeBe Shopp led the formers, blowing kisses from atop a light blue vintage Oldsmobile, followed by Judi Ford, fifty years out, in a petal-pink Thunderbird. Others trailed in hand-pushed rolling chairs. There were marching bands, baton twirlers, cheerleaders, and a penny-farthing bicycle brigade. Despite the soggy weather, the mood was celebratory; the parka-clad crowd whooped and cheered from folding chairs on the sidelines. The parade looked like it had marched right back to the boardwalk of the early 1920s before governors and celebrity marshals turned out for it, when it was still just one carnivalesque component of the Fall Frolic. Later, at my hotel, I asked the desk clerk, an Atlantic City native, what locals think of the pageant these days. "We like the parade," he said. "It brings out the community."

Even when it wasn't raining, a cloud hovered over pageant week. At a weekday welcome ceremony, Carlson and Mund had addressed contestants, but not each other. Carlson then disappeared mole-like into a windowless administrative office in Boardwalk Hall (formerly Convention Hall), not to be seen until Sunday's crowning. She skipped both the parade and the formers' autograph signing. On Thursday, a right-wing pro-Trump street art group plastered posters of Carlson's face around the city. PRIVATE BULLY, PUBLIC LIAR, they charged, predicting NO SWIMSUITS NO RATINGS. (It made me wonder if the swimsuit factions were divided along political lines, since some of Carlson's critics charged she was grafting her #MeToo activism onto the competition, but the divisions were more complicated, turning on differing views of pageant tradition and leadership.) Ominously, dozens of state directors met in a hotel conference room before the parade to address the Gretchen problem and how to solve it, possibly through legal action.

Though the preliminary competitions went smoothly, people were nervous about Sunday's live broadcast. "It's a mess," Suzette Charles (1984) said of the week's drama, speaking to *The New York Times*. "It feels like every day, it's another thing." The emcees, *Dancing with the Stars* judge Carrie Ann Inaba and roving TV personality Ross Mathews, were announced at the last minute, just a day before contestants arrived for their pageant orientation. On the eve of the broadcast, hoping to fill the house, volunteers gave out tickets on the boardwalk with a flier that read, "All you need to do is get dressed up, really nice, and show up to Boardwalk Hall."

Sheets of rain whipped Atlantic City Sunday night as people poured into the auditorium in suits or gowns with perilous stilettos, but when the lights went down, more than half the seats were empty. A preshow comedian warming up the crowd mentioned the missing swimsuit and was loudly booed, including by a clutch of formers.

Then the cameras rolled and . . . Miss America glided seamlessly, even gloriously, into the modern era—or at least the twenty-first century. The show was practiced and professional, and the contestants looked like real women, not the synthetic creations of years past. Sporting jumpsuits or jeans with loosely styled hair, clustered in groups of five and six, they announced in unison that they were smart, confident, strong, talented, accomplished, principled. In the Parade of States, they wore cocktail dresses and state sashes bearing no "Miss"; many eliminated the "Miss" in their introductions as well ("I am Katie Bouchard, KENtuckeee!"). A women's studies major from the University of Michigan threw down the political gauntlet: "From the state with 84 percent of the U.S. fresh water but none for its residents to drink, I am Miss Michigan, Emily Sioma," she said, setting Twitter abuzz about her boldness.

The talent was the usual—ballet, opera, classical piano (Liszt appeared twice), and—not again!—ventriloquism, but a feel-good poem performed by Miss Colorado was so ingenuously offbeat that I found myself clapping enthusiastically until I sensed a deafening silence around me. Clearly, this was not the stuff of Miss America talent; in fact, it had evidently just scuttled Colorado's candidacy for this "job." When I later recalled that she was a Harvard graduate heading for a PhD in neuroscience, I wondered if a mini TED-style talk on her chosen field wouldn't have shown her skills to better effect, though that too would likely have tanked in this resolutely frothy scholarship competition. One hopeful was even asked in her interview how 2.0 contestants should perform "when historically only stage talents have excelled." She encouraged women to "think outside the box." Well, maybe another year.

A red-carpet section allowed the top ten finalists to model whatever formal wear they wanted (most opted for gowns) as they identified their platforms: campus sexual assault, environmental awareness ("Let's talk trash"), and food insecurity among them. Before runners-up were announced in the countdown to the crowning, Cara Mund materialized wearing a shimmering emerald green gown with a full skirt, smiling and waving over her prerecorded valediction, having been forbidden from speaking live. It was part old-school bromides ("How can I say farewell when I know this is just the beginning?"), part 2.0 power talk ("As soon as I walk off this stage tonight I'm going to law school and become the first female governor of North Dakota"). She got a standing ovation.

Miss America truly reflected American racial diversity that year. Of the five finalists, four were women of color, and the fourth runner-up, Gabriela Taveras, was Afro Latina. (Taveras, who came close to making history, later told me she hadn't known that a Latina of color had never won.) Her story is remarkable. The first black Miss Massachusetts (she is of Dominican, Haitian, and Chinese descent), she's the daughter of a single mom. When she was one year old, her father was incarcerated, then deported. She worked four jobs starting at age fifteen to raise money to pay for a private college-prep high school, where she was the only girl on the boys' wrestling team. She was sexually abused as a small child, and her take on the swimsuit competition is like no other: she supports it partly *because* she was abused.

"I loved swimsuit because it allowed me to say, 'You can see my body on my own terms,'" she explains. She was raised to dress modestly—long shorts, high collars—from early childhood, which made her uneasy in her body. Competing in pageants helped her feel more comfortable, able to say, "My legs are not sexual objects, nor are my shoulders, nor is my belly. And nor is me in a swimsuit."

The winner, Nia Franklin (New York), enchanted the judges with her booming operatic voice and the kind of low-key poise that comes from confidence, not pageant coaching. She threw her hands up to thank God, then serenely walked back and forth across the stage, which nettled traditionalists who wanted to see their queen sashay down the runway to "There She Is," which had also been retired. They wanted pageantry. But this was no longer a pageant.

Miss America 2.0 was the best it could be, given the short history of its rebranding and its intrinsic constraints. What do you do with the name "Miss America" when you're pushing hopefuls toward a professional world without Misses, and when "Ms. America" is an established pageant for women over twenty-five? Once you remove the crown, which makes these driven women look like little girls playing dress-up, you have an honors ceremony fused to a talent show—which is why some people just wanted to see it die. Many members of the MAO Facebook Fan Forum liked the greater emphasis on academics but wished fewer traditions had been yanked. Some found it dull and unglamorous. Taveras told me most of the contestants wanted to keep the swimsuit. But Franklin supported its removal. "I'm more than just that," she said at a press conference afterward. "And all these women onstage are more than just that."

The pageant survived its overhaul—just barely. The ratings hit a historic low, and the media coverage was weary and perfunctory. Writing in *The Atlantic*, Megan Garber confessed to being both moved and confused by it, noting the numerous references to empowerment and not a single mention of feminism. (The same was true of the revamped website, whose front page quoted Mund saying, "Miss America does not focus on fitting into glass slippers. She's determined to shatter glass ceilings.") Commenters responded to *Washington Post* coverage with terse annoyance. "Even without the meat, it's still a meat market," one wrote. Another asked, incredulously, "Is this still on television?" Others, confusing it with Miss USA, made Donald Trump cracks.

While Miss America was advancing in half steps, the culture was taking giant leaps. That fall, a historic number of women ran and won in the 2018 midterm elections, including thirty-one first-time members of the House of Representatives. *These* were the achievers ambitious young women were celebrating as role models. As Christina Cauterucci wrote in *Slate*, "No matter how hard I try, I can't quite grasp . . . what's supposed to make sense about the act of publicly ranking a group of 51 women against one another based on a set of arbitrary, disparate skills. There's already a name for a competition where women compete against one another to prove their passion, ambition, intelligence, talent, and love for America: It's called an election."

Whatever the Miss America competition had gained in rebranding that night, it lost in leadership and sisterhood afterward. Mund took to Instagram to post thinly veiled jabs at Carlson and Hopper over the next year, then announced that she would study employment law at Georgetown University Law Center to "ensure no other woman feels the way I felt in the workplace." The MAO revoked the licenses of seven states because of procedural breaches. Four state pageants filed a lawsuit charging "an illegal and bad-faith takeover" by Carlson and Hopper, then dropped it later for lack of funds.

People took sides. Then the pageant became homeless. Atlantic City's Casino Reinvestment Development Authority, which had subsidized it for six years to the tune of $20 million, pulled the plug, which meant its eviction from Boardwalk Hall. For most of a century, save its eight-year exile in Las Vegas and its wartime move to the Warner Theater, the pageant had made its home by the sea in Boardwalk Hall. It was where fifteen-year-old Marion Bergeron had slipped a dress over her swimsuit before taking her title, where Bess Myerson walked the runway to shouts of "Mazel Tov!," where Mary Ann Mobley stripped and Bert Parks first crooned "There She Is." It was where Judi Ford did twenty-foot leaps and Vanessa Williams sang "Happy Days Are Here Again." The venue that for so long had welcomed America's "queen of femininity," as the theme song put it, now closed its doors in her pretty face.

———

WHAT HAD IT ALL MEANT? The pageant's symbolism evolved through history, but its meaning was purest during its bathing-beauty days in the 1920s, when Margaret Gorman and her successors won simply by getting the loudest cheers and the most votes. They were "red-blooded" Americans, poised for marriage and motherhood in post-suffrage America. When the pageant became Miss *America*, spangled in patriotism, complications arose. Who's entitled to say one American woman, whether the girl next door or the biggest glampot, is the finest? Miss America wasn't *elected* as a national "ambassador," in pageant parlance, though she has visited presidents and still entertains troops. As a testy *New York Times* reader complained, "You don't represent me, and you don't represent America." But to pageant fans, she does.

Adding talent in the 1930s had made sense by raising the bar, but it was always confusingly inconsistent. The strongest performers, with natural gifts or years of training, launched professional careers. The weakest sometimes achieved what Susan Sontag called "naïve" or "pure" camp, indulging "a seriousness that fails," like singing to a puppet in a wheelchair. (By contrast, Mobley's tongue-in-cheek striptease was knowingly cheesy—"deliberate" camp.) "Only that which has the proper mixture of the exaggerated, the fantastic, the passionate, and the naïve," according to Sontag, was pure camp—key ingredients of many pageant performances. But it was Bert Parks who brought true camp to the stage. Singing Paul McCartney's "Let 'Em In" in 1976, mincing as he danced with a pinky extended, affecting an inexplicable vocal blackface, backed by head-bobbing male dancers in bell-bottom tuxedoes—*this* was camp.

The scholarships compounded the confusion by trying to cover the skin show with a diploma. At this point Miss America began to look a bit like the military, where college funding motivates (at last count) 75 percent of enlistments. "[W]hether wearing a bikini or a beret, they all offer up their bodies to country in pursuit of their piece of the American Dream," wrote Chanté Griffin, who in 1996 was the first black Miss Teen of California.

The first in her family to go to college thanks to her win, Griffin, writing in *Dame* magazine, calls pageants "sexist at their core" but says, "I will never begrudge any woman for any (legal) way she chooses to support her college career," especially black women, who carry disproportionate college debt. Rather than focusing on the sexism of pageants, she proposes exploring "how we can change the climate that fuels them" and questioning the double standard that sustains them. Men, after all, don't enter pageants to win scholarships. "Pageantry's demands and rebukes live inside of us as a sort of gendered double consciousness where we partially see ourselves through pageantry's patriarchal gaze," she writes.

But though Griffin perceives pageants as a symptom, one could argue that Miss America perpetuates the problem. Its Princess Camp for five- to twelve-year-olds, for example, instills gendered social discipline early on. (It's also where the girl who raises the most money for Children's Miracle Network Hospitals receives an award.) At one camp, the girls get makeovers and manicures and learn "princess etiquette" at a tea party.

Even as a celebration of womanhood—and allowing that recognizing female beauty can be both pleasurable and meaningful—the pageant is rowing against a shifting tide. In the twenty-first century, trans, intersex, and genderqueer people have expanded definitions of femininity. So have athletes like Olympic runner Caster Semenya, forbidden from competing with women unless she takes drugs to suppress her naturally high testosterone levels, or Serena Williams, a powerhouse player who has transformed tennis. Of course, the femininity on display in Miss America was never "natural" anyway. As Jennifer Weiner wrote in *The New York Times*, the time has come to acknowledge that "nobody, much less a 19-year-old college student, wears evening gowns" and admit "if we're all being honest—that drag queens are doing this better." The point was driven home in the 2018 film *Dumplin'*, in which a drag queen teaches an overweight, alienated teen how to compete in a beauty contest.

Miss America has always operated on two frequencies. One reaches the general public; the other, a subculture of pageant people: generations of contestants and their families, state directors and volunteers, and the economic ecosystem they sustain—coaches, trainers, choreographers, makeup artists, photographers, and hairstylists. Local pageants, where it's easy to see the pageant community in action, offer a glimpse of why it's still a beloved, self-perpetuating tradition.

The 2019 Miss New York State competition, for example, staged in a restored 1930 Paramount Pictures movie palace in Peekskill, was low-key compared to the 2018 Miss America contest. It started late and chugged along in a state of convivial chaos, which nobody seemed to mind. Because the pageant's license had been revoked and only recently restored, it was planned in about two months by an entirely new fourteen-member volunteer staff and board, all of whom have full-time jobs and run the pageant in their spare time. There was no press list, no printed program. The families of the contestants, about 300 people, settled into their seats and chatted; little girls and teens in tiaras scooted up and down the aisles; formers sat together in a row in front, with seats reserved for their mothers. ("You'd think she was the mother of Jesus!" an usher exclaimed after seating and reseating one demanding matriarch.) Most of the New York state winners who'd won Miss America were absent (Tawny Godin Little, Nina Davuluri, Kira Kazantsev, and—no surprise—Vanessa Williams), but Mallory Hagan emceed, and reigning Miss America Nia Franklin both assisted and sang. Hagan was good-natured and professional in fielding procedural curveballs throughout.

The judges sat in the front row, with two auditors posted nearby, poised to count their votes. Peekskill's beamish young mayor made a brief and lively introduction, concluding, "God bless you all!" The ceremony opened with one of the male judges, an opera singer, delivering "The Star-Spangled Banner" at roof-rattling volume, with sustained vibrato and rolled *r*'s—deliberate camp, Sontag would surely agree.

The contestants appeared in black cocktail dresses—Miss Empire State, Miss Liberty, Miss Staten Island, Miss Thousand Islands. They included Stanford University, Brooklyn College, Duchess Community College, and NYU students and alums. One was refreshingly curvy for a beauty contestant. Another wore glasses throughout, even with her glittering jumpsuit. In the interview portion, they were asked if they support the Dream Act (yes), Representative Alexandria Ocasio-Cortez's initiatives (yes), requiring the measles vaccine (yes), legalizing assisted suicide (no), a "straight pride" parade (no), and legal abortion (yes, with hearty cheers from the audience). For talent, Miss Staten Island, a sanitation worker wearing her gray uniform, sang "I Feel Pretty" with a continental accent. Because about half of these contestants had won their titles before the 2.0 rule changes, they'd survived a swimsuit competition. Talking with one of their fathers later, I asked what he'd thought of his daughter competing in a swimsuit. He looked vaguely pained. "It was . . . pretty exploitative," he said.

First runner-up Sydney Park had written a dramatic monologue, "Sit Like A Lady," which she performed using a chair as a prop. It showed how far pageantry had come since Anna Stanley's 1989 guide devoted two full paragraphs to approaching a chair, turning, descending onto it, and organizing one's arms and legs attractively while occupying it. Park began:

When I was a little girl, I was told
to sit like a lady
Ankles crossed
Knees Together
Back straight
chin up

And ended:

If you tell me to sit like a lady
I will sit like a lady.
In the State House
in the Senate
in a courtroom
in a board room
in a corner office
in the Oval Office.
Because if you tell me to sit like a lady
then you best [be] prepared
for when I stand like one too.

It was one of many feminist sentiments expressed that night, though the F-word was never uttered, and despite newly issued judging guidelines dictating the use of "women," not "girls," for contestants, both terms were used onstage. The hybrid Evening Wear/ Social Issues Impact Initiative portion was also paradoxical in light of the 2.0 changes. The women emerged in their gowns, stood, then turned their backs to the audience—a vestigial gesture, it seemed, from the days when contestants in swimsuits and evening gowns were expected to pivot and show the judges their rears.

The winner, Lauren Molella, took home $10,000 for the title, bringing her cumulative total, as a veteran who'd competed in the Miss America system since she was a teen, to $84,000. Her $10,000 was among the lowest of the state jackpots. (The highest, in South Carolina, was a sobering $60,000—more than Miss America herself had won in scholarship money. This is why some women don't even want to win Miss America; they can get comparable purses without the punishing schedule and remain in their home states, in some cases continuing with college.)

State competitions like Miss New York were happening all over the country through May and June 2019 in anticipation of the ninety-ninth Miss America pageant, though entry numbers had fallen to about 4,000, down from 80,000 in the 1980s. It wasn't just that the pageant had dropped off young women's radar, or that reality TV delivered juicier drama, or that young activists like Parkland shooting survivor Emma Gonzalez didn't need a pageant to launch a platform, or that artist Tatyana Fazlalizadeh's viral "Stop Telling Women to Smile" campaign implicated Miss America by association, with its perpetually smiling contestants. ("A world full of women who smile on demand is a world where women's anger is irrelevant," wrote media critic Soraya Chemaly in *Rage Becomes Her: The Power of Women's Anger*.) It was also that social media had changed ideas of beauty, for better and worse. Instagram democratized it, enabling much more diversity, putting power in the hands of "influencers" themselves and granting marginalized women visibility. Women with unibrows, women wearing hijabs, women in wheelchairs now had a forum and didn't need a pageant stage to be seen. But there was a double edge. Instagram also hiked up beauty standards through the use of filters and editing apps like Facetune, reinforcing impossible ideals.

There was something charming about the real-world dynamic and in-progress image-making at these state contests, the genial acceptance of some of the more awkward talent, and the community connections fostered there. Whether or not the broader public cared anymore, they offered, on a small scale, the kind of regenerative affirmation that May Day celebrations of the early twentieth century had, in a coming-out ritual where women themselves designed their debuts. No one had the least idea if or where Miss America would take place that year (in a Connecticut casino on the Thursday before Christmas, it turned out). But they had faith that it would happen and hoped to see it reach its 2021 centennial.

That spring and summer, the state pageants were changing little by little as the 2.0 rules came into effect. In Virginia, a biochemist pursuing a doctorate in pharmacy, for example, had no stage talent and made no apology for it. Wearing a lab coat, safety goggles, and chandelier earrings, Camille Schrier performed a grade school science demonstration showing how the decomposition of hydrogen peroxide in a beaker creates a colorful shooting foam Vesuvius. She won, then repeated it at the Miss America competition, and took the crown.

But it seemed a little late in the game to be bringing applied skills to the pageant stage. Miss America was always late. The day after Pride week that July, in fact, after Americans had marched to celebrate the fiftieth anniversary of Stonewall (and many winners themselves had proclaimed their Pride support), the MAO quietly tweeted that trans women were eligible to compete. No press release. No 2.0 news flash. A fully supportive MAO Facebook fan forum discussion followed. Some said the rule had already been in effect for years; some wondered how "female" was being defined on entry forms at the state level. Then the tweet mysteriously disappeared. Weeks earlier, Gretchen Carlson, the key architect of Miss America 2.0—the biggest overhaul of the pageant in its history—stepped down without explanation. Fans in the forum were ecstatic; some hoped for a return to tradition. For nearly a century, the Miss America pageant had been trying to stop time. Now the past was tantalizingly within reach. "Bring back the swimsuit!" they said.

Acknowledgments

I T SEEMS EVERYONE HAS A pageant story. My thanks go
to the many people who shared them, both in and out of the
Miss America orbit. I'm grateful to the local, state, and national winners who took time to talk with me about a year that
shaped and changed their lives. I've identified them here by the
names they won with: Lee Meriwether, Miss America 1955; Marilyn Van Derbur, Miss America 1958; Debra Barnes, Miss America 1968; Judi Ford, Miss America 1969; Susan Supernaw, Miss
Oklahoma 1971; Lencola Sullivan, Miss Arkansas 1980; Elizabeth
Ward, Miss America 1982; Trelynda Kerr, Miss Oklahoma 1983;
Debra Deitering, Miss Iowa 1984; Marjorie Vincent, Miss America 1991; Deidre Downs, Miss America 2005; Ane Romero, Miss
New Mexico 2005; Gabriela Taveras, Miss Massachusetts 2018;
and Caroline Weinroth, Miss Northern Virginia 2018.

Yolande Dolly Fox was terrifically generous in reflecting on and sharing the papers of her legendary mother, Yolande Betbeze Fox.

For helping me understand the workings of state pageantry, thanks to Rachael Vopatek, board president of the Miss Iowa competition, and Mack Hopper, board chair of the Miss New York competition. Pageant judge Eric Cornell, who has served in three states, educated me about judging, as did Yolande Dolly Fox and Lencola Sullivan Verseveldt. Greg Petroff, a lawyer for the Miss America Foundation, walked me through the intricacies of the Miss America scholarship system. Thanks also to Liz Brown, promotions manager at the Miss America Organization.

Many friends and colleagues influenced this book. Jan Simpson, my beloved collaborator at CUNY's Craig Newmark Graduate School of Journalism, helped plant the seed of this idea years ago in a discussion we had just after the Miss America pageant. My Lehman College colleague Lise Esdaile shared her Vanessa Williams story, her 1984 photos, and many excellent resources during our marathon conversations. Mary Phillips, assistant professor of Africana Studies at Lehman, answered questions about the women of the Black Panthers even as she was busy writing her own book— about them. My chair, Paula Loscocco, has supported my scholarship and cheered me on with words of encouragement at a crucial juncture. My Lehman colleague Sondra Perl and her colleague Jennifer Lemberg, at the Olga Lengyel Institute for Holocaust Studies and Human Rights (TOLI), generously assisted me when I was researching Bess Myerson.

My friends Pam and Kevin Pariseau kindly shared contacts. Peggy Hazard helped with a curious bit of corporate research; Kerrie Chappelka advised on photo research and revealed a helpful secret that is safe with me; Michele McCarthy's Boardwalk Hall missives filled a gap in my research. Thanks to Kelvin Fichter for answering a last-minute SOS and rescuing my manuscript, and to Karin Schiesser for putting a pretty face on my book when it was just a proposal.

I thank Jackie Bright, executive director of the National Scholarship Providers Association (NSPA) for her help, and Mark Kantrowitz, publisher and vice president of research at Savingforcollege .com, for shedding light on the fine points of the non-profit scholarship world.

Jessica Bennett of *The New York Times* shared her files and thoughts during the 2018 competition. Karen Leader, associate professor of art history at Florida Atlantic University, reflected tenderly on her mother, Donna Sollars, Miss Nevada 1951. Historians Michelle Millar Fisher, Anna Burckhardt, and Stephanie Kramer directed me to fashion history resources. For forwarding notes on his interview with Philip Roth about his interview with Yolande Betbeze Fox, I'm grateful to Roth's biographer, Blake Bailey. Gary Jaffe of the Linda Chester Literary Agency helpfully reviewed an important section of this book. In licensing her 1968 pageant protest photo, Beverly Grant offered illuminating context about this action. Thanks also to Kathryn Cramer Brownell, associate professor of history at Purdue University, for assigning an early piece on Miss America at *The Washington Post*.

My sincere thanks to the outstanding independent researcher and historian Stephen (Skip) Moskey, who burrowed into the archives at the Smithsonian National Museum of American History, fact-checked sticky points, and gave me wonderful advice and encouragement.

I thank the reference librarians at the Nyack Library and at Lehman College, especially Lehman's chief librarian, Kenneth Schlesinger, whose vote of confidence helped secure my writing sabbatical. I'm grateful to the staff of the Atlantic City Free Public Library and the Atlantic City Historical Society, to Craig Orr, archivist at the Smithsonian's National Museum of American History, and to Marty Kane, president of the Lake Hopatcong Historical Museum.

CUNY has helped fund my research over the past twenty years, most recently through a 2018–2019 Shuster Fellowship that was crucial to the completion of this book. I thank the staff of the Office of Research and Sponsored Programs at Lehman College and CUNY's Research Foundation staff, including Paul Cole and Mary Irizarry.

I'm enormously grateful to my agent, Laurie Fox of the Linda Chester Literary Agency, whose wisdom, patience, professionalism, and charm is a balm to my soul. Just thinking about her when I hit trouble in writing this book made me feel calm. Megha Majumdar, my editor at Counterpoint Press, was so attuned to the spirit of *Looking for Miss America* that the first time we spoke I took notes to capture the way she so artfully articulated her understanding of it. I'm lucky to have worked with such a smart and insightful editor, and with her excellent team at Counterpoint Press.

My mighty sisters, Lawrie Mifflin and Lize Mifflin, who read parts of my manuscript, have influenced my thinking about women's history for as long as I can remember. My fierce daughter and periodic research assistant, Thea Dery, was key to the evolution of this book's stunning cover. Mark Dery was my constant sounding board. I knew it was just a matter of time before he would nail the connection between Miss America and Martin Heidegger. I'm grateful to him for helping me, for anchoring me, for encouraging me, and for many other reasons.

Notes

Introduction: American Beauties

3 "To a girl, to a girl": from "A Toast to Miss America" by William Richter, quoted in Ross, "Symbol of All We Possess" in Finder.

3 "just loud enough": Walker, "Beauty Winners ... Can Be Losers."

3 "She's a prom queen": Corliss, "Dream Girls."

3 "the body of the state": Deford, *There She Is*, 3.

3 "Miss Whatever She Wants to Be": Miss America 2.0 Judges' Manual 2019.

5 "stigma of pageantry": Lee, "My Miss California Past."

5 4,000—down from 80,000: Bauerlein, "Miss America's Finances Uncertain."

6 "I'm a huge feminist": interview with the author, March 24, 2019.

7 "in good health and of the white race": "1948 Pageant Contract," *American Experience*, PBS.org.

7 "We have nothing to apologize for": Roberts, "The Ugly Side of the Southern Belle."

8 "murdered those poor": quoted in Banner, *Marilyn: The Passion and the Paradox*, 196.

9 85 percent: author interview with Greg Petroff, Miss America Foundation attorney, July 11, 2019.

10 "The sooner you realize": "Miss America Doesn't Swing," *Alabama Journal.*

10 "Every day in a woman's life": Baxandall and Gordon, *Dear Sisters*, 186–7.

Chapter One: Bathing Beauties

11 "real rather than": "Judges to Pick," *Washington Herald.*

12 "madly in love": Deford, *There She Is*, 112.

12 "beauty maids": "Ranks of Beauty Augmented," *The Washington Post.*

13 "thousands of the most": "Maxim as Neptune," *New-York Tribune.*

13 "public performance of racial dominance"; "25 percent": Simon, *Boardwalk of Dreams*, 7, 69.

14 "Atlantic City is not a treat"; "From the howling": Huneker, *New Cosmopolis,* 315, 320.

15 "While I am": "King Neptune Opens," *The New York Times.*

15 "black slaves": "Tremendous Throngs"; "Second Annual Pageant Swings," *Atlantic City Daily Press.*

15 "charm and a knack": Banta, *Imaging American Women*, 210.

16 "from one end of the beach": "Night Carnival Draws," *Atlantic City Daily Press.*

17 "natty beach rig": "Miss Washington Lionized," *Washington Herald.*

17 "the censor ban": "1,000 Bathing Girls on View," *The New York Times.*

17 "beach cops"; "'Roll 'em up, sister'": "1-Piece Suits with a Skirt," *Atlantic City Daily Press.*

18 "lusty blow": "Keeps Her Knees Bare," *The New York Times.*

18 "I most certainly"; "bare feminine knees": "Bather Goes to Jail," *The New York Times.*

18 "beach lizards": "Bars Beach Lizards," *The New York Times.*

19 "As soon as the smaller swimsuit": Roberts, *Pageants, Parlors, and Pretty Women*, 114.

19 "not bold girls": "Defend 1-Piece Suit," *Atlantic City Daily Press.*

19 "newly enfranchised": "Now the Rotarians Ask," *The New York Times.*

20 "because they regard them": "Rotarians to the Rescue," *The New York Times.*

20 "The Bathers' Revue was remarkable": "Gorgeous Beauty Feature," *Atlantic City Daily Press.*

20 "blink, gasp": "Tremendous Throngs Greet King," *Atlantic City Daily Press.*

21 "Winner of [the] GRAND PRIZE": "Organizations May Enter," *Atlantic City Daily Press.*

21 "Congratulations": "Trip Cost 35 Cents," *Washington Herald.*

21 "were not interested": Hamlin in Watson and Martin, *There She Is, Miss America*, 35.

21 "She was very attractive"; "a little schoolgirl": Deford, *There She Is*, 113.

21 "the little Washington beauty": "Miss Washington Lionized," *Washington Herald.*

21 "little Margaret Gorman": "Miss Washington Will Rest," *Washington Herald.*

22 "Through pageantry": quoted in Glassberg, *American Historical Pageantry*, 135.

22 "The media maligned suffragists": Faludi, *Backlash*, 50.

23 "the first modern beauty contest": Banner, *American Beauty*, 255.

23 "of questionable reputation": quoted in Banner, *American Beauty*, 255. (Barnum sold his museum before his Congress of Beauty exhibition was mounted.)

24 "the most beautiful unmarried": Deford, *There She Is*, 110.

24 "supple body, well groomed and well dressed": Kellerman, *Physical Beauty*, 14.

25 "better breeding": "Parent Show Now," *Kansas City Kansan.*

25 "breeding": Deford, *There She Is*, 249.

25 "the boundaries between men's and women's spheres": Chauncey, *Gay New York*, 114.

26 "Look right up": quoted in Shteir, *Striptease*, 79.

27 "actively seeking sexual pleasure": Studlar, *The Perils of Pleasure?* 275–6.

28 "Hellow, Atlantic City": "Scores of Beauties Head for Pageant," *The New York Times.*

28 "fairly rocked": "Beauty Crown Won," *The New York Times.*

29 "'You're judging us?'" and other Rockwell quotes: Rockwell, *My Adventures as an Illustrator*, 204–5.

29 "a more popular taste": quoted in Banner, *American Beauty*, 256.

30 "Mother, what's a figure?": Deford, *There She Is*, 116.

31 "I don't use cosmetics": "Most Beautiful Girl," *The New York Times.*

31 "If Miss America comes to Atlantic City": Tosbell, "The Very Golden Apple," 32.

31 "natural"; "loaded dice": "Pageant Directors and Judges," *Atlantic City Daily Press.*

31 "piquant jazz babies": "Crowd Goes Wild," *Atlantic City Daily Press.*

31 "bobbed hair disqualifies": "Nature and Art," *The New York Times.*

32 "one of the many little shackles": Garden, "Why I Bobbed My Hair," 8.

32 "detrimental to the morality": "Women Condemn," *The New York Times.*

32 "The girls are exposed"; "vicious ideas": "YWCA Opens War," *The New York Times.*

32 "seemed to have been well primed": "Rain Stops Parade," *The New York Times.*

33 "Popular Favorite": Deford, *There She Is*, 131.

33 "made the long journey"; "My worth in future beauty contests": Dunn, "Arctic Venus."

34 "You have been my choice": Deford, *There She Is*, 122.

34 "a startling combination"; "as straight as a bullet": Sentner, "Beauty Queen Will Not."

34 "home girl": Dougherty, "Ruth Schaubel, Miss America of 1924."

35 "generally a shy woman": Deford, *There She Is*, 123.

35 "What chance has an ordinary girl": St. George, "Ruth M. Schaubel, Miss America 1924."

35 "This whole thing reeks": "Two More Spurn Beauty Pageant," *The New York Times.*

36 "How much are you getting"; "It had never been done": "'Miss California' Wins," *The New York Times.*

37 nearly 40 percent: Van Meter, *The Last Good Time*, 52.

37 "a slight nervous breakdown": "Beauty Aspirants Arrive," *The New York Times.*

37 "Ruler of the Sea": "Beauties in Parade for King Neptune," *The New York Times.*

37 "It's becoming hard now": Tosbell, "The Very Golden Apple," 30.

38 "guest of Honor": "Raise Fund for Jessie Jim," *Spokesman Review.*

38 "Tears trembled": "Oklahoma Girl Wins," *Pittsburgh Press.*

39 "her well molded throat"; "What kind of man": "Oklahoma Girl Wins," *Pittsburgh Press.*

39 "cook stoves are sometimes essential": "Prefers Stove to Husband," *The New York Times.*

39 "a type entirely apart": "Oklahoma Girl Wins," *Pittsburgh Press.*

39 a reported $60,000: "Miss America Quits Pageant," *San Jose Evening News.*

40 "that would be the envy"; "What for, then"; "thrilled to the eyebrows": Taaffe, "Indian Beauty Stops Here."

40 "I want to become a great artist": "Queen of Beauty," *Pittsburgh Press.*

41 "handling household weapons": "Miss America is 'A Great Help,'" *Pittsburgh Press.*

41 "There has been an epidemic"; "Many of the girls": Deford, *There She Is,* 129–30.

41 "Coney Island crowd": "Annual Display," *Pittsburgh Press.*

41 "an exposé of the bathing beauty": quoted in Louvish, 141–42.

42 "The basis of any industry": quoted in Louvish, 141–42.

42 "represents the type of womanhood": "Inter-City Beauty Picked," *The New York Times.*

42 "dainty girl": quoted in Roberts and Youmans, *Down the Jersey Shore,* 88.

43 "offered the possibility": Banner, *American Beauty,* 264.

43 "I got so tired": Wilson, "It Happened Last Night."

43 "never affected my life": St. George, "Ruth M. Schaubel."

43 "extremely kind": Mattiace, "First Miss America Disgusted."

Chapter Two: Dreamers

44 "Those days": Chapin, "Penalty," 51.

45 "I wonder if you know"; "You'll never catch me": Chapin, "Penalty," 128, 129.

45 "massively unhealthy": Shindle, *Being Miss America,* 133.

46 "fat individuals have always been considered a joke": Peters, *Diet and Health,* 4.

46 "The prize"; "Don't stand still out there": Chapin, "Penalty," 129.

47 $15 million: Johnson, *Boardwalk Empire,* 88.

49 "a funnier looking set of monkeys": Hellinger, "All in A Day," September 11, 1933.

49 "They have been conned": Hellinger, "All in A Day," September 12, 1933.

49 "Look, that's the way we run the contest": "Judges for the 1933 Miss America Pageant."

49 "Or else?": Deford, *There She Is,* 135.

50 "I felt like I'd been hit with a stun gun": Corliss and Sachs, "Dream Girls."

50 "She is a nice kid": Hellinger, "All in A Day," September 12, 1933.

51 "If I hadn't been Miss America": Eckerson, "Queen at 15."

51 "You're just a little bit special": "The Unique Sisterhood," *New Mexican.*

51 "Miss America of the Midway": "National Beauty Queen," *Daily Press.*

52 "go up there and show those Yankees": Bivans, *Miss America,* 14.

52 "I didn't like having nothing but swimsuits": Osborne, *Miss America,* 86.

53 "the most important thing in your lives": Deford, *There She Is*, 260.

53 "She was extremely articulate"; "It was awful": Dworkin, *Miss America, 1945*, 96.

53 "in good health and of the white race": "Allow Indians in Beauty Event," *Daily Plainsman*.

54 "non-confrontational ways of expressing racial pride": Craig, *Ain't I a Beauty Queen*, 19.

54 "We have eliminated the Negro": "Allow Indians in Beauty Event," *Daily Plainsman*.

55 "at least half of the girls"; "The People's Choice": Bivans, *Miss America*, 14, 16.

55 "a couple of ticket-takers": "Newly Crowned Beauty Queen Quits," *Daily Journal*.

56 "She's so young and we feel": Bivans, *Miss America*, 14.

56 "You realize, Bette": "'First Fancy' Sheltered Miss America," *Wisconsin State Journal*.

56 "to sacrifice my home life": "Miss Bertrand Island Talks Miss America Win," YouTube video.

57 "the incident": Deford, *There She Is*, 142.

57 "There is no Miss America here"; "a very dignified person": Tauber, et. al, "American Beauties."

57 "the Quakerest of the Quakers": Deford, *There She Is*, 270–71.

58 "We are past the time": Bivans, *Miss America*, 14.

59 "Because of its location": Van Meter, *The Last Good Time*, 79.

59 "emblematic of the spirit of America": Bivans, *Miss America*, 19.

60 57 percent: Faludi, *Backlash*, 51.

60 "This conundrum of glamour and grime": Schofield, "Miss America," 57.

60 "For the first time in history," Huhn, "War, Women and Lipstick."

60 $5,000; $2,500: "The History of the Miss America Pageant," *Official Yearbook of the Miss America Pageant, 1960*, 25.

60 $2.5 million: Deford, *There She Is*, 157-8.

61 80 percent; "The fact that I approached them": Deford, *There She Is*, 157–8.

61 $5 million: Parry, "1944 Miss America who inspired WWII effort."

61 "the girl we'd most like to bail out with": Schofield, "Miss America," 60.

61 "They try to keep us hidden"; "It wasn't Venus Ramey": "WW II Reunion: Miss America 1944," Library of Congress webcast.

62 "if the war had not interfered"; "Do not approve of beauty pageants": Board Report, 1–2.

62 "What better": Deford, *There She Is*, 154.

62 "properly wardrobed": Board Report, 3.

63 "entrée into oblivion": Dworkin, *Miss America, 1945*, 120.

63 "So What": Bud Burtson lyrics quoted in Jensen, "Miss America Disenchanted," 64.

63 "Miss America—So What?": Board Report, 4–5.

64 "no college girl"; "I wanted to go to college": Dworkin, *Miss America, 1945*, 98.

64 47 percent in 1920: Coontz, *A Strange Stirring*, 111.

65 40 percent in the 1940s: Coontz, *A Strange Stirring*, 111.

65 "What is Your Dream Girl Like?": Benjamin, "What is Your Dream Girl Like?"

65 3 percent of veterans: Hartmann, *The Home Front and Beyond: American Women in the 1940s*, 106.

Chapter Three: Seekers

67 "Nobody [there] cared about looks": Chaban, "At Bess Myerson's Former Home."

68 "The place resounded with music": Dworkin, *Miss America, 1945*, 16.

69 "I remember walking onto the stage": Dworkin, *Miss America, 1945*, 70.

69 "Official—Truman announces Japanese Surrender": Menand, 231.

69 "Buildings ablaze with parties": Dworkin, *Miss America, 1945*, 70.

69 "a bright woman": Dworkin, *Miss America, 1945*, 93.

70 "Bess Myerson is just not a very attractive name": Dworkin, *Miss America, 1945*, 93.

70 "I cannot change my name": Ades, "Miss America."

70 "I figured that if I could get her name": Preston, *Queen Bess*, 25.

70 "I was in a masquerade": Dworkin, *Miss America, 1945*, 94.

71 "Had champagne!": Dworkin, *Miss America, 1945*, 71.

71 "He asked me if the Miss America Pageant was": Dworkin, *Miss America, 1945*, 77.

71 "the first major national event": Dworkin, *Miss America, 1945*, 72.

73 "horseflesh": Dworkin, *Miss America, 1945*, 104.

73 "was legs": Deford, *There She Is*, 63.

73 "In a world ordered by sexual imbalance": Mulvey, "Visual Pleasure," 19.

73 "She had a Holy Roller way": Dworkin, *Miss America, 1945*, 106–7.

74 "the cheesecake that followed the flag": Dworkin, *Miss America, 1945*, 105.

74 "From a prison camp to this": "Veterans Select," *Central New Jersey Home News*.

74 "Turn around and smile": Dworkin, *Miss America, 1945*, 139.

74 "Watch yourself, Bess": Dworkin, *Miss America, 1945*, 124.

75 4,750,000; $45 million: Diner, *We Remember With Reverence and Love*, 110, 150.

75 "You've got to win, for all of us": Dworkin, *Miss America, 1945*, 108, 161.

75 "You have to show the world that we are not ugly": Ades, "Miss America."

75 "Beauty with brains": "Miss America 1945 Is Crowned," Paramount News.

76 "Mazel tov!": Dworkin, *Miss America, 1945*, 149.

77 "a colossal failure": Preston, *Queen Bess*, 37.

78 "Well, you didn't tell us she was Jewish": Preston, *Queen Bess*, 40.

78 "I realized this title was mine forever": quoted in Preston, *Queen Bess*, 41.

78 "They could have said, 'You speak well'": Dworkin, *Miss America, 1945*, 203.

79 "to do some kind of hosting on TV": DePaulo, "Miss America—Was Last Year's Voting Suspect?" 7.

79 "Our security": "Miss America Gives an Impassioned Speech," YouTube video.

80 "We were never taught as women or as girls": Preston, *Queen Bess*, 47.

80 "Bess Mess": Woo, "Bess Myerson."

80 "She was very, very busy": Wilke, "The Bess Mess."

81 "between the ascendance of Rosie the Riveter": Dworkin, *Miss America, 1945*, 103.

81 "[the] anomaly of the woman professional": Haskell, *From Reverence to Rape*, 133.

82 2 million women lost their jobs: Halberstam, *The Fifties*, 589.

82 "Are You Too Educated to be a Mother?": *Ladies' Home Journal*, 6.

82 "Only a sudden call for help": *Sensation Comics* #94.

82 "a deep illness"; "sexual disorder": Lundberg and Farnham, *Modern Woman: The Lost Sex*, 143, 270.

83 "Physician, heal thyself": Merrill, "Modern Woman: The Lost Sex," *Kirkus Reviews*.

83 "seemed rather stupid": Swarts, "Cloris Leachman."

83 "Having carefully publicized itself": "New Miss America," *Life*, 40.

84 "I'm only interested in one contract": Deford, *There She Is*, 167.

85 "BeBe is too young": "Youngsters Can Think Too," *Lebanon Daily News*.

85 "naïve": Deford, *There She Is*, 169.

85 "What fat?": Brown, "First Miss America from Minnesota."

86 "if they were high-school graduates": Ross, "Symbol of All We Possess," 204.

86 "I was repelled": Ross, *Reporting Back*, 105.

86 "Her act, as she planned it": Ross, "Symbol of All We Possess," 222.

87 "extravagantly cheerful"; "She smiled and told them"; "Some years you get a better-looking crop": Ross, "Symbol of All We Possess," 209–211.

87 "*She* doesn't giggle": Ross, "Symbol of All We Possess," 219.

87 "The MC asked the judges to examine the girls' figures": Ross, "Symbol of All We Possess," 217.

88 "Those poor, poor kids": Ross, "Symbol of All We Possess," 221.

88 "the Sweetheart of the U.S.A.": Ross, "Symbol of All We Possess," 216.

88 "'She's going to spend"; "because when you don't expect very much": Ross, "Symbol of All We Possess," 226–227.

88 "without moralizing": Ross, *Reporting Back*, 112.

89 "I had all this doped out," Deford, *There She Is*, 174.

90 "I'll be glad when this is over": Ross, "Symbol of All We Possess," 219.

90 "One is not born, but rather becomes, a woman": De Beauvoir, *The Second Sex*, 301.

90 "if you could learn to be a brain": Deford, *There She Is*, 172–3.

90 "the kind of girl you hope": Mercer, *How to Win a Beauty Contest*, 24.

90 "correctly"; "smiling at lamp posts": Mercer, *How to Win a Beauty Contest*, 79.

90 "Oh no, not her": Deford, *There She Is*, 174–5.

91 "She wasn't just a high strung kid"; "That year is so drastically superficial": Deford, *There She Is*, 174–5.

91 "You just don't come down off of it"; "She never quite recaptured": Leibowitz, "Pageant Swirl Has Arizona Roots."

Chapter Four: Achievers

93 "There was nothing but trouble": Raskin, "Miss America Was a Rebel."

94 "She was the sexiest, most glamorous": Deford, *There She Is*, 177.

94 "Let's Go"; "HAIRY SITS HERE": Deford, *There She Is*, 180.

94 "All those little girls": Raskin, "Miss America Was a Rebel."

95 "Don't you dare": Deford, *There She Is*, 180.

95 "I'm crazy about the southern accent": "Miss A Can Cook!" *Daily News*.

95 "I'm a singer, not a pinup": quoted in Boor Tonn, "Miss America Contesters," 162.

95　"strictly on the body": "The Bathing Suit is What Counts," *Business Week.*

96　"They were funny old men": Hoffman, *Alabama Afternoons*, 207.

96　"My mother was smart enough": All quotes by Yolande Dolly Fox (who goes by Dolly) are from an interview with the author on November 5, 2018.

97　"with the style of a local rug merchant"; "I was the only one": Deford, *There She Is*, 182.

97　"We no longer permit our Miss Americas": Hackett, "Talent Sidetracks Beauty."

98　"Well, I didn't smoke": "Miss Americas Used to Be Dumb," *Akron Beacon Journal.*

98　"the sweetest kid": Lenora Slaughter letter to Yolande Betbeze, December 13, 1951.

99　"I just didn't want to be an actress": Raskin, "Miss America Was a Rebel."

99　"I think I'll stay the old Yolande Betbeze": Stearn, "One Queen Who Will Be Happy."

99　"people expect"; "brings all the wrong types": Raskin, "Miss America Was a Rebel."

99　"people that are interested": Glover, "Newest, Prettiest Producer of Plays."

100　"It is a humiliation to every girl": "Beauty Queens Hit Bias in 'Miss America' Contest," *Jet.*

100　"There was (and still is) something baffling": Betbeze, "Miss America Cashes In."

100　"I'm a southern girl": "Bias Foes Picket Woolworth Here," *The New York Times.*

100　"That was against her dignity": Deford, *There She Is*, 182.

101　"Good Lord, no": Raskin, "Miss America Was a Rebel."

102　"For more than a year now": Cheshire, "War Disrupts Jet-Set Lovers."

103　"I would probably be in Mobile still": Hoffman, *Alabama Afternoons*, 209.

104　"wallflower roles": "Miss America A Wallflower?," *Courier News.*

104　"It was rather embarrassing": Bivans, *Miss America: In Pursuit of the Crown*, 132.

104　"a push by the derriere": Flint, "Albert A. Marks Jr. Is Dead."

104　"she murdered those"; "Surrounded by all those": quoted in Banner, *Marilyn: The Passion and the Paradox*, 196. (Monroe's comment was made to her friend Ralph Roberts and appeared in his unpublished memoir.)

105　"a young, healthy, simple girl": Fallaci, *The Egoists*, 98–99.

105 "Girls, show this great city": Ross, *Reporting Back*, 211.

105 "respectable families": Fallaci, *The Egoists*, 99.

105 "seemed to have stopped off": Halberstam, *The Fifties*, 575.

106 Twenty-seven million; 39 percent: Deford, *There She Is*, 193.

106 20,000 a day; nine in ten: cited in Ashby, *Amusement for All*, 296.

107 "I had no knowledge of the pageant": Ades, "Miss America."

107 "Yolande and Jean were there to support me": This and all other uncited quotes by Meriwether are from a December 31, 2018, interview with the author, facilitated by Elizabeth Gracen.

107 "He wasn't a celebrity flown in": Ades, "Miss America."

108 "No, no more": Deford, *There She Is*, 235.

108 "When you raise a family": "Miss America Pageant 1959," YouTube video.

109 "Mama, you could be a Miss America!": Jefferson, *Negroland*, 58.

109 "These men regarded beauty"; "They discussed race": Craig, *Ain't I a Beauty Queen?* 68.

110 "mere intentions": Craig, *Ain't I a Beauty Queen?* 66.

111 "many of whom": "Miss American Indian Facing Many Thrills," *Bismarck Tribune*.

111 "I'm afraid I may disappoint": "Miss Indian America Goes to Atlantic City," *The Billings Gazette*.

111 "The first few moments"; "Some of the . . . girls": Roth, "Coronation on Channel Two."

112 "People were saying": This and all other uncited quotes by Van Derbur in this chapter are from an interview with the author, October 3, 2018.

113 "Who is waiting?": Van Derbur, *Miss America by Day*, 61.

114 "a year of incredible loneliness": Van Derbur, *Miss America By Day*, 74.

115 "an ax embedded in my body": "Marilyn Van Derbur Addresses Healing from Trauma," YouTube video.

115 "the finest book"; "Me too": Van Derbur, *Miss America By Day*, back cover blurb, 329.

115 "I learned a lot from Lenora": Dworkin, *Miss America, 1945*, 183.

116 "I run the pageant": "Ex-WAC Repulsed in Battle," *Wilmington Morning News*.

117 "I'm tired of being proper and cultured": "Miss America 1959," CBS. All subsequent quotes from the broadcast of the 1958 pageant are here.

119 two-thirds of TV watchers; 60 million: Deford, *There She Is*, 194.

121 "highest number of lynchings"; "History of Lynchings": NAACP.org.

Chapter Five: Resisters

123 "assumed she was stupid": Deford, *There She Is*, 187.

123 "I felt like a freak": LeMieux, "Lookback: Montague's Miss America."

123 "this leg show"; "world events": Russell, *Suddenly Single*, 60, 67.

124 "Marilyn Buferd is twice divorced": "Official Preliminary of the Miss America Pageant," 1960, 7.

124 "T-E-A-M, Yay . . . football!": "Joleen Wolf—Miss Iowa 1962 Performs on Miss America 1963," YouTube video.

124 "our Cinderella queen": "Official Preliminary of the Miss America Pageant," 1961, 3.

124 "far from being a creature": Brown, *Sex and the Single Girl*, 5.

126 60 percent of men's salaries, black women just 42 percent: Coontz, *A Strange Stirring*, 10.

126 "America's Queen": Bradford, *America's Queen*, 473.

127 "I want them to see what they have done": "Selections from Lady Bird's Diary," PBS.org.

127 "She shouldn't have to answer": "Miss America Aide Avoids Rights Issue," *The New York Times*.

127 3 percent African American; "Miss America merely deals": Deford, *There She Is*, 154, 252.

127 "There they stood": Alvarez, *Something to Declare: Essays*, 38–42.

128 Highest ratings five times: Deford, *There She Is*, 196.

128 "I wanted to be Miss America for one reason": Van Dyke, *That Girl in Your Mirror*, 122.

128 "the greatest thing in my life": All quotes by Barnes Snodgrass in this chapter are from an interview with the author, December 12, 2018.

128 "May God Keep You in the Palm of His Hand": *Official Yearbook of the Miss America Pageant*, 1964.

128 "when more than half": cited in Tice, *Queens of Academe*, 167.

129 "Anyone who's had any doubts": Prewitt and Slattery, *A Bright Shining Place*, 235.

130 "I'd never even inquired": "Don't Grow Too Smart for Crown," *The Ogden Standard-Examiner*.

130 "I was so immature": Jayroe and Burke, *More Grace than Glamour*, 84.

131 "without embarrassment"; "Finally, the dinner conversation turned": Jayroe and Burke, *More Grace than Glamour*, 94, 86.

131 "I was truly a completely": Jayroe and Burke, *More Grace than Glamour*, 145.

132 "I was so disappointed in myself": Jayroe and Burke, *More Grace than Glamour*, 150.

132 "Our generation was raised"; "Yet here we were": Povich, *The Good Girls Revolt*, 11.

133 "It never occurs to anyone": Deford, *There She Is*, 282.

133 "left their calling cards": Moore, "Memories of Pageant Include Animals' Antics."

133 1,000 soldiers a month: Taylor and Morris, "The Whole World is Watching."

133 49 percent: "Gallup Poll Reports 49% Believe Involvement in Vietnam an Error," *The New York Times*.

133 60 percent: Seale, *A Lonely Rage*, 177.

134 "What's Going on Back Home"; "the last thing"; "cute little dresses": Jayroe and Burke, *More Grace than Glamour*, 114–15.

134 "The 1960s": Morgan, *Saturday's Child*, 263.

134 "why I might prefer attacking": Morgan, *Saturday's Child*, 245.

135 "of every political persuasion": Morgan, "No More Miss America!" 1–2.

135 "Women's Liberation," Robin Morgan letter to Richard Jackson, August 29, 1968.

136 "the best fun": Kennedy, *Color Me Flo*, 62.

136 "Welcome to the Miss America Cattle Auction": Cohen, *The Sisterhood*, 150–51.

136 "You can use her to push your products": Welch, *Up Against the Wall Miss America*.

136 "white beauty perpetuated racial"; Welch, *Up Against the Wall Miss America*, 91.

136 "rejected the civil rights ethos": Welch, *Up Against the Wall Miss America*, 82.

137 600 spectators: Curtis, "Miss America Pageant Is Picketed."

137 "Dykes, Commies, Lezzies!": Morgan, *Saturday's Child*, 261.

137 "If they were married": Giddens, "Atlantic City is a town with class."

137 "36-24-36 is hard to beat": Bishop, "Distaff Dissent."

138 "I think at one point": All quotes by Judi Ford Nash in this chapter are from an interview with the author, January 18, 2019, and followup emails.

138 "I'll grab her by the throat": Ades, "Miss America."

138 "Once Upon a Someday": *Official Yearbook of the Miss America Pageant, 1968*, 28–9.

139 "emanating a noxious odor"; "WOMEN'S LIBERATION!": Echols, *Daring to Be Bad*, 94–5.

139 "So many things seem wrong": Alexander, "Hooray! Getting Back to Normal."

140 "If the average American female": Buchwald, "The Bra Burners."

140 "As my father used to say": Van Horne, "Female Firebrands."

140 "the visual was insurmountable": Shindle, *Being Miss America*, 61.

141 "the opening salvo": Douglas, *Where the Girls Are*, 141–2.

141 "our leaflets, press statements": Morgan, *The Word of a Woman*, 23.

141 "Every day in a woman's life": Baxandall and Gordon, *Dear Sisters*, 186–7.

143 "like a way out": Ades, "Miss America."

144 "Real power to control our lives": Morgan, "No More Miss America!" 2.

144 "card-carrying feminist": Tonn, "Miss America Contesters and Contestants," 150.

145 "They waved white-gloved hands": Curtis, "Miss America Pageant Is Picketed."

146 "We want to be in Atlantic City": "Negroes Plan Show to Rival Contest," *The New York Times*.

146 "African Americans experienced it": Welch, *Up Against the Wall Miss America*, 76.

146 African American population had doubled: Simon, *Boardwalk of Dreams*, 73.

146 "Awareness": Antell, "Miss America Begins Reign."

146 "Miss America does not represent us": Klemesrud, "There's Now Miss Black America."

147 "but we understand the black issue": Curtis, "Miss America Pageant Is Picketed."

147 "No questions about": Antell, "Miss America Begins Reign."

147 "Miss Black America is of course an effort": Ades, "Miss America."

148 "[all] that same Atlantic City bullshit": Deford, *There She Is*, 255.

148 "You're such wonderful people": "Miss Black America Lyrics," Genius.com.

148 72 million: Ryan, "There She Is, Miss America."

148 "Miss America as run today": "Miss America Doesn't Swing," *Alabama Journal*.

148 pageant "no longer has big-city appeal"; $2 million: Ryan, "There She Is, Miss America."

149 "We are for normalcy": Ryan, "There She Is, Miss America."

149 "We are now integrated in every aspect": Deford, *There She Is*, 251.

149 "We didn't understand them": Osborne, *Miss America: The Dream Lives On*, 136.

149 "The Sound of Young": "'There She is, Miss America . . .'" *Times Herald.*

149 "When you're pregnant!": "Susan Anton on 1969 Miss America Final Question," YouTube video.

Chapter Six: Trailblazers

151 "Great dancers or singers do not show up": Deford, *There She Is*, 7.

152 "most people have no idea": interview with the author, February 27, 2019.

152 "What have I done?" George, *Never Say Never*, 23–4.

152 "Even though I'd won": George, *Never Say Never*, 18.

153 "which is good"; greatest accomplishment: "Phyllis George, Miss America of 1971," YouTube video.

153 "certain changes will be made": Klemesrud, "A Tradition On Way Out at Contest?"

153 "like a prostitute": "Girl Protests Beauty Pageant," *Ironwood Daily Globe.*

154 "poised and self-possessed": interview with the author, January 27, 2019.

154 "I am very, very happy": "Miss World Bob Hope Blooper 1970," YouTube video.

155 "We're not beautiful "; "Anybody that would try to break up": "Beauty Fete Disrupted by Women's Lib," *Los Angeles Times.*

155 Two thousand people: Judy Klemesrud, "For Miss America '75, the Questions Get Tougher."

156 50 million: Collins, *When Everything Changed*, 446.

156 "The sleepwalkers": Rich, "When We Dead Awaken: Writing as Re-Vision," 18.

157 "I'd like to see more women get involved": Goodman, "Sitting Mighty Pretty."

157 "men act and women appear": Berger, *Ways of Seeing*, 46–7.

158 "two kinds of Americans": Sanders, "Trump Champions Silent Americans."

158 "long, strange trip": Shindle, *Being Miss America*, 63.

159 "with dedication and perseverance": Takiff, "There She Goes."

159 "I didn't think it was strange at all"; "I think that a large number of people began not watching": Ades, "Miss America."

160 half were on dean's lists: Fallon, "Atlantic City: Betty, Bella, and 50 Fabulous Femmes."

163 "Here were girls": Ebert, "Smile."

163 "Who doesn't get stuck": Kael, *For Keeps*, 647.

164 "We're eliminating the robe": "Miss America Pageant Due for Modernization," *The Victoria Advocate.*

164 70,000 women entering: Dobkin, "Once Upon a Someday."

165 1 percent; "I know all the reporters want me to say": Klemesrud, "Miss Iowa, the Black Girl from Queens."

165 "show the radicals": "Negro Beauty Shocked," *Long Beach Independent.*

166 "I'm sure that": Simpson, "Ex-Iowa Queen: U.S. Not Ready for Black Queen."

167 "The boys who have returned": Supernaw and Hobson, *Muscogee Daughter*, 105–6.

167 "Well, that's OK": Barron, "Miss Oklahoma Hits School Bias."

168 "It's so dehumanizing"; "To study the white man": Supernaw and Hobson, *Muscogee Daughter*, 135, 154.

168 "I didn't know whether he meant"; "looking like a drowned rat": Supernaw and Hobson, *Muscogee Daughter*, 159–60.

169 "You must fight yourself": Supernaw and Hobson, *Muscogee Daughter*, 39–41.

170 "endured the prejudice of the majority population": Supernaw and Hobson, *Muscogee Daughter*, 174.

170 "Our so-called stealing of this country": "John Wayne: Playboy Interview," *Playboy.*

171 "War Cry": "War Cry," *Piqua Daily Call.*

171 "more like an oddity"; "Princess Soft Sunshine"; "so ratted and rigid": Supernaw and Hobson, *Muscogee Daughter*, 187–9.

171 65 percent of women: Finer, "Trends in Premarital Sex in the United States, 1954–2003."

172 "would not have believed"; "We're the Miss America girls"; "something inside gnawed": Supernaw and Hobson, *Muscogee Daughter*, 190, 194, 196.

173 "Ticket Back to Africa": "Miss America Beauty Takes Slur," *The Afro-American.*

173 "I'm no women's liberationist": "Miss Wyoming: Proud Black Beauty Queen," *Jet.*

174 "discovering things about myself": All quotes by Sullivan in this chapter are from an interview with the author, February 20, 2019.

174 "Oh go take a bath": "Pageant Breaks Traditions," *Palm Beach Post.*

175 "We Want Bert"; "I wouldn't sing that lousy song": Rieker, "There He Was."

Chapter Seven: Iconoclasts

177 "Here She Is—Miss America!": Williams, *You Have No Idea*, 31.

177 "I never had any desire"; "girls who had starved": Williams, *You Have No Idea*, 7, 27.

178 "I had no emotion—I wasn't happy": Williams, *You Have No Idea*, 30.

178 "I was not the kind of girl": Gay, *Bad Feminist: Essays*, 61.

178 "Wow, she looks like me": Ades, "Miss America."

178 "We went, my wife and I": Early, "Life with Daughters," 136, 300.

179 "that this nation has been able": "Black Leaders Praise Choice," *The New York Times*.

179 "a society which is still profoundly racist": "Movin' On Up," *The Nation*, 261–2.

179 "in a historical moment": Banet-Weiser, *The Most Beautiful Girl in the World*, 132.

180 "I'm not an activist": "Miss America 1983," YouTube video.

180 "Look at Her": "Miss America 1974 - Judy Hieke, 1st Runner up - Rebecca King, Winner," YouTube video.

180 "Are you ready to go to Harlem now?"; "Did you hear"; "Well, we can't shelter you": Williams, *You Have No Idea*, 44–46.

181 "We had no idea": Williams, *You Have No Idea*, 33.

181 "Vanessa is a lovely young woman": Fein, "Miss America Gives Up Her Crown."

181 "Remember, you will always be a Miss America": Williams, *You Have No Idea*, 59.

181 $24 million: Darrach, "Vanessa Fights Back."

181 $2 million: Williams, *You Have No Idea*, 62.

181 "the wholesome American image": Fein, "Miss America Gives Up Her Crown."

182 "They just wiped their hands of her": Williams, *You Have No Idea*, 69.

182 "moral turpitude": Williams, *You Have No Idea*, 39.

182 "no specific language": Darrach, "Vanessa Fights Back."

182 "One gives us the Whore"; "The most interesting thing": Jefferson, "Vanessa Williams," 250.

183 "I don't want that whore in my play": Williams, *You Have No Idea*, 67.

184 "the only winner anyone remembers": Ades, "Miss America."

184 "really hurt my brand": Strzemien, "Vanessa Williams: Winning."

184 Suzette Charles wondered: "1984 Miss America Winner Says," *Inside Edition*.

184 "It can be so boring": Mattiace, "First Miss America Disgusted with Pageant."

185 "A fit body reflects a fit mind": Williams, *You Have No Idea*, 26.

185 20 percent: Ades, "Miss America."

185 74 million: Baxandall and Gordon, *Dear Sisters*, 184.

185 "would make us a neuter society": Dew, *Sharlene Wells, Miss America*, 4.

185 against abortion and premarital sex: Spotnitz, "Sharlene Wells, a Mormon."

185 "I follow the flag"; "What a relief": Toscano, "Miss America 1985."

186 $26.5 million lawsuit: Sitomer, "LIBEL: More than Ever, It's a Tightrope for the Press."

186 "the girly-type competitions": Dew, *Sharlene Wells, Miss America*, 71.

186 "I think what has happened": Spotnitz, "Sharlene Wells, a Mormon."

187 "illegal babies" (and the rest of her story): posted on Facebook December 23, 2017, with follow-up clarification with the author in July 2019.

187 "feel uncomfortable": Diaz, "Miss America Has a Latina Problem."

187 "I grew up with friends": "Charlene [sic] Wells Miss America 1985 Will Judge," YouTube video.

188 "struggles with these same issues": Deitering Maddox, "The Miss America Pageant's Influence," 83. (She goes by Deitering Maddox, but the thesis is attributed to Maddox Deitering.)

188 "a little side trip"; "It just wasn't the right time": Deitering Maddox, "The Miss America Pageant's Influence," 51, 65.

189 "She's so religious": Dew, *Sharlene Wells, Miss America*, 101.

189 "Every former contestant interviewed": Deitering Maddox, "The Miss America Pageant's Influence," 37.

189 "depression, indescribable pain": Deitering Maddox, "The Miss America Pageant's Influence," 77.

190 "The whole thing about being yourself": Deitering Maddox, "The Miss America Pageant's Influence," 57.

190 "wonderful opportunity": Deitering Maddox, "The Miss America Pageant's Influence," 68.

190 "They assume you're here": Deitering Maddox, "The Miss America Pageant's Influence," 53.

191 "she would have done a lot more": Deitering Maddox, "The Miss America Pageant's Influence," 65.

191 "unexpectedly positive"; "interact with others": Ruwe, "I Was Miss Meridian 1985," 139, 148–9.

192 "I was from Oklahoma": interview with the author, January 11, 2019.

192 "I consider my pageant career": Gracen, "The Battle for Miss America."

193 "a viable way of paying for school"; "the showbiz bug"; $150,000; "trains you to be 'on'": interviews with the author, October 6 and October 15, 2018.

193 "to shake off": Gracen, "The Battle for Miss America."

193 "a goal she strove for": *Official Yearbook of the Miss America Pageant, 1982*, 28.

193 "I guess I was brainwashed": "There She Is: Elizabeth Ward Gracen," *Playboy*, 147.

194 "Don't Miss the Playboy Fantasy": *Official Yearbook of the Miss America Pageant, 1982*.

195 five 1989 contestants: Goodman, "Silicone, Suction and Miss America."

195 "the American way": DiGirolamo, "Cosmetic Surgery OK by Miss America Judges."

196 the average Miss America: Etcoff, *Survival of the Prettiest*, 201.

196 "if your behind is flabby": Hall, "The Rear Guard."

196 "I'll admit to a boob job": Goodman, "Silicone, Suction and Miss America."

196 "That's absolutely the most ridiculous thing": Carlson, *Getting Real*, 81–7.

197 "Suck-and-Tuck Glide": Stanley, *The Crowning Touch*, 63.

198 "dampen" a "Mexican" accent; "Christian music": Stanley, *The Crowning Touch*, 84, 18.

198 "so outclassed the winner": Goldman, *Hype and Glory*, 281.

198 "[a] true winner is made": Stanley, *The Crowning Touch*, 78.

198 "[o]ne is not born, but rather becomes, a woman": De Beauvoir, *The Second Sex*, 301.

199 claimed she was "robbed": Chapman, "Miss America Rides a Rancorous Wave."

199 a "turn-off"; "That panicked me": Osborne, *Miss America: The Dream Lives On*, 119.

199 "A friend and I were trying": Vespa, "Crowning Moments."

200 "Pageants Hurt All Women": Patrice, "The Law Dean Who Became an Undercover Beauty Queen."

200 "Hear me out": Carlson, *Getting Real*, 76.

201 "These weren't celebrities": Goldman, *Hype and Glory*, 285.

201 by 25 percent between 1940 and 1970; 80 percent surge: Simon, *Boardwalk of Dreams*, 100, 194.

201 "You mean porn, right?": Goldman, *Hype and Glory*, 230–31.

202 "You don't want to just go": Deford, *There She Is* (revised edition), 302.

203 "I can't imagine doing anything else": Collins, "Miss America's an R.N."

203 "You're dying well, my dear": Goldman, *Hype and Glory*, 292.

204 $150,000: Venezia, "Miss Minnesota Becomes Miss America 1989."

204 "I'm Debbye Turner": DiGirolamo, "Miss Missouri Debbye Turner."

204 "not [to] be limited": Roberts, "Miss America: Debbye Turner Fits Her Crown."

205 "it's funny"; "a father's": Early, "Life With Daughters," 140, 137.

Chapter Eight: Believers

206 "When I was competing": interview with the author, July 24, 2019.

207 "to places where AIDS activists": Pressley, "Actor and 1998 Miss America Kate Shindle."

207 "How do you talk about practicing safe sex": Marin, "Ms. America."

207 "I'd learned that carrying": Whitestone and Hunt, *Listening with My Heart*, 120.

208 "more women were choosing to go to college": Shindle, *Being Miss America*, 115.

208 "45-year-old Stepford Wives": Marin, "Ms. America."

209 "the look on a woman's face": "Courtney Love—Cover of 'Live Through This,'" YouTube.

209 leapt 66 percent, and women were getting 89 percent: "Quick Facts," Surgery.org.

210 "[W]e hope to engage the American people": Miss America Organization, "American Public to Decide on Swimsuit Competition."

210 Seventy-nine percent: Shindle, *Being Miss America*, 121.

210 forty-one of the contestants: Corliss and Sachs, "Dream Girls."

210 "I was embarrassed for so many years": Roberts, "Beauty is as Beauty Does."

210 "Are you kidding?": Nemy and McDonald, "Bess Myerson, New Yorker of Beauty."

210 "What a happy surprise": letter from Lenora Slaughter to Yolande Betbeze, September 15, 1995.

212 "she just opened up whole ideas for me": Roth, "Researching Miss America."

212 "the household Apollo"; "shiksa": Roth, *American Pastoral*, 3–4, 15.

213 "Do you know what"; "I hated them"; "They put you up"; "How can I back out of this this?": Roth, *American Pastoral*, 178–80.

213 "Why is it that if a girl": Roth, *American Pastoral*, 363.

214 "I walked out on that runway": Roth, *American Pastoral*, 386.

214 "I worked so hard": Ades, "Miss America."

215 "a new crown": Roth, *American Pastoral*, 385.

216 8.8 million viewers (by comparison to 22 million): Kuczynski, "State Pageants at War."

216 "We're so proud of you!": Baraquio, *Amazing Win, Amazing Loss*, 99.

217 "Losers' Lounge": Shindle, *Being Miss America*, 187.

217 decreased by 12 percent: Rubinstein and Caballero, "Is Miss America an Undernourished Role Model?": 1569.

217 "a tale of American girlhood": Baraquio, *Amazing Win, Amazing Loss*, Introduction.

218 "Don't worry—I'll get your back": Pearlman, *Pretty Smart*, 10.

218 "I love a well-sculpted body": Baraquio, *Amazing Win, Amazing Loss*, 127.

218 "By the time it comes out": Strow, "Miss America Slot Plan Debated."

218 "the rebellion of the beauty queens": Kuczynski, "State Pageants at War."

219 $10 million "reserve"; $1 million in the red: Shindle, *Being Miss America*, 152.

219 "the bodies that won the swimsuit": Schneider and Carswell, "Off-again Romance."

220 close to $110,000: interview with the author, December 1, 2018.

222 "The liberal Miss America judges": Hafiz, "Nina Davuluri's Miss America 2014 Win."

222 "feeling like I could never": "The first Indian-American to be crowned," *Times of India*.

222 "to suggest that Davuluri's win": Mukhopadhyay, "Miss America Nina Davuluri."

223 "I did lots of things": "Become a Contestant." MissAmerica.org, 2014.

224 "fat as fuck": Duboff, "Let's Get to Know Our New Miss America."

224 "The pressure of having to wake up every morning": Cantrell, *Miss Unlikely*, 151.

225 "was tired of mind and body": "Miss America Hiding Away," *Scranton Republican*.

225 "There were times": Whitestone and Hunt, *Listening with My Heart*, 161.

225 "wanted me to be the same": Baraquio, *Amazing Win, Amazing Loss*, 164.

225 "Miss America was all about the big picture": Shindle, *Being Miss America*, 136.

225 "pay to play"; "balancing the books": Shindle, *Being Miss America*, 197, 211.

226 85 percent of Miss America's scholarships, totaling, in 2019, $1.3–$1.4 million: author interview with Greg Petroff, July 11, 2019.

226 "[T]hrough it all, the swimsuits" and all other John Oliver quotes: "Miss America Pageant," *Last Week Tonight with John Oliver*.

227 young mothers, statistically, come from: "The American Family—Older And Smaller," *Innovation Hub*, NPR.org.

227 $50,000: Suddath, "Getting Rid of the Swimsuit."

229 "I was determined": Haskell and Rensin, *Promises I Made My Mother*, 128.

229 "a pile of malcontents" and other comments in the exposé: Yashir, "The Miss America Emails."

229 "Trying to live a principled life": Haskell and Rensin, *Promises I Made My Mother*, 207.

230 "highly conflicted": Weiner, "My Guilty Pleasure."

230 "[I]t's really hard for me": "The 'White Lady Tears' Edition," *The Waves.*

230 "We will no longer judge": Jensen, "Miss America Axes Swimsuit Competition."

231 "Instead of trying to change its spots": Bishop, "Beauty Pageants Should Die Out."

231 "It's a beauty pageant ... period": Kuperinsky, "Miss America Torn Apart."

232 "Our chair and CEO": Rosenberg, "Miss America Cara Mund Says She Has Been 'Silenced.'"

232 "If you can dream it": "Cara Mund Chats Miss America Win," *Live With Kelly and Ryan.*

Chapter Nine: Survivors

235 "Private Bully, Public Liar": Carroll, "Anti-Political Correctness Group."

236 "It's a mess"; "All you need": Bennett, "Here's What You Didn't See."

238 "I loved swimsuit because": interview with the author, May 29, 2019.

239 "I'm more than just that": Parry, "Miss America Glad She Didn't."

239 "Miss America does not focus": MissAmerica.org, retrieved September 6, 2018.

239 "Even without the meat"; "Is this still on television?": Citizen 451; Boxcar 10, comments on Argetsinger, "Stripped of Bikinis."

239 "No matter how hard I try": Cauterucci, "Even Without the Swimsuit Competition."

240 "ensure no other woman": Mund, Instagram.

240 "an illegal and bad-faith takeover": Parry, "Lawsuit on 'takeover.'"

240 $20 million: Auble and Carroll, "Miss America likely returning to A.C."

241 "You don't represent me": comment on Friedman, "There's Big Money to Be Made in Beauty Pageants."

241 "naïve" or "pure" camp: Sontag and Hardwick, *A Susan Sontag Reader*, 112–14.

241 75 percent: "War and Sacrifice in the Post-9/11 Era," Pew Research Center.

241 "[W]hether wearing a bikini": Griffin, "Celebrating Blackness in Beauty Pageants."

242 "princess etiquette": Johnston, "Miss Ohio's Outstanding Teen."

242 "nobody, much less a 19-year-old college student": Weiner, "The End of Miss America."

245 "women," not "girls": *Miss America 2.0 Judges' Manual 2019.*

245 $84,000: Farrell, "Miss New York is a Millbrook native."

245 $10,000: author interview with Mack Hopper, June 24, 2019.

245 $60,000: Wilkinson, "New Miss South Carolina crowned for 2019."

246 4,000, down from 80,000: Bauerlein, "Miss America's Finances Uncertain."

246 "A world full of women who smile": Chemaly, *Rage Becomes Her*, 123.

Bibliography

Ades, Lisa. "Miss America." *American Experience*, PBS, January 22, 2002.

Aggarwal-Schifellite, Manisha. "The Long, Strange Life of the Mrs. America Pageant." *Jezebel*, January 5, 2016.

"Alabama Entry Wins Miss America Title." *Evening Star*, September 10, 1950.

Alexander, Shana. "Hooray! Getting Back to Normal." *Life*, September 20, 1968, 28.

———. *When She Was Bad: The Story of Bess, Hortense, Sukhreet, and Nancy*. New York: Random House, 1990.

Ali, Yashir. "The Miss America Emails: How the Pageant's CEO Really Talks About The Winners," HuffPost.com, December 21, 2017.

Allen, Robert, C. *Horrible Prettiness: Burlesque and American Culture*. Chapel Hill: University of North Carolina Press, 1991.

"Allow Indians in Beauty Event." *Daily Plainsman,* April 25, 1948.

Altschuler, Glenn C., and David I. Grossvogel. *Changing Channels: America in TV Guide.* Urbana: University of Illinois Press, 1992.

Alvarez, Julia. *Something to Declare: Essays.* Chapel Hill, NC: Algonquin Books of Chapel Hill, 1998.

"The American Family—Older and Smaller." *Innovation Hub,* NPR.org, June 28, 2019.

"American Public to Decide on Swimsuit Competition," press release. Miss America Organization, July 12, 1995.

"Annual Display of Pulchritude has Opposition." *The Pittsburgh Press,* September 9, 1928.

Antell, Len. "Miss America Begins Reign; Black Queen Charges Bias." *Philadelphia Inquirer,* September 9, 1968.

"Antiwar Miss Montana Gave Up Title Gladly." *The New York Times,* July 20, 1970.

Antler, Joyce. *You Never Call! You Never Write!: A History of the Jewish Mother.* New York: Oxford University Press, 2007.

Arco, Paul Anthony. "There She Is, Miss America: Catching up with Judi Ford Nash." NorthwestQuarterly.com, Spring 2014.

"Are You Too Educated to be a Mother?" *Ladies' Home Journal,* June 1946, 6.

Argetsinger, Amy. "Stripped of Bikinis, Miss America Teeters On." *The Washington Post,* September 6, 2018.

Ashby, LeRoy. *With Amusement for All: A History of American Popular Culture Since 1830.* Lexington: University Press of Kentucky, 2006.

Auble, Amanda, and Lauren Carroll. "Miss America likely returning to A.C., but with big changes." *Press of Atlantic City,* May 31, 2019.

"Authoress Goes on 'Attire' Strike." *Atlantic City Daily Press,* September 5, 1921.

Banet-Weiser, Sarah. *The Most Beautiful Girl in the World*. Los Angeles: UC Press, 1999.

Banner, Lois W. *American Beauty*. New York: Knopf, 1983.

———. *Marilyn: The Passion and the Paradox*. New York: Bloomsbury Press, 2012.

Banta, Martha. *Imaging American Women: Idea and Ideals in Cultural History*. New York: Columbia University Press, 1987.

Baraquio, Angela Perez. *Amazing Win, Amazing Loss: Miss America Living Happily, EVEN After*. Anaheim, CA: APB Publishing, 2014.

Barron, Donna. "Miss Oklahoma Hits School Bias." *Lawton Constitution*, June 28, 1971.

"Bars Beach 'Lizards': Long Beach Also Rules Women Must Not Wear One-Piece Bathing Suits." *The New York Times*, May 27, 1921, 14.

"Bather Goes to Jail; Keeps Her Knees Bare." *The New York Times*, September 4, 1921.

"The Bathing Suit Is What Counts." *Business Week*, March 17, 1951.

Battelle, Phyllis. "Early Miss America Winners Got Only Fame." *The Washington Post and Times Herald*, September 2, 1956.

Bauerlein, Valerie. "Miss America's Finances Uncertain as it Fights for Relevance." *Wall Street Journal*, August 3, 2018.

Baxandall, Rosalyn, and Linda Gordon. *Dear Sisters: Dispatches from the Women's Liberation Movement*. New York: Basic Books, 2000.

"Beauties in Parade for King Neptune." *The New York Times*, September 10, 1926.

"Beauty and Grace Reign Supreme as Merry Mermaids Revel in One-piece Bathing Suits Before Great Gallery Along the Beachfront." *Atlantic City Daily Press*, September 9, 1921.

"Beauty Aspirants Arrive at Shore." *The New York Times*, September 8, 1926.

"Beauty Crown Won by 'Miss Columbus.'" *The New York Times*, September 9, 1922.

"Beauty Fete Disrupted by Women's Lib." *Los Angeles Times*, November 21, 1970.

"Beauty Pageant Viewership." Nielsen Media Research Inc., 2007, TVbythenumbers.com.

"Beauty Queens Hit Bias in 'Miss America' Contest." *Jet*, May 22, 1952, 5.

"Become a Contestant." MissAmerica.org, 2014. Accessed July 12, 2014, web.archive.org/web/20150316132053/http:/www.miss america.org/competition-info/become-a-contestant.aspx.

Benjamin, Louise Paine. "What is Your Dream Girl Like?" *Ladies' Home Journal*, May 1942, 28.

Bennett, Jessica, and Sara Simon. "Here's What You Didn't See on Miss America." *The New York Times*, September 10, 2018.

Betbeze, Yolande. "Miss America Cashes In." *Look* (n.d.), 1951 (in Miss America 1951 Papers, 1949–2000, Archives Center, National Museum of American History).

"Bias Foes Picket Woolworth Here." *The New York Times*, June 16, 1960.

Bishop, Betty. "Distaff Dissent." *Kingsport Times-News*, September 8, 1968.

Bishop, Tricia. "Beauty Pageants Should Die out Like the Dinosaurs They Are." *Baltimore Sun*, June 7, 2018.

Bivans, Ann-Marie. *Miss America: In Pursuit of the Crown*. New York: MasterMedia Limited, 1991.

Black, Edwin. *War Against the Weak: Eugenics and America's Campaign to Create a Master Race*. New York: Four Walls Eight Windows, 2003.

"Black Leaders Praise Choice of First Black Miss America." *The New York Times*, September 19, 1983.

"Board Report, November 10, 1944." Archives Center, Lenora Slaughter Papers, National Museum of American History (Collection No. 1227), National Museum of American History, Washington, D.C.

Boucher, John L. "Bra-Burners Blitz Boardwalk." *Atlantic City Daily Press*, September 8, 1968.

Bradford, Sarah. *America's Queen: The Life of Jacqueline Kennedy Onassis*. New York: Penguin Books, 2000.

Brand, Peggy Zeglin. *Beauty Matters*. Bloomington: Indiana University Press, 2000.

Brown, Curt. "First Miss America from Minnesota, Now 87, Looks Back on the Trials of Instant Celebrity." *Star Tribune*, December 24, 2017.

Brown, Helen Gurley. *Sex and the Single Girl*. Fort Lee, NJ: Barricade Books, 2004.

Brownmiller, Susan. *Femininity*. New York: Linden Press/Simon and Schuster, 1984.

Buchwald, Art. "The Bra Burners." *New York Post*, September 12, 1968.

Buszek, Maria Elena. *Pin-up Girls: Feminism, Sexuality, and Popular Culture*. Durham, NC: Duke University Press, 2006.

Butler, Judith. *Gender Trouble: Feminism and the Subversion of Identity*. New York: Routledge, 1990.

Campbell, W. Joseph. *Getting It Wrong: Debunking the Greatest Myths in American Journalism*. Berkeley: University of California Press, 2016.

"Cara Mund Chats Miss America Win." *Live with Kelly and Ryan*, September 12, 2017.

Carlson, Gretchen. *Be Fierce: Stop Harassment and Take Your Power Back*. New York: Penguin Books, 2016.

———. *Getting Real*. New York: Center Street, 2017.

Carroll, Lauren. "Anti-Political Correctness Group Claims Responsibility for Miss America Sign." *Press of Atlantic City*, September 7, 2018.

Cauterucci, Christina. "Even Without the Swimsuit Competition, Miss America Is Indefensible." *Slate*, June 5, 2018.

Chaban, Matt A. V. "At Bess Myerson's Former Home, Shades of a Bronx Utopia." *The New York Times*, January 12, 2015.

Chapin, George. "The Penalty of Beauty." *The New Movie Magazine*, July 1930, 51.

Chapman, Stephen. "Miss America Rides a Rancorous Wave into the Future." *Chicago Tribune*, September 19, 1986.

"Charlene [sic] Wells Miss America 1985 Will Judge Miss America in 2017." YouTube video, posted June 2, 2017. www.youtube .com/watch?v=fTfdx9kVn3U.

Chauncey, George. *Gay New York: Gender, Urban Culture, and the Makings of the Gay Male World, 1890–1940*. New York: Basic Books, 1994.

Chemaly, Soraya L. *Rage Becomes Her: The Power of Women's Anger*. New York: Atria Books, 2018.

"Cheryl." Iowa Public Television, 1970. YouTube video, posted January 15, 2019, www.youtube.com/watch?v=EI2wDqyzT5o.

Cheshire, Maxine. "War Disrupts Jet-Set Lovers," *The Boston Globe*, June 8, 1967.

Cohen, Coleen Ballerino, Richard Wilk, and Beverly Stoeltje, eds. *Beauty Queens on the Global Stage*. New York: Routledge, 1996.

Cohen, Marcia. *The Sisterhood: The True Story Behind the Women's Movement*. New York: Simon and Schuster, 1988.

Collins, Gail. *When Everything Changed: The Amazing Journey of American Women from 1960 to the Present*. New York: Little, Brown, 2009.

Collins, Helen. "Miss America's an R.N. Will It Make a Difference?" *RN*, December 1987, 35.

Coontz, Stephanie. *A Strange Stirring: The Feminine Mystique and American Women at the Dawn of the 1960s.* New York: Basic Books, 2011.

Corliss, Richard, and Andrea Sachs. "Dream Girls." *Time*, September 18, 1995, 146.

"Courtney Love—Cover of 'Live Through This.'" YouTube video, posted November 27, 2010, www.youtube.com/watch?v=UxzZcvcdOxk.

Crain, Maxine Leeds. *Ain't I a Beauty Queen? Black Women, Beauty, and the Politics of Race.* New York: Oxford University Press, 2002.

Crawford, Bill. "Miss America Can Claim New Record for Tears." *Lawton Constitution*, September 13, 1971.

"Crowd Goes Wild Over Marvelous Spectacle Two Miles in Length." *Atlantic City Daily Press*, September 8, 1922.

Cummings, Cary. "Cinderella Story Includes a Crown." *Los Angeles Times*, June 28, 1984.

Curran, John. "Miss America Pageant Features Even Greater Cultural Diversity." *Daily Record*, September 16, 2002.

"Cursed by Their Fatal Gift of Beauty." *Milwaukee Sentinel*, November 1, 1925.

Curtis, Charlotte. "Miss America Pageant Is Picketed by 100 Women." *The New York Times*, September 8, 1968.

"Curvy Coed Miss Black America." *Dayton Daily News*, September 9, 1968.

Darrach, Brad. "Vanessa Fights Back." *People Weekly*, September 10, 1984, 36.

De Beauvoir, Simone. *The Second Sex.* New York: Vintage Books, 1974.

"Defend 1-Piece Suit." *Atlantic City Daily Press,* June 7, 1921.

Deford, Frank. "Confessions of a Miss America Judge." *TV Guide,* September 2–8, 1978, 22.

———. *There She Is: The Life and Times of Miss America.* New York: Viking Press, 1971, revised edition, 1978.

DePaulo, Lisa. "Miss America—Was Last Year's Voting Suspect?" *TV Guide,* September 2, 1989, 5–7.

Dew, Sheri L. *Sharlene Wells, Miss America.* Salt Lake City, UT: Deseret Book Co., 1985.

Diaz, Thatiana. "Miss America Has a Latina Problem." *Refinery29,* September 12, 2018.

Didion, Joan. "On the Morning After the Sixties." *The White Album.* New York: Simon and Schuster, 1979.

DiGirolamo, Michelle. "Cosmetic Surgery OK by Miss America Judges." UPI, September 15, 1989.

———. "Miss Missouri Debbye Turner, a marimba-playing veterinary student, was . . ." UPI, September 17, 1989.

Diner, Hasia R. *We Remember with Reverence and Love: American Jews and the Myth of Silence after the Holocaust, 1945–1962.* New York: New York University Press, 2009.

Diprete, Thomas A. *The Rise of Women: The Growing Gender Gap in Education and What It Means for American Schools.* New York: The Russell Sage Foundation, 2013.

Dobkin, Robert A. "Once Upon a Someday is Miss America Theme." *Santa Cruz Sentinel,* September 4, 1968.

"Don't Grow Too Smart for Crown." *The Ogden Standard-Examiner,* September 7, 1961.

Dougherty, Frank. "Ruth Schaubel, Miss America of 1924." *Philadelphia Daily News,* May 27, 1988.

Douglas, Susan J. *Where the Girls Are: Growing up Female with the Mass Media.* New York: Times Books, 1994.

Dow, Bonnie J. "Feminism, Miss America, and Media Mythology." *Rhetoric and Public Affairs* 6, no. 1 (2003): 127–49.

Duboff, Josh. "Let's Get to Know Our New Miss America, Nina Davuluri." VanityFair.com, September 16, 2013.

Dunn, Geoffrey. "Arctic Venus: The first Miss Alaska." *Anchorage Press*, August 24, 2011.

Dworkin, Susan. *Miss America, 1945: Bess Myerson's Own Story*. New York: Newmark Press, 1987.

Early, Gerald. "Life with Daughters: Watching the Miss America Pageant." *The Kenyon Review* 12.4 (1990): 132–145.

———. "Waiting for Miss America." *The Antioch Review* 42, no. 3 (1984): 291–305.

Ebert, Roger. "Smile." RogerEbert.com, January 1, 1975.

Echols, Alice. *Daring to Be Bad: Radical Feminism in America, 1967–1975*. Minneapolis: University of Minnesota Press, 1989.

Eckerson, Alice. "Queen at 15; Miss America 'Too Young.'" *Press of Atlantic City*, September 11, 1983.

Erling, John. "Jane Jayroe Gamble." *Voices of Oklahoma*, March 11, 2017.

Etcoff, Nancy L. *Survival of the Prettiest: The Science of Beauty*. New York: Anchor Books, 2000.

"Ex-WAC Repulsed in Battle to Enter Miss America Contest." *Wilmington Morning News*, September 7, 1954.

Fair, John D. *Mr. America: The Tragic History of a Bodybuilding Icon*. Austin: University of Texas Press, 2015.

Fallaci, Oriana. "Hugh Hefner: I am in the Center of the World." In *The Egoists*. Milan: Rizzoli Editore, 1963.

Fallon, Beth. "Atlantic City: Betty, Bella, and 50 Fabulous Femmes." *Daily News*, September 4, 1974.

Faludi, Susan. *Backlash: The Undeclared War Against American Women*. New York: Crown Publishers, 1991.

———. "Miss Teen Covina's Revenge." *Mother Jones*, April 1988, 32.

Faragher, John Mack, Florence Howe, and Mount Holyoke College. *Women and Higher Education in American History: Essays from the Mount Holyoke Sesquicentennial Symposia*. New York: Norton, 1988.

Farrell, Barbara Gallo. "Miss New York is a Millbrook Native, Dutchess Community College Instructor." *Poughkeepsie Journal*, June 19, 2019.

Fein, Esther B. "Miss America Gives Up Her Crown." *The New York Times*, July 24, 1984.

Finer, Lawrence B. "Trends in Premarital Sex in the United States, 1954–2003." *Public Health Reports* 122, no. 1 (2007): 73–78.

"'First Fancy' Sheltered Miss America in 1937." *Wisconsin State Journal*, September 11, 1981.

"The First Indian-American to be crowned Miss America." *Times of India*, n.d.

"1st Miss America, Margaret Gorman Cahill, Dies." Associated Press, October 3, 1995.

"1st Miss America Margaret Gorman Cahill Dies." *Deseret News*, October 3, 1995.

"1st 'Miss Black America' Pageant to be Staged in Atlantic City." *Chicago Daily Defender*, August 31, 1968.

Flint, Peter B. "Albert A. Marks Jr. Is Dead at 76; Ex-Chief of Miss America Pageant." *The New York Times*, September 25, 1989.

Foley, Brenda. *Undressed for Success: Beauty Contestants and Exotic Dancers as Merchants of Morality*. New York: Palgrave Macmillan, 2005.

Friedman, Hilary Levey. "There's Big Money to Be Made in Beauty Pageants." *The New York Times*, September 13, 2013.

Friedman, Myra. *Buried Alive: The Biography of Janis Joplin.* New York: Three Rivers Press, 1992.

Funnell, Charles E. *By the Beautiful Sea: The Rise and High Times of that Great American Resort, Atlantic City.* New Brunswick, NJ: Rutgers University Press, 1983.

Gaar, Gillian G. *She's a Rebel: The History of Women in Rock and Roll.* Seattle: Seal Press, 2002.

"Gallup Poll Reports 49% Believe Involvement in Vietnam an Error." *The New York Times,* March 10, 1968.

Garber, Megan. "I'm Still Confused About 'Miss America 2.0.'" *The Atlantic,* September 10, 2018.

Garden, Mary. "Why I Bobbed My Hair." *Pictorial Review,* April 1927, 8.

Gay, Roxane. "Fifty Years Ago Protestors Took on the Miss America Pageant and Electrified the Feminist Movement." Smithsonian.com, January 2018.

George, Phyllis. *Never Say Never: Yes, You Can!* Louisville: Butler Books, 2009.

Giddens, Suzanne. "Atlantic City is a town with class, they raid your morals and judge your ass," unidentified clipping, most likely from *New York Free Press,* 1968. Women's Liberation Movement Print Culture collection, Digital Repository, Sallie Bingham Center for Women's History and Culture, Duke University Libraries.

Gill, Brendan. "The Miss America Uproar: What it Says About Us All." *TV Guide,* September 15–21, 1984.

"Girl Protests Beauty Pageant." *Ironwood Daily Globe,* March 28, 1970.

Gitlin, Todd. *The Sixties: Years of Hope, Days of Rage.* New York: Bantam Books, 1993.

Glassberg, David. *American Historical Pageantry*. Chapel Hill: University of North Carolina Press, 1990.

Glover, William. "Newest, Prettiest Producer of Plays is Former Miss America." *San Bernardino Sun*, October 18, 1955.

Goldman, William. *Hype and Glory*. New York: Villard Books, 1990.

Goodman, Ellen. "Silicone, Suction and Miss America." *The Washington Post*, September 19, 1989.

Goodman, Mark. "Sitting Mighty Pretty." *People*, September 20, 1976, 1.

Gordon, Linda. *Feminism Unfinished*. London: W. W. Norton, 2014.

"Gorgeous Beauty Feature of Climaxing Spectacles in City's Great Pageant." *Atlantic City Daily Press*, September 9, 1921.

Gracen, Elizabeth. "The Battle for Miss America." *Flapper Press*, August 23, 2018.

Griffin, Chanté. "Celebrating Blackness in Beauty Pageants: It's Complicated." *Dame*, May 28, 2019.

Gould, Jack. "Crowning a Beauty." *The New York Times*, September 9, 1968.

Gourley, Catherine. *Flappers and the New American Woman*. Minneapolis: Twenty-First Century Books, 2008.

Hafiz, Yasmine. "Nina Davuluri's Miss America 2014 Win Prompts Twitter Backlash Against Indians, Muslims." *Huffington Post*, September 16, 2013.

Halberstam, David. *The Fifties*. New York: Fawcett Columbine/Ballantine Books, 1994.

Hall, Carla. "The Rear Guard." *The Washington Post*, September 18, 1985.

Hall, Harold. "Why Beauty Winners Fail in the Movies." *Motion Picture Magazine*, April 1927, 32.

Hamlin, Kimberly A. "Bathing Suits and Backlash: The First Miss America Pageants, 1921–1927." In *There She Is, Miss America*, edited by Elwood Watson and Darcy Martin, 27–51. New York: Palgrave Macmillan, 2004.

"Harding Greets Gorman Before Crowd of 10,000." *The Washington Herald*, September 12, 1921.

Hartmann, Susan M. *The Home Front and Beyond: American Women in the 1940s*. Boston: Twayne Publishers, 1982.

Haskell, Molly. *From Reverence to Rape: The Treatment of Women in the Movies*. Chicago: University of Chicago Press, 1987.

Haskell, Sam, and David Rensin. *Promises I Made My Mother*. New York: Ballantine Books, 2009.

Hellinger, Mark. "All in a Day." King Features Syndicate, September 11, 1933.

———. "All in a Day." King Features Syndicate, September 12, 1933.

Hirshey, Gerri. *We Gotta Get Out of This Place: The True, Tough Story of Women in Rock*. New York: Atlantic Monthly Press, 2001.

"History of Lynchings." NAACP, www.naacp.org/history-of-lynchings.

"The History of the Miss America Pageant." *Official Yearbook of the Miss America Pageant, 1960*.

Hoffman, Roy. *Alabama Afternoons: Profiles and Conversations*. Tuscaloosa: University of Alabama Press, 2011.

"Hudson Maxim at Beach Carnival: 'Miss New York' Is a Favorite at Atlantic City's Autumn Beauty Contest." *The New York Times*, September 8, 1921.

Hund, Constance Luft. "War, Women and Lipstick." *Ladies' Home Journal*, August 1943, 73.

Huneker, James. *New Cosmopolis, A Book of Images: Intimate New York: Certain European cities before the war: Vienna, Prague, little*

Holland, Belgian etchings, Madrid, Dublin, Marienbad: Atlantic City and Newport. New York: Scribner, 1915.

Huus, Kari. "Miss America Seeks Relevance and Ratings." MSNBC.com, September 17, 2004.

"Indian Princess Prize Beauty is Thrilled by S.L." *Deseret News,* September 17, 1926.

"Inter-City Beauty Picked." *The New York Times,* September 8, 1921.

Jayroe, Jane, with Bob Burke. *More Grace than Glamour: My Life as Miss America and Beyond.* Oklahoma Heritage Association, 2006.

Jefferson, Margo. *Negroland.* New York: Pantheon Books, 2015.

———. "Vanessa Williams." *Vogue,* November 1984: 250–251.

Jensen, Erin. "Miss America axes swimsuit competition; Gretchen Carlson says 'We are no longer a pageant.'" *USA Today,* June 5, 2018.

Jensen, Oliver. "Miss America Disenchanted." *Life,* September 16, 1946, 64.

Jewell, K. Sue. *From Mammy to Miss America: Cultural Images and the Shaping of US Social Policy.* New York: Routledge, 1993.

Jobin, Taylor. "Miss America Pageant Proves Beauty Is Only Skin Deep." DAonline.com, September 25, 2014.

"John Wayne: Playboy Interview." *Playboy,* May 1971.

Johnson, Nelson. *Boardwalk Empire: The Birth, High Times, and Corruption of Atlantic City.* Medford, NJ: Plexus Publishing.

Johnson, Nicole. *Living with Diabetes.* Washington, D.C.: Lifeline Press, 2001.

Johnson, Thomas A. "'Keep Pressure On,' Negroes Are Urged in Atlantic City Talk." *The New York Times,* August 28, 1967.

Johnston, Jessica. "Miss Ohio's Outstanding Teen hosting Beauty Boot Camp for local 'princesses.'" Y-CityNews.com, July 8, 2019.

"Joleen Wolf—Miss Iowa 1962 Performs on Miss America 1963." YouTube video, posted Feb. 18, 2013, www.youtube.com /watch?v=dhxocCgUC-M.

Jones, Charles E., ed. *The Black Panther Party (reconsidered)*. Baltimore, MD: Black Classic Press, 2005.

"Judges for the 1933 Miss America Pageant in Atlantic City." Miss America 1933.com, missamerica1933.com/judges.html.

"Judges to Pick District Queen from Group of 6." *Washington Herald*, August 28, 1921.

"Jury Inquiry Due in Atlantic City." *The New York Times*, August 24, 1967.

Kael, Pauline. *For Keeps: 30 Years at the Movies*. New York: Plume, 1996.

"Keeps Her Knees Bare in Atlantic City Jail: Authoress Holds Out for 'Constitutional Rights'—Policeman to Push Assault Charge." *The New York Times*, September 5, 1921.

Kellerman, Annette. *Physical Beauty: How to Keep It*. New York: George H. Duran Company, 1918.

Kennedy, Florynce. *Color Me Flo: My Hard Life and Good Times*. New York: Simon and Schuster, 2017.

Kent, Bill. "Mr. Miss America." *The New York Times*, September 13, 1998.

KGW and AP Staff. "PSU Students Oppose Miss America Speech." KGW-TV.com, May 15, 2002.

"King Neptune Opens Seashore Pageant." *The New York Times*, September 7, 1922.

Kitch, Carolyn. *The Girl on the Magazine Cover: The Origins of Visual Stereotypes in American Mass Media*. Chapel Hill: University of North Carolina Press, 2009.

Klemesrud, Judy. "For Miss America '75, the Questions Get Tougher." *The New York Times*, September 9, 1974.

———. "Miss America: She's Always on the Road." *The New York Times*, July 4, 1974.

———. "Miss Iowa, the Black Girl from Queens." *The New York Times*, June 30, 1970.

———. "There's Now Miss Black America." *The New York Times*, September 9, 1968.

———. "A Tradition on Way Out at Contest?" *The New York Times*, September 10, 1970.

Kuczynski, Alex. "State Pageants at War with Miss America Organization." *The New York Times*, February 16, 2002.

Kuperinsky, Amy. "Miss America Torn Apart: How the Pageant Cut the Swimsuits and Started a Civil War." NJ.com, n.d., 2018.

———. "Miss America Organization Responds to John Oliver's Segment on Pageant." NJ.com, September 22, 2014.

"Last Week Tonight with John Oliver: Miss America Pageant." HBO, September 21, 2014.

Latham, Angela J. *Posing a Threat: Flappers, Chorus Girls, and Other Brazen Performers of the American 1920s*. Hanover, NH: Wesleyan University Press, 2000.

LeBaran, Gaye. "When 'Smile' Made Santa Rosans Do Anything But." *The Press Democrat*, January 15, 2016.

Lee, Crystal. "My Miss California Past Doesn't Mean I'm Not A Great Employee." *Refinery29*, October 31, 2017.

Leibowitz, David. "Pageant Swirl Has Arizona Roots." *Arizona Republic*, September 17, 1999.

LeMieux, Dave. "Lookback: Montague's Miss America." MLive.com, September 9, 2013.

Lenček, Lena, and Gideon Bosker. *Making Waves: Swimsuits and the Undressing of America*. San Francisco: Chronicle Books, 1988.

Lenora Slaughter Papers. Smithsonian Museum, Archives Center, National Museum of American History.

Letter, Lenora Slaughter to Yolande Betbeze, December 13, 1951. Yolande Betbeze Papers, Smithsonian Museum, Archives Center, National Museum of American History.

Letter, Lenora Slaughter to Yolande Betbeze, September 15, 1995. Collection of Dolly Fox.

Letter, Robin Morgan to Richard Jackson, Mayor of Atlantic City, August 29, 1968. Robin Morgan Papers, Digital Repository, Sallie Bingham Center for Women's History and Culture, Duke University Libraries.

Levi, Vicki Gold, and Lee Eisenberg, Rod Kennedy, and Susa Subtle. *Atlantic City, 125 Years of Ocean Madness: Starring Miss America, Mr. Peanut, Lucy the Elephant, the High Diving Horse, and Four Generations of Americans Cutting Loose*, 2nd ed. Berkeley: Ten Speed Press, 1994.

Lim, Shirley Jennifer. *A Feeling of Belonging: Asian American Women's Public Culture, 1930–1960.* New York: New York University Press, 2006.

Lord, M. G. *Forever Barbie: The Unauthorized Biography of a Real Doll.* New York: William Morrow, 1994.

Louvish, Simon. *Mae West: It Ain't No Sin.* New York: Thomas Dunne Books, 2005.

Lundberg, Ferdinand, and Marynia Foot Farnham. *Modern Woman: The Lost Sex.* New York: Harper and Brothers, 1947.

MacWilliams, Byron. "There She Is, Miss Akademia." *Chronicle of Higher Education* 48, no. 3 (September 14, 2001): A64.

Maddox Deitering, Debra. "The Miss America Pageant's Influence on the Self-Construction of its 1985 Contestants." Master's thesis, University of Nebraska at Omaha, 2001, Digital Commons@UNO, digitalcommons.unomaha.edu/studentwork/1815.

Margolis, Charles J. *Did I Really Say That?: The Complete Pageant*

Interview Guide. South Windsor, CT: Interview Image Assoc, 2011.

"Marilyn Van Derbur Addresses Healing from Trauma," YouTube video, posted November 4, 2017, www.youtube.com/watch?v=Aj477j3ynhU.

Marin, Rick. "Ms. America." *The New York Times*, September 12, 1993.

Martin, Richard, and Harold Koda. *Splash!: A History of Swimwear.* New York: Rizzoli, 1990.

Mattiace, Peter. "First Miss America Disgusted with Pageant." *Daily Kent Stater*, September 5, 1980.

"Maxim as Neptune, Rules Fall Pageant at Atlantic City." *New-York Tribune*, September 8, 1921.

Maxwell, Betty. *Miss Unlikely: From Farm Girl to Miss America.* Savage, MN: BroadStreet Publishing, 2019.

May, Lary. *Screening Out the Past: The Birth of Mass Culture and the Motion Picture Industry.* New York: Oxford University Press, 1980.

McNutt, K. S. "Jane Jayroe: Oklahoma Native Reflects on her Miss America Win." *The Oklahoman*, September 11, 2016, oklahoman.com/article/5517456/jane-jayroe-oklahoma-native-reflects-on-her-miss-america-win.

Menand, Louis. "A Note by Louis Menand." In *The 40s: The Story of A Decade*, edited by Henry Finder with Giles Harvey, 231–34. New York: Modern Library, 2014.

Mercer, Jacque. *How to Win a Beauty Contest.* Phoenix: Curran Publishing Co., 1960.

Merrill, Anthony F. "Modern Woman: The Lost Sex." *Kirkus Reviews*, n.d.

Miss America 2.0 Judges' Manual 2017. misslanecounty.org/wp

-content/uploads/2017/03/MAO-Judges-Manual-Revised
-Feb-2017.pdf.

Miss America 2.0 Judges' Manual 2019.

"Miss America 1945 is Crowned." Paramount News (Getty Images).

"Miss America 1945." Paramount News (Getty Images).

Miss America 1951 Papers, 1949–2000. Archives Center, National Museum of American History.

"Miss America 1974 - Judy Hieke, 1st Runner up - Rebecca King, Winner." YouTube video, posted November 10, 2018, www .youtube.com/watch?v=-7Uip0rxlyI.

"Miss America 1983." YouTube video, posted February 14, 2016, www.youtube.com/watch?v=UqsNJQ8TmOw.

"Miss A Can Cook! But She'll Skip Love for Her 4G Bonus." *Daily News*, September 11, 1950.

"Miss America a Wallflower? Marilyn Monroe Makes It So." *Courier News*, September 3, 1952.

"Miss America Against Mixed Marriages." *The Journal News*, September 17, 1985.

"Miss America Aide Avoids Rights Issue." *The New York Times*, September 14, 1965.

"Miss America Beauty Takes Slur Without Tears." *The Afro-American*, September 14, 1974.

"Miss America Doesn't Swing." *Alabama Journal*, January 23, 1970.

"Miss America Gives an Impassioned Speech" (Filmed 1972). YouTube video, posted March 9, 2018, www.youtube.com /watch?v=jk4zDHmA_h0.

"Miss America Hiding Away at Resort in the Poconos." *Scranton Republican*, September 26, 1924.

"Miss America Is Great Help About the House." *Pittsburgh Press*, September 26, 1927.

"Miss America Pageant 1959." CBS, YouTube video, posted February 14, 2017, www.youtube.com/watch?v=12fCmQ3TIyg.

"Miss America Pageant Due for Modernization." *Victoria Advocate*, September 3, 1974.

"Miss America Quits Pageant Over Quarrel in Coin Demand." *San Jose Evening News*, September 9, 1927.

"Miss America Whistleblower Who Revealed Insulting Emails: 'I Wish I'd Said Something Sooner.'" InsideEdition.com, December 28, 2017.

"Miss American Indian Facing Many Thrills at Atlantic City." *Bismarck Tribune*, September 4, 1954.

"Miss Americas Used to Be Dumb, But Not Now." *Akron Beacon Journal*, January 18, 1951.

"Miss Bertrand Island Talks Miss America Win." NorthJersey.com, posted August 14, 2018, www.northjersey.com/videos/news/morris/2018/08/14/video-miss-bertrand-island-talks-miss-america-1937-win/925204002.

"Miss Black America." Curtis Mayfield, Genius.com.

"Miss Black America Chosen." *Arizona Republic*, September 9, 1968.

"Miss California—Shattering the Myth." *Off Our Backs*, October 1983.

"'Miss California' Wins Beauty Title." *The New York Times*, September 12, 1925.

"Miss Indian America Goes to Atlantic City." *The Billings Gazette*, September 4, 1955.

"Miss Indianapolis is Prettiest Girl." *The New York Times*, September 8, 1922.

"Miss Iowa's Joy Dimmed by Father's Vietnam Tour." *The Fort Scott Tribune*, September 5, 1968.

"Miss New York Winner of Black Beauty Pageant." *The Miami News*, August 23, 1969.

"Miss Washington Lionized by Huge Crowds at Shore." *Washington Herald*, September 9, 1941.

"Miss Washington Will Not Rest Until She Starts Trip." *Washington Herald*, September 04, 1921.

"Miss World Bob Hope Blooper 1970." YouTube video, posted May 5, 2008, www.youtube.com/watch?v=reCX3_OAkv8.

"Miss Wyoming: Proud Black Beauty Queen." *Jet*, June 6, 1974.

Mockridge, Norton. "About Squeezing into That Title." *The Evening Sun*, September 5, 1969.

Monty, Shirlee. *Terry*. Waco, TX: Word Books, 1982.

Moore, Pat. "Memories of Pageant Include Animals' Antics." *La Crosse Tribune*, September 8, 1982.

Morgan, Robin. "No More Miss America!" press release and open letter inviting women to attend the Miss America protest, August 22, 1968. Robin Morgan Papers, Digital Repository, Sallie Bingham Center for Women's History and Culture, Duke University Libraries.

———. *The Word of a Woman: Feminist Dispatches*. New York: Norton, 1992.

———. *Saturday's Child: A Memoir*. New York: W. W. Norton, 2001.

———. ed. *Sisterhood Is Powerful: An Anthology of Writings from the Women's Liberation Movement*. New York: Random House, 1970.

Morrison, Toni. *The Bluest Eye*. New York: Plume, 1994.

Moses, W. W. "Blackfeet Adopt Princess of Siwashes, Selected for Eastern Beauty Pageant." *Great Falls Tribune*, September 5, 1926.

"Most Beautiful Girls Avoid All Cosmetics." *The New York Times*, September 13, 1922.

"Movin' On Up." *The Nation*, October 1, 1983, 260–61.

Mukhopadhyay, Samhita. "Miss America Nina Davuluri Is Not a Symbol of Progress." *The Nation*, September 18, 2013.

Mulvey, Laura. "Visual Pleasure and Narrative Cinema." In *Visual and Other Pleasures*, 2nd ed. New York: Palgrave Macmillan, 2009.

Mund, Cara. Instagram, August 17, 2019, www.instagram.com/p /B1RsoM0Aeg0.

"National Beauty Queen." *Daily Press*, July 8, 1935.

"Nature and Art." *The New York Times*, September 10, 1922.

"Negro Beauty Shocked." *Long Beach Independent*, June 16, 1970.

"Negro Girls Sought to Enter Contests for Miss America." *The New York Times*, August 15, 1968.

"Negroes Plan Show to Rival Contest for Miss America." *The New York Times*, August 29, 1968.

Nemy, Enid, and William McDonald. "Bess Myerson, New Yorker of Beauty, Wit, Service and Scandal, Dies at 90." *The New York Times*, January 5, 2015.

"New Miss America." *Life*, September 16, 1946, 40.

"New Trend Toward Black Beauties: Darker Girls are Winning in Bids for Titles." *Ebony*, December 1967, 164–170.

"Newly Crowned Beauty Queen Quits Pageant in Disgust." *Daily Journal*, September 13, 1937.

"News Flashes." *Southeast Missourian*, September 15, 1927.

"New York Model Named Miss Black America." *Press and Sun-Bulletin*, August 23, 1969.

Niemark, Jill. "Why Do We Need Miss America?" *Psychology Today*, October 1998, 40–46.

"Night Carnival Draws Great Crowds to 'Walk.'" *Atlantic City Daily Press*, September 8, 1921.

"1984 Miss America Winner Says Vanessa Williams Apology Was

for Ratings." *Inside Edition*, posted September 14, 2015, www
.youtube.com/watch?v=yUlqviZJgac.

"1948 Pageant Contract: Miss America." *American Experience*,
PBS.org,www.pbs.org/wgbh/americanexperience/features/miss
america-1948-pageant-contract/.

"Now the Rotarians Ask One-Piece Suit: Atlantic City Club Re-
quests Officials to Ease the Curb on Beach Mermaids." *The
New York Times*, June 8, 1921.

Official Preliminary of the Miss America Pageant, 1953, 1954, 1957–
62, 1967. Miss America Pageant National Headquarters.

Official Yearbook of the Miss America Pageant, 1945–1965, 1967–68,
1971–72, 1974, 1977–78, 1982, 1984, 1990–1992, 1996–98,
2003–2004. Miss America Pageant National Headquarters.

"Oklahoma Girl Wins National Beauty Prize." *Pittsburgh Press*,
September 11, 1926.

"1-Piece Suits with a Skirt on the Beach." *Atlantic City Daily Press*,
June 13, 1921.

"1,000 Bathing Girls on View in Pageant." *The New York Times*.
September 9, 1921.

"On the Rhode to Miss America for Miss RI." Eventbrite.com.
www.eventbrite.com/e/on-the-rhode-to-miss-america-for
-miss-ri-tickets-72445497433.

"Organizations May Enter if Bathing Costumes Worn." *Atlantic
City Daily Press*, September 3, 1921.

Osborne, Angela Saulino. *Miss America: The Dream Lives On: A 75-
Year Celebration*. Dallas: Taylor Publishing Company, 1995.

"Pageant Breaks Traditions: Two Black Women are Top Contenders." *Palm Beach Post*, September 7, 1980.

"Pageant Directors and Judges Make Discovery That Starts
Something." *Atlantic City Daily Press*, September 4, 1922.

"Parent Show Now." *Kansas City Kansan*, September 2, 1920.

Parry, Wayne. "Lawsuit on 'takeover' of Miss America Pageant is Withdrawn." Associated Press, March 5, 2019.

———. "New Miss America Glad She Didn't Have to Don Swimsuit to Win." Associated Press, September 10, 2018.

———. "1944 Miss America who inspired WWII effort dies at 92." *Business Insider*, June 19, 2017.

Patrice, Joe. "The Law Dean Who Became An Undercover Beauty Queen." *Above the Law*, May 16, 2016.

Paumgarten, Nick. "The Death and Life of Atlantic City." *The New Yorker*, September 7, 2015.

Pearlman, Penny. *Pretty Smart: Lessons from Our Miss Americas*. Bloomington, IN: AuthorHouse, 2008.

Peiss, Kathy. *Hope in a Jar: The Making of America's Beauty Culture*. New York: Metropolitan Books, Henry Holt and Company, 1998.

Peters, Lulu Hunt. *Diet and Health, With Key to the Calories*. Chicago: Reilly and Lee Co., 1918.

"Philadelphia Girl Wins Negro Beauty Pageant." *Green Bay Press-Gazette*, September 9, 1968.

"Phyllis George, Miss America of 1971, Was Interviewed Briefly While in Roanoke." March 13, 1971, YouTube video posted September 28, 2016, www.youtube.com/watch?v=sy2K88pwqLo.

Pierpont, Claudia Roth. *Roth Unbound: A Writer and His Books*. New York: Farrar, Straus and Giroux, 2013.

Plummer, William. "Haunted by Her Past." *People Weekly*, August 6, 1984, 80.

Polk, Anthony. "$26.5 Million Libel Award." *The Washington Post*, February 21, 1981.

Povich, Lynn. *The Good Girls Revolt: How the Women of Newsweek Sued their Bosses and Changed the Workplace*. New York: Public Affairs, 2016.

"Prefers Stove to Husband." *The New York Times*, September 13, 1926.

Pressley, Nelson. "Actor and 1998 Miss America Kate Shindle on LGBT Rights, NEA and 'Fun Home,' and Running for Office Someday." Washingtonpost.com, May 8, 2017.

Preston, Jennifer. *Queen Bess: An Unauthorized Biography of Bess Myerson*. Chicago: Contemporary Books, 1990.

Prewitt, Cheryl, and Kathryn Slattery. *A Bright Shining Place: The Story of a Miracle*. Cathedral City, CA: Salem Family Ministries, 1981.

"Princess America." *Milwaukee Sentinel*, August 31, 1927.

"Queen of Beauty Would Be Artist." *Pittsburgh Press*, September 10, 1927.

"Quick Facts: Highlights of the ASAPS 1999 Statistics on Cosmetic Surgery." Surgery.org.

"Rain Stops Parade in Beauty Pageant: King Neptune Arrives in Atlantic City, but Boardwalk Display Is Postponed." *The New York Times*, September 4, 1924.

"Raise Fund for Jessie Jim: Indian Princess Off for New Jersey Tuesday." *The Spokesman-Review*, August 24, 1926.

Randolph, Sherie M. *Florynce "Flo" Kennedy: The Life of a Black Feminist Radical*. Chapel Hill: University of North Carolina Press, 2018.

"Ranks of Beauty Augmented by 2 Visiting Maidens." *The Washington Herald*, September 2, 1921.

Raskin, Barbara. "Miss America Was a Rebel (and Still Is)." *The Washington Post*, November 2, 1969.

"Remembering 1968: When Miss America met women's liberation." CBSNews.com, September 30, 2018.

Rich, Adrienne. "When We Dead Awaken: Writing as Re-Vision." *College English* 34, no. 1 (1972): 18–30.

Rieker, Jane. "There He Was—After 25 Years the Miss America Pageant Tells Bert Parks to Take a Walk." *People Weekly*, January 21, 1980, 96.

Riverol, A. R. *Live From Atlantic City: A History of the Miss America Pageant*. Bowling Green, OH: Bowling Green University Popular Press, 1992.

Roberts, Blain. *Pageants, Parlors, and Pretty Women: Race and Beauty in the Twentieth-Century South*. Chapel Hill: University of North Carolina Press, 2014.

——. "The Ugly Side of the Southern Belle." *The New York Times*, January 16, 2013.

Roberts, Roxanne. "Beauty is as Beauty Does." *The Washington Post*, September 16, 1995.

——. "Miss America: Debbye Turner Fits Her Crown." *Orlando Sentinel*, October 7, 1989.

Roberts, Russell, and Rich Youmans. *Down the Jersey Shore*. New Brunswick, NJ: Rutgers University Press, 1993.

Rockwell, Norman. *My Adventures as an Illustrator*. Garden City, NY: Doubleday, 1960.

Rosenberg, Amy S. "Miss America Cara Mund Says She Has Been 'Silenced, Bullied' by Gretchen Carlson." *Philadelphia Inquirer*, August 17, 2018.

Ross, Lillian. *Reporting Always: Writing from The New Yorker*. New York: Scribner, 2015.

——. "Symbol of All We Possess." In *Reporting Back: Notes on Journalism*. Washington, D.C.: Counterpoint, 2002.

——. "Symbol of All We Possess." In *The 40s: The Story of a Decade*, edited by Henry Finder with Giles Harvey. New York: Modern Library, 2014.

"Rotarians to the Rescue." *The New York Times*, June 10, 1921.

Roth, Philip. *American Pastoral*. New York: Vintage International, 1998.

——. "Coronation on Channel Two." *The New Republic*, September 23, 1957, 21.

——. "Researching Miss America." WebofStories.com, n.d., www.webofstories.com/play/philip.roth/101.

Rubinstein, Sharon, and Benjamin Caballero. "Is Miss America an Undernourished Role Model?" *JAMA* 283 (March 22, 2000): 1569.

Russell, Miriam S. *Suddenly Single: A Life After Death*. Manchester Center, VT: Shires Press, 2017.

Ruwe, Donelle R. "I Was Miss Meridian 1985: Sororophobia, Kitsch, and Local Pageantry." In *There She Is, Miss America*, edited by Elwood Watson and Darcy Martin, 137–152. New York: Palgrave Macmillan, 2004.

Ryan, Pat. "There She Is, Miss America." *Sports Illustrated*, October 6, 1969.

St. George, Donna. "Ruth M. Schaubel, Miss America 1924." *Philadelphia Inquirer*, May 28, 1988.

Sanders, Sam. "Trump Champions The 'Silent Majority,' But What Does That Mean In 2016?" NPR, January 22, 2016.

Sardella, Carlo M. "Miss America Faces Ms." *The New York Times*, September 1, 1974.

Savage, Candace. *Beauty Queens: A Playful History*. New York: Abbeville Press, 1998.

"Says Miss America Should Give Up Pageant Crown if Family Has Ties to KKK." *Jet*, October 21, 1985, 14–15.

Schneider, Karen S., and Sue Carswell. "Off-again Romance." *People Weekly*, October 7, 1991, 46.

Schofield, Mary Anne. "Miss America, Rosie the Riveter, and

World War II." In *There She Is, Miss America: The Politics of Sex, Beauty and Race in America's Most Famous Pageant*, edited by Elwood Watson and Darcy Martin, 53–66. New York: Palgrave Macmillan, 2004.

Schulman, Bruce J. *The Seventies: The Great Shift in American Culture, Society, and Politics*. New York: Free Press, 2014.

"Scores of Beauties Head for Pageant." *The New York Times*, September 5, 1922.

Seale, Bobby. *A Lonely Rage: The Autobiography of Bobby Seale*. New York: Bantam Books, 1978.

"Second Annual Pageant Swings Off to Auspicious Start as 'His Bosship of the Seas' Lands On Beach with Inter-City Beauty Court—Crowds, Gun Salutes, and Siren Chorus Welcome." *Atlantic City Daily Press*, September 8, 1921.

"Selections from Lady Bird's Diary on the Assassination, Nov. 22, 1963." *At the Epicenter*, Part 3, PBS.org, www.pbs.org/ladybird /epicenter/epicenter_doc_diary.html.

Sensation Comics #94, November/December 1947.

Sentner, David. "Beauty Queen Will Not Let It Affect Her Head." *Nevada State Journal*, September 17, 1924.

Sherrow, Victoria. *Encyclopedia of Hair: A Cultural History*. Westport, CT: Greenwood Press, 2006.

Shindle, Kate. *Being Miss America: Behind the Rhinestone Curtain*. Austin: University of Texas Press, 2014.

Shteir, Rachel. *Striptease: The Untold History of the Girlie Show*. New York: Oxford University Press, 2004.

Simon, Bryant. *Boardwalk of Dreams: Atlantic City and the Fate of Urban America*. New York: Oxford University Press, 2006.

Simpson, Judy. "Ex-Iowa Queen: U.S. Not Ready for Black Queen." *Atlantic City Press*, September 11, 1971.

Sitomer, Curtis. "LIBEL: More than Ever, It's a Tightrope for the Press." *The Christian Science Monitor*, May 15, 1984.

Solomon, Barbara Miller. *In the Company of Educated Women: A History of Women and Higher Education in America*. New Haven, CT: Yale University Press, 1985.

Sontag, Susan, and Elizabeth Hardwick. *A Susan Sontag Reader*. New York: Farrar, Straus and Giroux, 1982.

Spotnitz, Frank. "Sharlene Wells, a Mormon Sunday School Teacher, Began Her . . ." UPI, September 17, 1984.

Staihar, Janet. "Sound of Young: Miss America Pageant Shifts to a Rock Beat." *The Courier-Journal*, August 31, 1969.

Stanley, Anna. *The Crowning Touch: Preparing for Beauty Pageant Competition*. San Diego, CA: Box of Ideas Publishing, 1989.

Stearn, Jess. "One Queen Who Will Be Happy When Reign Ends." *Daily News*, September 2, 1951.

Steele, Valerie. *Fashion and Eroticism: Ideals of Feminine Beauty from the Victorian Era to the Jazz Age*. New York: Oxford University Press, 1985.

"Stink Bombs and Racial Protests Enliven Miss World '71 Contest." *Tucson Daily Citizen*, November 21, 1970.

Strow, David. "Miss America Slot Plan Debated." *Las Vegas Sun*, February 20, 2002.

Strzemien, Anya. "Vanessa Williams: Winning Miss America Hurt My Brand." *Huffington Post* (video), posted May 6, 2013.

Studlar, Gaylyn. "The Perils of Pleasure? Fan Magazine Discourse as Women's Commodified Culture in the 1920s." In *Silent Film*, edited by Richard Abel. New Brunswick, NJ: Rutgers University Press, 1996.

Suddath, Claire. "Getting Rid of the Swimsuit Was Just the Beginning." *Bloomberg Businessweek*, September 21, 2018.

Supernaw, Susan, and Geary Hobson. *Muscogee Daughter: My Sojourn to the Miss America Pageant.* Lincoln: University of Nebraska Press, 2006.

"Susan Anton on 1969 Miss America Final Question." YouTube video, posted October 9, 2017, www.youtube.com/watch?v=g9X7Cqq35QM.

Swarts, Tracy. "Cloris Leachman: Leaving Northwestern for Pageants 'Seemed Rather Stupid.'" *Los Angeles Times*, December 20, 2016.

Taaffe, Agnes. "Indian Beauty Stops Here; Thrilled by Trip to Atlantic City Fete." *Minneapolis Star*, August 29, 1927.

Takiff, Jonathan. "There She Goes in 2 Directions at Any Time." *Philadelphia Daily News*, October 28, 1971.

Tauber, Michelle, et. al. "American Beauties: 80 Years." *People*, October 16, 2000.

Taylor, David, and Sam Morris. "The Whole World is Watching: How the 1968 Chicago 'Police Riot' Shocked America and Divided the Nation." *The Guardian*, August 19, 2018.

"There She Is: Elizabeth Ward Gracen, Miss America 1982, Moves Back Into the Spotlight." *Playboy*, May 1992, 70.

"'There She is, Miss America ...'" *Times Herald*, September 5, 1969.

Thompson, Erica. "Miss Black America at 50: A Look Back at the Pageant's History of Protest and Pride." Mic.com, August 17, 2018.

Tice, Karen. *Queens of Academe: Beauty Pageantry, Student Bodies, and College Life.* New York: Oxford University Press, 2012.

Tittle, Walter. "Ziegfeld of the Follies." *World's Work* 53, March 1927, 562–8.

Tonn, Mari Boor. "Miss America Contesters and Contestants: Discourse about Social 'Also-Rans.'" *Rhetoric and Public Affairs* 6, no. 1 (2003): 150–60.

Tosbell, E. A. "The Very Golden Apple." *The New Yorker*, September 3, 1927, 28–33.

Toscano, Louis. "Miss America 1985, Sharlene Wells of Utah, projected . . ." UPI, September 16, 1984.

"Tragedy or Obscurity Comes to Beauty Queens; Disaster Follows Scores of Winners; None Has Made Good as Actress." *Milwaukee Journal*, March 19, 1931.

"Tremendous Throngs Greet King of the Seas as He Lands on Beach." *Atlantic City Daily Press*, September 8, 1921.

"Trip Cost 35 Cents to Miss Gorman." *Washington Herald*, July 19, 1922.

"Two More Spurn Beauty Pageant." *The New York Times*, September 10, 1925.

"The Unique Sisterhood of Miss America." *New Mexican*, September 11, 1983.

Up Against the Wall Miss America. Newsreel (collective), 1968, YouTube video, posted September 5, 2018, www.youtube.com /watch?v=dffBFG9xgYY.

Van Derbur, Marilyn. *Miss America by Day: Lessons Learned from Ultimate Betrayals and Unconditional Love*. Denver, CO: Oak Hill Ridge Press, 2004.

Van Dyke, Vonda Kay. *That Girl in Your Mirror*. Old Tappan, NJ: F. H. Revell Co., 1966.

Van Horne, Harriet. "Female Firebrands." *New York Post*, September 9, 1968.

Van Meter, Jonathan. *The Last Good Time*. London: Bloomsbury, 2003.

Venezia, Joyce A. "Miss Minnesota Becomes Miss America 1989." Associated Press, September 11, 1988.

Vespa, Mary. "Crowning Moments." *People Weekly*, September 15, 1986, 82.

"Veterans Select Queen of Beauty." *Central New Jersey Home News*, September 5, 1945.

Walker, Gerald. "Beauty Winners . . . Can Be Losers." *Cosmopolitan*, June 1960, 50–56.

Walker, Nancy A., ed. *Women's Magazines 1940–1960: Gender Roles and the Popular Press*. Boston and New York: Bedford/St. Martin's, 1998.

"War Cry." *Piqua Daily Call*, September 4, 1971.

"War and Sacrifice in the Post-9/11 Era." Pew Research Center Social and Demographic Trends, October 5, 2011.

Watson, Elwood, and Darcy Martin, eds. "The Miss America Pageant: Pluralism, Femininity and Cinderella All in One." *Journal of Popular Culture* 34, no. 1 (Spring 2000): 105–126.

———, eds. *There She Is: Miss America: The Politics of Sex, Beauty, and Race in America's Most Famous Pageant*. New York: Palgrave Macmillan, 2004.

Waxman, Olivia B. "'I Was Terrified': Inside a History-Making Protest with the Women Who Took on the Miss America Competition." Time.com, September 7, 2018.

Weiner, Jennifer. "The End of Miss America." *The New York Times*, December 23, 2017.

———. "My Guilty Pleasure." *The New York Times*, September 13, 2015.

Weinstock, Tish. "How Instagram is Redefining our Understanding of Beauty." I-D.Vice.com, June 11, 2018.

Welch, Georgia. "'Up Against the Wall Miss America': Women's Liberation and Miss Black America in Atlantic City, 1968." *Feminist Formations* 27, no. 2 (2015): 70–97.

West, Mae. *The Wicked Age*. 1927. MS. Library of Congress.

"What Has Befallen the 6 Beauties Who Won the Title 'Miss America'?" *Milwaukee Journal*, June 23, 1934.

"The 'White Lady Tears' Edition." *The Waves*, Slate.com, May 24, 2018.

Whitestone, Heather with Angela Elwell Hunt. *Listening with My Heart*. New York: Galilee, 1998.

Wilke, Deborah. "'The Bess Mess': How a 1940s Beauty Queen Inspired 'Miss America's Ugly Daughter.'" *Hollywood Reporter*, July 11, 2018.

Wilkinson, Jeff. "New Miss South Carolina Crowned for 2019. Here's the Winner." TheState.com. June 29, 2019.

Williams, Vanessa, and Helen Williams, with Irene Zutell. *You Have No Idea: A Famous Daughter, Her No-Nonsense Mother, and How They Survived Pageants, Hollywood, Love, Loss (and Each Other)*. New York: Gotham Books, 2012.

Wilson, Earl. "It Happened Last Night." *Central New Jersey Home News*, September 9, 1958.

Wiltse, Jeff. *Contested Waters: A Social History of Swimming Pools in America*. Chapel Hill: University of North Carolina Press, 2007.

Wolf, Naomi. *The Beauty Myth: How Images of Beauty Are Used against Women*. New York: William Morrow, 1991.

"Women Condemn Beauty Parades." *The New York Times*, May 9, 1924.

Woo, Elaine. "Bess Myerson, Miss America Who Rose in Politics and Fell in Scandal, Dies at 90." *Los Angeles Times*, January 5, 2015.

Woollacott, Angela. *Race and the Modern Exotic: Three Australian Women on Global Display*. Melbourne: Monash University Press, 2011.

"World War II Reunion: Miss America 1944." Library of Congress webcast, filmed May 28, 2004.

Yockel, Michael. "Lenora Slaughter Frapart, the Doyenne of the American Beauty Pageant." NYPress.com, January 31, 2001 (updated February 16, 2015).

Yolande Betbeze Papers (Collection 0888), Smithsonian Museum, Archives Center, National Museum of American History.

"Youngsters Can Think Too." *Lebanon Daily News*, August 19, 1949.

"YWCA Opens War on Beauty Contests; Calls Atlantic City Parade Peril to Girls." *The New York Times*, April 18, 1924.

Zhorov, Irina. "Years Later, Miss Indian America Pageant Winners Reunite." *Code Switch*, NPR, July 12, 2013.

Zorn, Eric. "Crowning Glories: Illinois' Last Miss America Looks Back at 1969 and a World of Difference." *Chicago Tribune*, September 17, 1990.

© Thea Dery

The author of *Bodies of Subversion: A Secret History of Women and Tattoo* and *The Blue Tattoo: The Life of Olive Oatman*, MARGOT MIFFLIN has written for *The New York Times*, *Vogue*, *VICE*, *Elle*, *O*, *The Oprah Magazine*, *The New Yorker*, and many other publications. Mifflin is a professor at Lehman College of the City University of New York (CUNY) and the Craig Newmark Graduate School of Journalism at CUNY. Find out more at margotmifflin.com. You can follow her on Twitter at @msmifflin and on Instagram at @mmifflin.